The
REAL ESTATE OFFICE
SECRETARY'S
HANDBOOK

by

LILLIAN DORIS

FORMER EDITOR, PRENTICE-HALL REAL ESTATE SERVICE;
CO-AUTHOR: COMPLETE SECRETARY'S HANDBOOK

Revised by the

EDITORIAL STAFF OF PRENTICE-HALL, INC.

Englewood Cliffs, New Jersey
PRENTICE-HALL, INC.

LIBRARY OF CONGRESS CATALOG CARD NUMBER: 66–13039

PRINTED IN THE UNITED STATES OF AMERICA: 76505—B & P

Seventh Printing . . . . . March, 1975

A Word About This Revised Edition

With the many changes and the tremendous activity in the real estate field in recent years, today's real estate office secretary needs the latest help at her fingertips. The Real Estate Office Secretary's Handbook has now been revised to incorporate the most modern practices, not only in real estate but in secretarial skills, too.

Special attention has been paid to the many forms that our readers have found so useful. Forms have been replaced or revised wherever changes in practices or the nature of agreements have made a new form a necessity, or even just a good idea.

In countless places the text has been changed to up-date it, or new material has been added because of a new situation or trend in the industry. A glossary of real estate terms also has been added as a special help to the secretary whose experience in this exciting field in limited.

Several chapters are entirely new. There is a longer, more complete telephone chapter that includes new equipment a secretary might find useful in today's real estate office. There is also a brand-new treatment of mail handling in the real estate office, again reflecting new equipment and procedures. Coverage of the correct form in business correspondence has been changed for easier and clearer reference.

We believe you will find that this revision gives you up-to-date information in extremely practical form, and with a greater concentration than ever on the problems peculiar to the real estate office. We are again indebted to many of the same people who made the original edition so valuable to so many thousands of secretaries over the years.

EDITORIAL STAFF OF PRENTICE-HALL INC.

Author's Preface to the Original Edition

The purpose of this book is to help the secretary in a real estate office perform easily, quickly, and independently whatever work is assigned to her. The book covers in detail the usual duties in a real estate office, such as meeting the public, using the telephone expertly, maintaining reminder systems, filing, and other everyday tasks. In moves along to show how to do, in a craftsmanslike way, any kind of work that may turn up in a real estate office, whether it is letter writing, preparing advertisements, typing real estate instruments, assisting salesmen, keeping records, or helping in any of the office phases of real estate work.

With the help of the numerous people to whom acknowledgment is made on the following page, the author has been able to make this book meet the needs of secretaries in all parts of the country. The practices and techniques given are approved methods based on the way successful secretaries do their work in large and small organizations from coast to coast. Research, experience, and close consideration of what is best for today's business world lie behind the information offered here as authoritative. The user of the book must remember, however, that the employer has the prerogative of determining how a certain task shall be done and what responsibilities his secretary shall assume.

Among the people to whom acknowledgment is made are several whose cooperation merits special mention. Miss Mercedes K. Kerwin cheerfully supplied the author with information on numerous phases of real estate office practice. Mr. William MacRossie, outstanding appraiser, and his secretary, Mrs. Janet Wehnes, helped considerably to make the chapters on assisting the appraiser and writing the appraisal report completely practical. Mr. Charles Woessner, realtor, made numerous expert suggestions and carefully read many of the chapters of the manuscript. To all of these people, to those named in the list of acknowledgments, and to those who are credited in the text, the author expresses deep gratitude.

LILLIAN DORIS

Acknowledgments

Elaine Adler, Pease & Elliman, Inc., New York, N.Y.
Alexander Summer Co., Realtors, Teaneck, N.J.
Brita H. Allan, Hamline Twin City Real Estate Co., St. Paul Minn.
J. D. Atwell, Atlanta Federal Savings & Loan Association, Atlanta, Ga.
Ford S. Barrett, Jr., F. S. Barrett & Co., Inc., Realtors, Spokane, Wash.
Ann Bartels, Frazier Eales Co., Sioux City, Iowa
Marcella Bishop, Albert B. Ashforth Co., New York, N.Y.
Beverly A. Black, Margaret Caradine Wright Real Estate, Clayton, Mo.
Polly Black, Moseley & Company, Kansas City, Mo.
Lloyd J. Boice, Realtor, Germantown, N.Y.
Stuart Bondurant, The Stuart Bondurant Realty Co., Winston-Salem, N.C.
C. R. Christian, Byron Reed Company, Inc., Realtors, Omaha, Neb.
Beatrice Clark, Dwight-Helmsley, Inc., New York, N.Y.
John M. Cullerton, Realtor, Irvington, N.J.
Ramona M. Eberhart, Badger Realty Service, Madison, Wis.
Lorella Eidsmoe, Wood Shol Company, Minneapolis, Minn.
Florence E. Elzey, Arthur J. Parsons, Upper Darby, Pa.
N. Lee Foster, Foster & Barnard, Inc., Denver, Colo.
Mary Warren Geer, Glendale, Calif.
Earl Godwin, Godwin & Strauss, Inc., Realtors, Philadelphia, Pa.
E. W. Hague, E. W. Hague & Co., Realtors, Elizabeth, N.J.
John Marvin Herman, Realtor and M. A. I., North Muskegon, Mich.
Betty Hieber, Suburban Realty Company, Perrysville, Pa.

Elva Jasmann, Frank L. McGuire, Inc., Portland, Oreg.

Fred O. Jones, Fred O. Jones Agency, Gt. Falls, Mont.

Ben A. Kagay, Realtor, Kagay Realty Co., Effingham, Ill.

Mercedes K. Kerwin, r. e. Scott Co., Realtors, Elizabeth, N.J.

Harris N. Kroll, Harris N. Kroll & Co., St. Louis, Mo.

Mark Levy, Realtor, Mark Levy Realty Company, Chicago, Ill.

Carroll Lucas, S.S. Walstrum-Gordon & Forman, Ridgewood, N.J.

William MacRossie, Wm. A. White & Sons, New York, N.Y.

James B. McAfee, Hawes & McAfee, Inc., Realtors, Manasquan, N.J.

Mary G. McCaffrey, Wood, Dolson & Co., New York, N.Y.

Marie T. A. McCardle, Frank G. Binswanger, Inc., Philadelphia, Pa.

Lois P. Melton, Warren A. Reeder, Jr., Hammond, Ind.

Helen V. Mulligan, Pease & Elliman, Inc., New York, N.Y.

Frank S. O'Hara, Realtor, Frank O'Hara, Inc., Jackson Heights, N.Y.

Edna K. McKeown, Blanchard & Calhoun Realty Co., Augusta, Ga.

Agnes M. Parrott, Douglas Van Riper, Manhasset, L.I., N.Y.

Russel A. Pointer, Pointer, Coon, and Wood, Saginaw, Mich.

Gerald O. Pratt, Waguespack Pratt Co., Realtors, New Orleans, La.

Thomas K. Procter, Codwell, Banker & Company, San Francisco, Calif.

Myrle W. Spicer, Jackson-Cross Co., Philadelphia, Pa.

Mary E. Swift, John A. Linnett, Newark, N.J.

Margaret Tucker, Albert B. Ashforth Co., New York, N.Y.

Lester D. Wallerstein, Morton G. Thalhimer, Inc., Realtors, Richmond, Va.

Janet Wehnes, Wm. A. White & Sons, New York, N.Y.

Richard E. Weiss, Realtor, Hammond, Ind.

Charles Woessner, Realtor, Fresno, Calif.

Table of Contents

9. **Writing Letters Without Dictation** *(Continued)*

appointment 130. You ask someone to come in to see your employer 130. Reply to request asking your employer for an appointment 130. Letters calling attention to omission of enclosures 132. Letters making plane and train reservations 132. Letters making hotel reservations 133. Reply to notice of meeting 134. Follow-up letters 134.

Letters the Secretary Writes for Her Employer's Signature: Kinds of letters the secretary composes 135. The signature 136. Letters of transmittal 136. Letters acknowledging receipt of papers 139. Letters asking for additional information 139. Letters transmitting information 140.

Model forms for letters written without dictation 143. Processed form letters 143. Letters seeking listings 143. Adaptable form letters for increasing sales 146. Adaptable good will letters 150.

Kinds of papers to be discussed 153. Caution to secretary 154.

Listing Agreements: What is a listing 154. Form of exclusive listing agreement 155. Who signs the listing agreement? 158.

Deposit Receipts and Memoranda of Agreements so Sell and Purchase: What is a deposit receipt? 158. Offer to purchase 158. Use of deposit receipt as memorandum of sale 162. Disposition of deposit receipt and signed offer to purchase 162.

Contract of Sale: What is a contract of sale 162. Who signs the contract of sale 167. Disposition of the contract of sale 167.

Deeds: What is a deed 167. Kinds of deeds 168. Forms of deeds 168. Who signs the deed 168. Disposition of the deed 169.

Mortgages: What is a mortgage 169. Assuming a mortgage and acquiring property subject to a mortgage 170. Forms of mortgages 170. Who signs a mortgage 171. Disposition of the mortgage or trust deed 171.

Leases: What is a lease 171. Classification of leases 172. Form of lease 172. Who signs the lease 173. Disposition of the lease 173. Assignment and sublease 173.

Real Estate Closings: What is a closing 173. Broker's part in the closing 174. The closing statement 175. Practice where real estate broker prepares the closing statement 175. Preparation of the closing statement 175.

Calculation of Adjustments for Closing Statement: How to

13. Helping the Salesman *(Continued)*

master file of listings 210. Inactive listings file 210. Control of the master file 210. Listings folder files 211. Multiple listing of exclusives 211. Duties relating to multiple listing 212. Checking the Multiple Listing Service bulletins 212. Notifying the Multiple Listing Service of bulletin items 213. Keeping track of payments due other brokers 213. Keeping track of expirations and activity 213.

Helping with Sales Office Routine: Sales management and the secretary 215. Assisting at sales staff meetings 215. Carrying out routines for equalizing salesmen's opportunities 216. Salesman's report 216. Clipping items for sales and other purposes 216. Watching the appointment calendar 217. Keeping track of salesmen's whereabouts 217.

Taking Care of Signs, Windows, and Displays: Sign duties 217. Window duties 218. Maps and photographs as selling tools 219.

Eliminating Selling Distractions: Keeping children occupied 219. Keeping track of keys 219.

14 How You Can Help with the Firm's Advertising   **221**

The secretary's part in advertising 221. Getting acquainted with the local newspaper's advertising work 222. Kinds of advertising undertaken 222. Advertising media 223.

Newspaper Advertising: Kinds of newspaper advertising 223. Uses of classified and display ads 224. What the secretary should know about classified advertising 224. Obtaining essential data from the newspaper 224. The importance of timing 225. Typing the classified ad 225. Getting the classified ad to the newspaper 227. Checking the classified ads 228. What the secretary should know about display advertising 228. How the layout is marked for the printer 229. How art work is handled 230. Rules for handling art work 230. How to type the copy for a layout 231. How display space is purchased 231. Preferred position 232. Clipping and filing display ads 232. File of cuts and mats 232.

Direct Mail Advertising: What the secretary should know about direct mail advertising 232. Building and maintaining mailing lists 233. The physical care of mailing lists 233. Classification of mailing list 233. Cleaning out the mailing list 234. Checking the results of mailings 234. Mailing list typed on gummed paper 235.

Working with an Advertising Agency: The secretary's duties in dealing with an agency 235. Advertising files 236. Records of classified ads placed with agency 236.

Chapter 1

Introducing the Real Estate Business

THIS CHAPTER gives you a brief explanation of the various aspects of real estate operations. Throughout this book, as the work of the secretary is explained, you will become more familiar with the nature of the real estate business.

License required. In most states, to be a real estate broker or salesman you must first obtain a license. The laws vary from state to state, and the requirements sometimes differ for residents and non-residents of the state. The general purpose of these laws is to protect the public from incompetency, irresponsibility, and dishonesty in real estate transactions, and to protect those practicing real estate against the unfair competition of unscrupulous and fraudulent operators. The requirements are designed to assure the authorities that the applicant has had adequate training, possesses a working knowledge of the real estate business, is honest and morally sound, and enjoys a good reputation. For proof of competency, the law may require the applicant to pass a written or oral examination. For proof of good reputation, the recommendations of two or more citizen property owners may be required by the state.

Unless a secretary is licensed, her work cannot include selling. No license is required to do secretarial work in a real estate office. You must be on guard not to violate the license laws in carrying out your duties in meeting the public, writing to prospects, and talking to them on the telephone. More will be said about this subject at appropriate places in the book.

Functions of real estate practice. Real estate brokers and their salesmen serve the public in the following ways:

1. By getting seller and buyer together (page 2)
2. By exchanging properties (page 6)
3. By leasing various types of properties (page 6)
4. By managing properties (page 7)
5. By appraising (page 7)
6. By financing and refinancing (page 8)
7. By subdividing and home building (page 9)
8. By remodeling and modernizing (page 9)
9. By removal of blight areas (page 10)
10. By insurance (page 10)

Getting Seller and Buyer Together

Kinds of property that are sold. In the real estate business, the various kinds of property that may be sold include:[1]

1. Homes. This is residential property of one-family units.

2. Multiple dwellings. This is residential property of multiple-family units and includes various kinds of apartment houses.

3. Home sites, subdivisions, lots. This is property that professional builders, land speculators, and home buyers purchase for the purpose of building homes.

4. Industrial property. This includes property that is to be used for manufacturing, storage, or distribution purposes.

5. Commercial property. This includes office buildings, hotels, theaters, stores, garages, gas stations, and parking lots.

6. Farms.

In the sale of any of these types of property the steps for completing the deal are similar. The legal data, points, and papers to be checked in the preparation for the closing vary according to the type of sale made.

Function of the real estate man. The real estate man acts

---

[1] Zoning ordinances regulate and control the character and use of property. The classification given here may be different from that prescribed by the zoning ordinances of a particular locality.

as a broker in finding a buyer for real estate owned by someone else. When the buyer and seller are brought together and a deal is made, the broker becomes entitled to a fee called a commission, which is usually a percentage of the purchase price and is ordinarily paid by the seller. The customary rate of commission is usually set by the local real estate board.

To have properties to show to prospective buyers, the real estate man must have listings. These are his "stock in trade" just as groceries are the stock in trade of the grocer. A large part of the work of the real estate office entails getting listings and keeping records of them. They must be kept in such form that when a prospective buyer walks into the broker's office and describes what he wants, the real estate salesman can quickly produce from among his listings information about properties that might interest his prospect.

Selling property means finding buyers, or "prospects," as they are called in the trade. The real estate man does not sit and wait for prospects to come to him. He looks for them in a number of places, and he maintains records of prospects' names. The owners of listed properties might themselves be prospects for the purchase of other listed properties. People who came to buy but could not be satisfied at that particular time are prospects for sales later on. Names on various lists, such as automobile owners, income tax payers, association member, and others, may be prospects. News stories about births, deaths, marriages, promotions, are all filled with prospects for the alert real estate broker. His personal contacts bring him prospects. He or one of his salesmen may make house-to-house canvasses to find prospects. And, of course, he finds buyers by advertising what he has for sale.

Once the real estate broker has a prospect for a particular property, he must show that property and sell it. Since our purpose is merely to acquaint you with the aspects of selling that touch your work, we shall skip the subject of how a sale is made. However, it is vitally important that you know the steps that take place from the signing of a deposit receipt to the actual transfer of ownership of the property from the seller to the buyer.

Steps from signing of deposit receipt to transfer of ownership. Let us assume that the salesman has taken a prospect to look at a home, and the prospect is interested. In some cases, the salesman has a buyer who is willing to purchase at a lower price than the seller is asking, or who wants possession before the seller can give it to him, or who hesitates about the cost of financing. In that case there will be considerable negotiation between the buyer and seller, and perhaps others, in which the broker will play an important part. For simplicity, however, let us assume we have an ideal situation in which the prospect is completely "sold" on the house and is willing to pay in exact accord with the price, terms, and conditions of the listing.

From this point on the steps vary with the real estate practice in the locality. The procedure explained below applies generally where the services of an escrow department are not used. What happens in the case of an escrowed deal will be described in detail at pages 6 and 179.

1. The broker will receive a deposit from the buyer, and will have him sign a written offer (usually in the form of a deposit receipt) to purchase the property. In most offices, printed forms that have been prepared by an attorney for the broker, or adopted by the local board of realtors, and approved by a counselor at law of the state, will be used for the purpose. The deposit receipt and the written offer of purchase will be explained in Chapter 11.

2. The broker gets in touch with the seller, shows him proof that he has found a buyer, and has him sign the written offer of purchase, which was signed by the buyer.

Instead of signing a deposit receipt, the buyer and seller may enter into a formal contract of sale of the property. In many cases this contract will be prepared by either the seller's attorney or the buyer's attorney, and will be signed at a meeting between the two attorneys and their principals. The contract of sale includes the terms of the purchase, which usually call for a certain amount of cash on execution of the contract, an additional amount of cash on delivery of title, and the amount that will be paid in the form of a bond or note secured by a mortgage (in some states, a trust deed) on the property. This contract will be treated fully in Chapter 11.

The agreement of purchase and sale provides for a closing of title about thirty days later. In that period steps 3 through 8 will generally be taken.

3. Financing may have to be arranged. We shall see how the broker helps in this problem when we describe the financing function at page 8.

4. Title must be searched by the buyer's attorney to be sure that the

seller owns the property and has the right to sell it.[2] The bank or other financial institution that makes a mortgage loan insists on evidence of title by title insurance or an abstract of title. In some cases an attorney's opinion is used instead of title insurance or an abstract.

Title insurance means that a title insurance company issues a title policy to the new owners, binding the insurance company to indemnify the insured (owner) for losses sustained by reason of defect in title to the property. The policy is issued only if the title is found to be clear after an examination of the recorded title is made by the title insurance company or an attorney.

An abstract of title is a chronological history of the property from its original grant to the present time. Because this method of handling title is costly and cumbersome, it is rapidly being replaced by title insurance.

5. A survey of the property may have to be made to get the exact dimensions of the land and to clear up the boundaries. An engineer or surveyor is employed by the buyer or seller for this purpose. The surveyor furnishes a certified map of the property with a description of the courses, distances, and quantity of land.

6. The broker, attorney, or title company checks to see that everything is ready for the closing of title. The closing is a meeting of the parties and their attorneys and broker, at which the legal steps necessary to transfer the ownership of the property are taken. Closings are described more fully in Chapter 11.

7. The broker or the attorneys for the buyer and seller prepare a closing statement. This statement shows in detail the money that is due the seller and the credits that are due the buyer for all of the items that make up the terms on which the property is changing hands. The closing statement is described in Chapter 11.

8. The closing is held. The broker collects any commission still due him from the seller at the closing.

---

2 When you hear the term "Torrens certificate" you should know that it refers to the registration of title under the Torrens system of land registration. The system is used extensive in only a few states. Under it, a persons in whom the fee simple is vested may apply to have the land placed on the register of titles. After certain legal formalities are complied with, a certificate of registration is issued, and the registered owner has good title to the property. Subsequent transfers of the certificate of title registration can be readily effected at slight expense, because it is not necessary to go beyond the registry to effect transfer after the first registration.

Procedure where escrow service is used. Some brokers use the services of an escrow department of a bank, abstract company, title company, or private company organized for the purpose, to close their real estate deals. Where this practice is followed, a seller about to transfer a property to a purchaser, either directly or through his broker, agrees to escrow the deal. He will deposit his deed, furnish a title, and make delivery to the escrow office. The purchaser at the same time agrees to deposit his funds with the escrow office with the understanding that they will be conveyed to the seller when good title is created in him, as the buyer. Both the buyer and the seller agree to pay a portion of the escrow expense. Generally, it is not necessary for the buyer and seller to engage their own attorneys. The escrow department closes the transaction.

In escrowed deals, the escrow department orders a title company to make a search of the title of the real estate being transferred.

The commission of the broker is collected by the escrow department and turned over to the broker.

Serving the Public in Other Ways

Exchanging properties. Every real estate broker has occasion at some time to act for a client who wants to exchange his property for some other property. Someone who owns a city home may want to trade it for a country estate or farm. The owner of a farm may find that he is not cut out to be a farmer and may want to exchange his farm for city property. An executive in the east may be moved to the West and want to exchange his eastern home for one in the locality of his new work.

Many brokers specialize in exchanges. On deals that are made under rules of a real estate board, the broker is entitled to a full commission from each of the parties to the deal. Often, however, each of the parties to a deal is represented by his own broker.

Leasing various types of properties. Practically all brokers lease property at one time or another. A few brokers devote all their time to leasing as a general practice and become known as lease brokers. They are generally located in cities where there is a good deal of business property. Among these specialists are chain-store brokers who know how to deal with the representatives of the chains and how to group certain types of business in the shopping centers.

Leasing as generally practiced involves getting rental listings, finding tenants, negotiating the transactions, and completing the deals. The real estate man brings about the agreement between landlord and tenant as to terms and length of the lease, but the actual writing of the lease agreement is usually left to an attorney. The agreement, or lease contract, defines the relationship between the landlord (called the owner or lessor) and the one who is to occupy the premises (called the tenant or lessee). It sets forth the terms and conditions, known as covenants, describes what and where the property is, the rent and when it is to be paid, what the tenant is required to do, and other stipulations imposed by the landlord and required to be met by the tenant.

The broker may also arrange for assignments of leases and for subleases. In an assignment, the tenant surrenders all his interest in a lease, not to the landlord, but to a third party. The new tenant is called the assignee. The assignee then takes the place of the original tenant in his relations with the landlord. In a sublease, the original tenant finds a new tenant for part or all of the premises, but remains obligated to the landlord for the rent and for the terms of the lease. The subtenant is obligated to the original tenant.

Leases are described more fully in Chapter 11.

Managing properties. Property management is a highly specialized field of real estate activity. It involves entering into an agreement with the owner of income-producing property to relieve him of renting the premises, taking care of the building, servicing tenants, collecting rents, hiring superintendents and other help, and maintaining good tenant relations. For this service, the property manager gets a regular commission for leasing to new tenants or for renewing leases, plus a percentage of the annual income of the property.

Not all real estate offices go into the management business. Those that do usually set up a property management department equipped to handle as many separate properties as they can get to maintain. A secretary in an office that manages property will have a great variety of duties. These will be brought out in the chapters on collecting rent and keeping records of managed properties. Other duties will be mentioned from time to time throughout the book.

Appraising. It takes a wealth of experience, tremendous knowledge of facts and basic valuation principles, and rare qualities of judgment to be able to appraise the value of property. That is why appraisal is a specialized field of real estate operations that only a few real estate men undertake. The real estate appraiser may have to appraise for a number of different purposes, like buying, selling, condemnation, financing, and inheritance taxes. The appraisal he makes is presented in the form of a written report. The work of the appraiser is discussed in Chapter 19, the appraisal report in Chapter 20.

A qualified appraiser may be called as witness in a court case involving a dispute as to the value of property, or in hearings involving questions of rezoning. For expert testimony a fee is charged on a per day basis.

Financing. Almost all buyers of real estate pay only a small fraction of the purchase price in cash; the balance is financed through some kind of loan. Every real estate man must know how to help his prospect work out the financing of the property he wants to buy. He must know the loan sources of his community—the banks, mortgage companies, savings and loan associations, insurance companies, and individuals who might be interested in investing in mortgages. He must know the lending policies of each. This means that you will hear talk about trust deeds, first mortgages, second, or junior mortgages, amortized mortgages, straight-term mortgages, construction loans, purchase money mortgages—all having to do with financing the purchase of property. You will be told more about these financing instruments in Chapter 11.

The broker ordinarily does not earn a separate fee or commission for helping his client to arrange the financing. However, there are times when a buyer will gladly pay a commission to the real estate broker who helps him obtain a loan. Sometimes lenders will come to the real estate man and ask him to find some good real estate mortgages for them. They may be willing to pay a commission to the broker for the service, especially when good investments are hard to find because money is plentiful..

A few real estate firms specialize in mortgage banking or brokerage. In that case, someone will be designated to handle all the financing problems that come up in real estate transactions. Or there may be a mortgage loan department that offers mortgage financing as part of the firm's real estate service. Such a department might serve individuals, firms, contractors, and other real estate men.

There are also mortgage bankers, established principally to finance real estate. They act as correspondents or representatives for financial institutions. Although they are not essentially real estate brokers, they may have a licensed real estate brokerage department to handle sales that arise out of their financing transactions. They do not usually go into property management though they may be qualified to handle rent collections temporarily. One of their functions is to service loans. This means that they perform certain duties for the lender. For example, they send out notices of interest, installment payments on mortgages, taxes, and insurance, and see that these debts are paid. They may even inspect properties that have been mortgaged to make sure that they are being maintained in accordance with the loan agreement. Fees are charged for the various services rendered.

Subdividing and home building. Years ago, communities were created by a promoter of subdivisions. He bought a tract of land, divided it into lots, and sold them. The buyers built their own homes on them. Today, the developer makes plans for acquiring a tract of land and lays it out into a community with streets, utilities, water, sewage disposal, shopping centers, and homes. He buys the land and carries out his plans, building homes with all the modern equipment that today's home-buyer wants. The developer may set up his own selling organization to dispose of the homes and the land that goes with them, or have a broker handle the sales.

Many housing projects in large industrial cities have been developed with little thought to furnishing shopping facilities. In some cases, the original plans include vacant land for the building of stores; in others, they do not, and the promoter of business property must fit his plans into the picture. Thus, business property development as well as home development is an important activity in the real estate field.

Some real estate men still promote subdivisions for the sale of lots, but most of those who go into subdividing usually become home builders also. Some real estate men specialize as brokers for subdividers. They scout around for tracts suitable for development and help the developer acquire the property at a better price than if the developer approached the owner himself. Many real estate organizations have subdivision departments and some have building departments in connection with the subdivision department.

When you are secretary to a developer you are secretary to a real estate man, a builder, and a financier.

Remodeling and modernizing. A great deal of attention is given to substantial, old structures—homes, apartment houses, stores, hotels, and other kinds of buildings—by some real estate men. They see the opportunities of increasing rentals and attracting new tenants if the property is modernized, and the possibility of selling the property at a profit after the improvement has been made. Real estate firms with management departments are frequently active in planning remodeling operations for owners. If the real estate organization has a building department, it assists the management department in the repair and alteration of the properties.

Real estate brokers also serve professional building modernizers who count upon the real estate man to locate in good neighborhoods old run-down buildings that can be acquired and improved.

Removal of blight areas. In large cities and small towns alike there are areas affected by blight. Reclaiming such districts for higher and better use has interested municipal authorities and housing experts for years. The National Association of Real Estate Boards has sponsored a movement for redeeming depressed areas by the establishment of voluntary neighborhood associations. It urges such associations to get control of declining areas and to rejuvenate them by repairs, rebuilding, and rehabilitation. This method of attacking the blight problem is preferred by real estate boards to government-inspired slum clearance. The boards would have the financing of rehabilitation guaranteed by government agencies, just as the Federal Housing Administration (FHA) now guarantees home mortgages.

Few real estate men are interested in selling and renting shacks and business properties in slum areas. But many are vitally interested in assisting associations of property owners with the problem of rehabilitating the blighted portions of their territory. The real estate man helps to sell and manage properties in areas that have been reconstructed to remove the blight.

Insurance. Insurance is a business separate from real estate. However, many real estate offices operate insurance departments with a trained and experienced insurance man in charge. Or, if there is no insurance department, they have relations with an insurance agent through whom they can serve their clients' need for insurance. The connection between real estate and insurance is obviously close. Owners of property and those who have an interest in it, like mortgagees, must be protected against numerous property risks. They need insurance against fire, lightning, sprinkler damage, cyclone, hail, smoke, explosion, water damage, and other hazards. They require liability insurance to protect them against claims for injuries to people sustained on their properties, and for damages to other people's property. They frequently want burglary and robbery insurance, plate glass insurance, elevator insurance, and rent insurance. A real estate firm with an insurance department furnishes these and other kinds of insurance policies. It may even extend its operations to include all branches of insurance protection, like life, health insurance, surety bonds, and others.

It is not the purpose of this book to cover the work of a secretary in the insurance department.

The real estate investor. So far we have explained the activities through which the real estate business serves the public. Some brokers also engage in buying and selling property for their own account. Sometimes they have an investor associated with them, the investor supplying the money and the real estate man the practical knowledge of the opportunities for making money in real estate. With a knowledge of trends in real estate generally as well as in special areas, with alertness in recognizing a good buy, and with imagination in ferreting out possible uses of property that the average owner cannot see, the real estate broker makes a good teammate for an investor. In some cases, the real estate man becomes an investor as a side line to his real estate business.

Chapter 2

Meeting the Public[1]

Brokers and salesmen are busy people, shuttling in and out of the office, showing or inspecting property, or calling on the various people involved in a real estate transaction. As a result, the secretary is often the front-line representative of her office, faced with the problem of handling the public to the best interests of her employer.

In most communities, the real estate business is highly competitive. Each office tries to attract and interest the unknown individuals who will need their services. These people may choose to do business with your firm. If something displeases them, either with the reception they receive or with the service they are offered, they are at liberty to take their business elsewhere.

The public does business with a real estate office on a voluntary basis. The skill with which you handle the public plays a significant part in the total picture of a smoothly running business.

Background for Meeting the Public Adequately

Know the needs of your office. The real estate office is primarily a sales organization. Incidental to your secretarial duties, you are

[1] Acknowledgment for this chapter is made to Mary Warren Geer, licensed real estate broker, Glendale, California, author of *Selling Home Property* (Englewood Cliff N.J.: Prentice-Hall, Inc., 1951).

13

expected to do everything you can to make selling easier. You must therefore know the needs of your office.

Your office needs comprehensive information on tap. Most of the people who come to your office are, at the outset, strangers to your employer and his salesmen, who need a lot of information in order to serve these potential clients well. They need facts, such as names, addresses, and phone numbers. Equally important, they need a slant on the impending business. Friendliness and genuine interest in your callers are the short cut you use to gain the most information in the shortest time. Facts are important in transacting business. Such things as the human or personal reasons for the proposed business, or the way the caller feels toward what is ahead, or scraps of information about his family problem are invaluable to the salesman in starting to deal with a stranger.

Your office needs goodwill. In the small office, you are usually the single contact between the outside world and your employer. You are receptionist, bookkeeper, telephone operator, and secretary all in one. But busy as you are, one of the most important jobs you have goes beyond these duties; it is to make the public *like your* office. The smaller the organization, the longer the caller is apt to have to wait for your often absent employer. Your friendliness, your interest in the caller, your pride in the office in which you work, are the best possible means to hold his interest and goodwill until he can meet your employer.

In the larger organization, a receptionist is usually the first contact the public has with your firm. The receptionist in your case may or may not be an asset to the firm. Your task is to reinforce the caller's desire to do business with your office and no other. Your knowledge of your employer, his ideas, the achievements of the office, and the things he wants his clientele to know are your tools for making your firm's services seem outstanding.

Understand your public. You will be better able to understand your public if you keep the following points in mind:

1. The majority of your callers are comparatively inexperienced in the buying or selling of property and in other real estate deals. To most of them a real estate transaction is a major undertaking, attempted only a few times during a lifetime.

2. The clientele of a real estate office is comparatively sensitive.

Because the business at hand seems both personal and tremendously important, they expect you to regard it as important, too.

3. People get "keyed up" about the details of a major financial move. They may come in exuberant, upset, very talkative, or down-right angry. It is necessary for you to recognize these temporary moods for what they are—manifestations of nervousness. These outbursts of emotion are not directed against you. So far as the callers are concerned, you are simply a sounding board. If you permit yourself to become upset with them, you add considerably to the salesman's problem in resolving their difficulties.

4. No two individuals are alike; therefore, no single policy on handling them is totally effective. One caller is businesslike, another is sociable. Serving the caller in accordance with his needs makes him think more of your firm.

5. Callers often ask searching questions about your office and the people in it. Usually they are simply satisfying a perfectly normal curiosity. A courteous, casual answer to the seemingly silly or personal question often serves to reassure them in a strange undertaking.

6. Despite the fact that you try to make it clear that you are the secretary, many people will mistake you for a partner in the firm. Your statements to them will be interpreted as official policy. Your way of handling them will be the basis for a large part of their impression of your firm.

Follow established policy on handling callers. No two real estate offices share exactly the same opinion as to which callers should receive personal attention from one of the sales force and which should not. It is vitally important that you and your employer have a complete understanding in this matter.

Usually the employer's policy is flexible. In general, it is good business for the broker or a salesman to talk to every possible caller. The personal contact with a salesman may turn an unlikely prospect into a likely one. When business is slow, or when the broker is breaking in a new salesman, even the least promising caller might provide an opportunity to reinspect some listings or give a new salesman some experience. When business is brisk, serving such customers is often postponed in favor of more probable business.

Some brokers want to meet personally all callers who plan to use the firm's services. This enables them to allot the callers to the proper members of the staff.

In many offices that employ a number of salesmen, prospective customers who do not ask for a specific person are referred to the salesmen in rotation. An understanding with your employer is needed here in the event that the person usually in charge of this phase of operations is not present. The employing broker sets up a program in which on certain days, or at certain hours, or in certain order, each salesman takes his turn "on the floor." You, representing your employer, should understand the setup, keep tabs on whose turn it is, and be prepared to arbitrate if any question arises in his absence.

Role of the Secretary in Meeting the Public

Twofold duty of secretary. In meeting the public you carry a double duty. You serve the public by acting as a gracious and thoughtful hostess. You serve your employer by trying to bring to him only the people he will want to see, by gathering information about the people he will see, and by turning these people over to him in a pleasant frame of mind.

Services common to employer and public. You meet the public adequately when your activity results in both a satisfied employer and a satisfied clientele. The needs of both employer and public have certain touchstones of similarity.

1. Both expect prompt, pleasant attention to their needs. You drop whatever you are doing to serve them graciously.

2. You are expected to know the exact time of appointments, and the exact spelling and pronunciation of names. Your familiary with the names of both the caller and the person with whom he is dealing precludes any possibility of misunderstanding between the people involved or the other salesmen.

3. Both expect your knowledge of their business to remain confidential.

4. Both want to make the best possible use of their time. Your employer wants to handle the maximum amount of business, in comfortable time order, every day. Your callers want ample time for their appointments, as soon as possible, in terms of their convenience.

5. Each wants the undivided attention of the other. Avoidable interruptions, or even the customer's children, can render it almost impossible to do business. You protect them from unnecessary distractions (see page 219).

6. Both are primarily concerned with themselves. You refrain from burdening them with your problems, your ailments, or your woes, even when they go out of their way to tell you of theirs.

Greeting the caller. Greet *every* caller hospitably. Nothing is more trying than having to stand aimlessly in a strange office, waiting to be noticed. Look up and smile the moment a caller enters. Say, "How do you do?" or, "Good morning" or, "Good afternoon." Rise and go to meet the caller if he doesn't approach your desk. If he does not immediately tell you what he wants, offer your service. When you ask, "May I help you?" let your facial expression and the lift of your head show that you are really interested in him.

Learning the purpose of a call. Often the caller will volunteer the nature of his business with the firm after your friendly reception. If he does not, quiz him gently. Here are some usable questions, to be asked with a gracious, interested smile:

"Do you need help in finding a property, or disposing of one?"

*   *   *

Or: "Our staff is momentarily tied up. Would you like me to take down the information on your needs? This will save time when one of the men is free."

*   *   *

Or: "Mr. White is one of our best salesmen. Mr. Green is our specialist on takings listings. Which one would you like to see?"

*   *   *

Or: "I am secretary to Mr. Folger, manager of the firm. I wonder if you would be good enough to tell me what you wish to see him about."

Legitimate buyers and sellers are usually willing to answer such questions frankly. Other callers with real reason to see a member of the firm will usually smile and state their mission.

Handling the caller unwilling to state his business. A few people have confidential business to transact with your employer or one of his salesmen. Others use a touch of mystery to gain a welcome they might not otherwise enjoy. Here are some suggestions for discovering the type of mission without antagonizing the caller:

"Mr. Folger is extremely busy right now. He asked me to postpone everything except the most necessary appointments. If you will tell me what you wish to see him about, I will find out how soon he can see you."

*   *   *

Or: "If you need service, I'm sure one of our men can help you very soon. It *is* property you wished to see us about, isn't it?"

*   *   *

Or: "If your business is of a confidential nature, perhaps you would like to write a note to my employer and put it in a sealed envelope. I will give it to him at the earliest possible moment."

Once in a great while you will be faced with the alternative of being actually rude to the caller, or of having the caller "camp" in your office to wait for the person he wishes to see. If that person is in the office, it is sometimes best to offer the caller a two- or three-minute audience with him in which to state his case. Inform the salesman or your employer of the problem you have. Offer to break up the conference after a few moments if he signals you to do so (see page 22).

Making the caller comfortable. If the caller is someone your firm will want to see, show him where to leave his hat, coat, parcels, and the like. Do not help a man with his coat, since this might embarrass him. If the caller is a woman, help her remove her wraps and hang them up for her. If the caller has to wait any length of time, offer him a newspaper or magazine. Then watch him unobtrusively. A lot of people are so absorbed in the impending business that they cannot settle down to read. If you catch him glancing toward you, lay aside what you are doing and indicate a willingness to talk or listen. A simple question like, "Is there anything I can do for you?" or a statement such as, "It must be wonderful to be able to buy (or sell) a property right now," is usually enough to allow him to express his pent-up thoughts about the proposed business.

If the caller seems content to read or to just sit and wait, do not insist on talking. He may need this respite to prepare his thoughts for the coming appointment.

When the caller wants to talk, guide as much of the conversation as possible toward subjects that might reveal his attitude, his ideas, and his reservations on the business to be undertaken. For the rest, stay with happy generalities, non-controversial news of the day, and favorable statements about your office and your associates. Let the caller do most of the talking. Stay away from anecdotes that your employer or his salesman might later want to tell.

Getting the minimum necessary information. Different employers will expect different amounts of information about callers before talking to them directly. Be sure to know exactly how much information your employer expects you to obtain for him.

In greeting the caller you have a fine opportunity to get the minimum necessary information, which is his name, address, and phone number. When the caller has disclosed that he is a buyer or a seller, you can immediately say, "Let me make a note of your name and address and phone number in case we need to reach you later." Or, "Will you let me know how to reach you in case you do not find what you want today? We are constantly getting fine offerings." Or, "I am responsible for the records of the office. Let me get the necessary information while you are waiting. This will save you time later."

Take a clean sheet of paper, or a file card. Start at the top with a notation of what the caller wants, such as "in market for store building," or, "wishes to sell residence in Brookdale district." Then fill in his name, address and phone number. (Be sure your notation is accurate. Check initials, spelling, and numbers.)

Some customers, particularly complete strangers or people unfamiliar with the firm, are unwilling to give you a means of following them up. In that case, make a notation of what they want at the top of the slip or card, and add the notation, "No information on address or phone number." Give this to your broker or his salesman. Then he is alerted to seek it himself during the interview. Have an understanding with the members of the sales force so that they will either ask the seller to leave this information with you at the end of the visit, or will secure the information themselves and turn it over to you.

Getting additional information. Your employer may prefer to leave additional questions to the sales force. But if his orders are for you to find out everything you can before passing a caller on to him or his salesman, try to find out as much as you can on the following matters

Buyers	*Sellers*
Probable size of investment	Approximate location of property
Approximate down payment	Approximate sales price
Approximate monthly payment	Terms required
Business connections	Condition of property
Preferred type of property	Description of property
Accommodations needed	Legal description
Preference on location	Income from property (if any)
Attitude toward buying	Taxes, assessments (if any)
Any special prejudices	Reason for selling
	Attitude toward selling

Write down all the information you get on an information form or listing form, which your employer will undoubtedly have.

Usually you can gather a lot of useful information by being sincerely friendly and interested in your callers and their proposed move. Amost any conversation that takes place between you will contain fragments of the information your employer wants. A few moments of talk will reveal whether you can question the caller directly.

Introducing the caller. Very often you will have the job of introducing an office caller to the person he will see. You should know at least the basic rules for correct introductions.

It helps to remember that in most introductions you are showing deference to one person by presenting or introducing the other person to him. The rules for doing this are simple: Present a man to a woman; Present a younger person to an older one of the same sex, unless rank or official position is important. As an illustration of this second rule, ordinarily a younger man in a company will be introduced to an older one, showing deference to age, but if the younger man were company president the older man would be introduced to him, showing deference to rank.

Usually, you mention first the person to whom deference is shown; in other words, you mention the woman first if a man and woman are being introduced, the older person first if they are the same sex. Some examples:

> Miss Jones, this is Mr. Smith.
> Mr. Elder, Mr. Younger.
> Mrs. Brown, this is Miss Jones.
> Miss Jones, this is Mr. Elder.

If two people are equal in sex and rank, the name you mention first makes little difference.

If you have not had a chance to speak to your employer or the salesman before you introduce him to a caller, try to brief him on why the caller is there as you are making the introduction. For example: "Mr. Folger, this is Mr. Stewart, who will help you. Mr. Folger is interested in the property advertised in the Gazette this morning." This approach saves having to repeat some questions, and gets the interview started in a definite direction.

If you don't have the caller's name—which should be unusual—you can manage the introduction this way: "This is Mr. Bailey, our manager. Mr. Bailey, this is...I'm sorry, I didn't get your name," or "...this gentleman would like to speak to you about..."

If the caller gives you a business card with his name and company on it, give this to your employer, either before you introduce the caller or as the introduction is being made.

Handling the caller with an appointment. If you have a receptionist, give her a list of appointments each day, and amend it through the day as new appointments are made. This makes it easier for her to handle callers courteously and efficiently.

When a caller with an appointment arrives, notify your employer (or his salesman) immediately unless he is in a conference that cannot be interrupted. Your firm may or may not have private offices for your employer and his salesmen. If there is no reception desk and the caller is already in your immediate presence, it is better to leave him a moment to announce his arrival privately to the broker or salesman. When the office member is ready to see the caller, say, "Will you come with me, Mr. Stewart."

Getting the salesman back to the office for an appointment. It is not uncommon for a caller to arrive for an appointment, only to find the salesman not there. If he is delayed very long, the caller is apt to get impatient and want to leave. After a short time it is permissible to inquire of other people in the office if they know of his whereabouts. If they do, try to reach him by phone. If you cannot reach him, consult your employer about the advisability of having someone else serve the caller. Since a division of commission might be involved if the second salesman transacted business with the caller, this is a decision for the employing broker.

Handling the caller without an appointment. In most offices, the bulk of callers will be people who drop in, either in response to an advertisement, or simply to state their needs. They should be greeted as cordially as the callers who have appointments.

When the broker wants to meet and allot each caller to a salesman, you make the caller comfortable until he can be interviewed. In offices where the broker is himself selling actively, the salesmen usually come forward in rotation to handle the caller. If your office is made up of salesmen specializing in different phases of the business, it is customary to turn the caller over to the man who specializes in the appropriate field.

Interrupting conferences. When an emergency arises that requires you to interrupt a conference, make your interruption as unobtrusive as possible. If you must enter a room, do so quietly. Do not knock at the door.

Type on a slip of paper any message that must be delivered to someone in the conference room. If you need instructions, type the questions. The matter can then be handled with a minimum of distraction of either party from the business at hand.

Terminating a conference. When a visitor overstays his appointment time, so that other business is threatened with neglect, call the member of your office and notify him of his other appointment. Often the broker or salesman himself loses track of time, or is so engrossed in the matter at hand that he is oblivious of the fact that he should be somewhere else, or that someone is waiting for him. If a phone call does not terminate the conference, go to the door (or desk) and, at the first break in the conversation, say, "Your next customer is waiting. Shall I tell him that you will be delayed, or will you tell him yourself?"

Pinch-hitting for your employer. Occasionally it is necessary for your employer or his salesman to leave the caller temporarily for other business. Be ready to step in and act as hostess (not sales person) when such departures are necessary. Leave your desk and go to the caller. Say, "Is there anything I can do for you while you are waiting? Mr. Folger will not be away very long, but perhaps you would like to look around the office (or step outside for a breath of air, or have me bring you a cup of coffee) while he is gone." This bridges the delay in business. It also prevents a group of callers from getting their heads together to think up new problems for the salesman. If they choose to confer, you are near enough to observe their apparent reaction to the matter at hand, and able to report to your employer at once, before he returns to them.

Sidetracking the unwanted caller. The most important thing to remember about the unwanted caller is that some day he may have a real estate need your firm might want to handle. Also consider that it is almost impossible to get rid of the caller sharply without being seen and heard by others. Show that your firm is a fine one by couching your dismissals in kind and understandable language.

Rounding out a good impression. Whenever the opportunity presents itself, add a pleasant note to the call as the visitor leaves. This need not be effusive. If you are busy at your desk, simply look up and say, "Thank you for coming in." Regardless of the nature of their call, this note of appreciation, quietly offered, is pleasing to the caller.

Types of Callers and How to Treat Them

Classification of callers. The callers at your office will divide naturally into distinct classifications, worthy of special treatment in the interest of the business. It is important to know what to look for and how to make the most of your time with them. They fall into three main divisions: (1) people who want to use the firm's services, (2) people who want to sell you something, (3) visitors, solicitors and nuisance callers.

People who want to use the firm's services. In this group are four kinds of callers: (1) the people with whom your firm is working at present (buyers, sellers, loan people, attorneys, escrow officers, advisers, insurance representatives, appraisers, surveyors, architects, building trades people, or anyone else directly concerned with pending business) ; (2) new or strange buyers and sellers; (3) people whose indefinite plans or peculiar needs render them possible rather than probable customers or clients; (4) nuisance callers.

The people in process of doing business with your firm Whether you have actually met these people with whom your firm is dealing or not, they are apt to identify themselves to you by their apparent familiarity with the firm, and a general sort of fellowship and friendliness in their approach to you. It is particularly worth while to try to remember them and place them, through your familiarity with why they are there. Your acceptance and welcome of them makes the contact with your firm just that much more binding.

New buyers or sellers. New buyers and sellers, intent on doing business soon, are the bread and butter of the business. We have already demonstrated how you get minimum and additional information from such callers, and how you handle those who will not state their business. (See pages 19–20.)

Any seller commands special attention. Prime listings are the core of a successful real estate business. No seller should ever be permitted to leave your office feeling that your firm is indifferent to his potential listing. With a little experience you will come to recognize many locations and types of property as readily salable. When a seller comes in to list such a property, or even to consult with your broker about it, it is important to inform your broker or whatever salesman is available, even if he is in conference, that the seller is in the office. If he tells you to get the data, go back to the seller and explain why a member of the sales force cannot see him now. Take down all the information he will give you. Make a definite appointment, at the earliest possible time, for someone to talk to him. Thank him sincerely for coming in, and assure him that your firm is really interested in the property. Tell him you hope he will wait to talk to them before he lists his porperty elsewhere.

How to decide on priority. It takes considerable experience in a real estate office before you learn to spot the people the sales force might prefer to postpone handling. No salesman wants to spend time on deals that cannot be made. On the other hand, most salesmen want to find out for themselves whether a deal is possible or not. There is, of course, no problem if a member of the sales force is in the office and free—in this case all potential buyers or sellers are referred to him for attention.

The problem of selecting the time order in which callers should receive attention arises when business is brisk and the whole force busy. Should you ask the caller to wait? Should you make a future appointment? One of the best ways to determine whether other business should be sidetracked in his favor is to consider the time element. Ask him how soon he needs to find what he is looking for, or how quickly he needs to sell, as the case may be. A need for action within the next ninety days indicates that the caller should receive prompt attention. You can further verify the urgency of his call by asking if his proposed tranaction falls within the firm's usual financial brackets. "About what price and terms do you want to stay within?" and "What sort of price do you expect to get for your property?" are the questions that yield the most revealing answers. If he needs prompt action on a normal piece of business, put him in immediate touch with one of the sales force, even if only long enough to arrange a later appointment. If the caller seems really disappointed that he cannot be served immediately, or if you sense that, lacking service here, he will proceed directly to another office, your next move is to start getting more information on his needs. If the quality of his information indicates that he is on a more or less exploratory mission, you will be able to alert the salesman quite fully before the actual appointment. If the caller is in earnest about getting quick action, you have an opportunity to show him to some extent the advantages of dealing with your office.

Sometimes the best solution in handling callers that cannot be crowded into a busy schedule is to arrange to have your employer talk to them by phone outside of business hours. He, then, can judge whether to rearrange the office schedule to accommodate them.

People who want to sell you something. You see representatives that sell your firm office supplies and maintenance items, or that furnish it with linen service, cleaning service, and the like. You know the needs of the office and therefore do not have to trouble your employer with such matters.

You dismiss in a friendly way all other salesmen unless they handle something worthy of the attention of your employer. If an appointment should be arranged, make it for an hour when you employer is not usually busy. If the item or service is something about which you are in doubt, allow the salesman to demonstrate it to you first, so that you can take the matter up with your employer before granting the salesman time with him.

Visitors. Visitors include friends, relatives, business or club associates, or other people who come on purposes of a social, rather than a business, nature. Upon learning the purpose of the visit, extend the caller a hospitable welcome. If your employer wants to see the caller but is engaged, find out if the caller can wait until your employer is free. If he can, make him comfortable. If your employer does not wish to see the caller, you must cause the visitor to leave. Tell him, "Mr. Folger is extremely busy on a very important deal, and probably will be tied up for a long time. The chances are he cannot see you at all until this business is completed. Is there some way he can get in touch with you then?"

If your employer is unable to see the caller but wants to contact him later, find out where the caller can be reached. Make duplicate slips containing the name, address and phone number of the caller, the preferred time and/or place of contact, and the nature of the call if this is important. Give the caller and the employer each a copy.

A caller soliciting a contribution. You may know from previous experience with your employer the charitable causes to which he contributes. If you do not have this information, ask your employer to give you such a list, with the appropriate donation entered against each item. When a caller asks for a contribution that does not fall within the prescribed limits, tell the caller, "Our firm contributes regularly to a number of charitable causes, up to the limit of its budget. I am sorry that your project does not fall within our program."

If the call is for a donation to a cause on the list, tell the solicitor that you will bring the request to your employer's attention. When your employer signs the check for the donation, give it to the caller and accept whatever receipt or token is offered (stickers, buttons, and the like) and display it during the remaining time of the drive to forestall further requests.

The nuisance caller. Occasionally you will encounter individuals who habitually use any business office unfairly. They repeatedly borrow your phone, or lounge in the comfortable chairs in your waiting room, or they make a habit of dropping in to read your newspaper or to use your stationery for their private correspondence. This is one of the hazards of a street-level office. It can be distracting or embarrassing to both your callers and the sales force, even though the offender does not realize it. It is your job to discourage these nuisance callers as tactfully as possible.

Chapter 3

Your Telephone Technique

THE PROPER USE of the telephone is one of our most important secretarial skills. The successful real estate secretary knows just how to save her employer time and money and how to build good will by the proper use of the telephone.

Telephone Courtesy and Cooperation

People who speak to you over the telephone form a mental picture of you, your personality, and the kind of person you are from the tone of your voice and your manner of speaking to them. From judgment of you they go on to judgment of your employer and your company. The caller who is kept waiting while the telephone rings, who finally hears an uninformative "Hullo," and then is kept waiting again while someone searches for information gets the impression that neither the person he is talking to nor her employer knows very much about business. Help to maintain your employer' reputation for efficiency and cooperation by using the proper telephone techniques.

Your telephone voice. Let the phrase "the voice with a smile" be an accurate description of your telephone voice. It should apply to secretaries even more than to telephone operators. Your voice alone over the telephone must do for you what you can convey by gestures and facial expression in face-to-face conversation. What you could say to a friend by a shrug of the shoulders or a raised eyebrow, you must convey to someone on the telephone by variations in the pitch of your voice and by other means of emphasis.

Do you always remember to keep your voice pleasant? A simple way to help you do so is to take an instant, just as you pick up the telephone, to sit up straight and smile. This small conscious effort makes a world of difference in how your voice comes across to the person on the other end of the line.

Here are a few additional pointers to help you convey your meaning and improve your telephone voice:

1. *Speak distinctly with good pronunciation.* Try to say every syllable of every word properly so that your listener will have no trouble understanding you. If you find that some words are difficult to enunciate, speak those words more slowly to make sure you get them right. Don't be afraid to use your jaw, your tongue, and your lips to form sounds properly. The proper use of your speaking apparatus is the only road to proper speech.

2. *Avoid speaking too slowly or too rapidly.* Did you know that the person speaking at an average rate says about 126 words a minute? Time yourself and see if you are near that average. If you speak much too slowly or rapidly, correct the fault. Naturally, you do not have to say 126 words *every* minute.

3. *Avoid monotony.* Your voice is capable of more than 1,000 inflections: Use them. Vary the pitch of your voice to give certain words emphasis. For example, take the sentence:

"Mr. Jones, I'm so glad you called."

Try emphasizing the words *Mr. Jones* and *so* by speaking them at a slightly higher pitch. This lends your voice variation and makes it much more interesting to the listener.

4. *Do not vary the volume of your voice.* While you want to have variation in the pitch of your voice, you do not want to change the volume too much. Shouting into the phone will annoy the person you are speaking to, and letting your voice drop too low will make it difficult for him to understand you. You should strive to speak in a normal conversational tone with plenty of inflections but not too much variation in voice level

5. *Pause for emphasis after important words.* Some suitable places to pause are after a personalized word of address, after the name of your company and after mentioning special servicer your employer offers.

6. *Keep your voice cheerful as well as businesslike* and remember to say "please" and "thank you." Do not use too cold a tone, but on the other hand do not let your voice seem over-familiar. Strive for a happy medium.

Answer promptly. Always try to answer the telephone on the first ring. The most important reason, of course, is the courtesy toward the caller that this prompt action represents. However, another important reason not often mentioned is the fact that when you let the telephone ring you are tying up a line and wasting not only your employer's time but the caller's as well.

On those occasions when you are unable to answer promptly, you should offer some apology to the caller. A person who calls during the business day knows there is someone in your office and he will insist on letting the phone ring until it is answered. The longer he has to wait, the more irritated he will become.

The apology does not have to be effusive or complicated. Just say, "Mr. Brown's office. I'm sorry to have kept you waiting. I was not at my desk when the phone began to ring." Or perhaps, "I'm sorry to have kept you waiting. I had a call on the other line." A short statement of what kept you is enough.

The wrong number. Basic politeness is essential in the business world, but sometimes it is forgotten in telephone conversations because the caller is unseen. Keep in mind the niceties of social conversation—do not interrupt or cut off the caller's speech abruptly.

A *test* of your good manners is the caller who has the wrong number. You want to be as courteous to such callers as you are to anyone calling on business. Inform the caller politely that he has reached a wrong number, and ask him to check if he has dialed correctly. You might say:

1. "We have no Mr. Barry in this office, sir. This is WInfield 3–1765. Are you sure this is the number you wanted?"

2. "This is WInfield 3–1765. Are you sure you dialed the right number, sir?"

3. "This is not the Prime Manufacturing Company. This is WInfield 3–1765. Is this the number you were trying to reach, sir? This is a real estate office."

One secretary who made the mistake of answering a wrong number in an impatient and rude manner discovered to her dismay that the caller was a good client who had dialed the number by mistake from his list of frequently called numbers. It is good business practice to be polite at all times.

Suppose you get the wrong number when you are placing a call. Check the number immediately, but do not say, "What is your number?" or "Who is this?" Instead ask a tactful question that is likely to get the information you want, such as, "I beg your pardon, but is this REgency 7–4367?" If the reply shows some error was made, express regret in some way, even if you were not responsible. For example, "I am sorry you were disturbed."

Be ready to speak. Have you ever seen someone in the office pick up a telephone to stop its ringing and then hold it in mid-air for several seconds while he continued a conversation with someone in the office before answering? This reduces the person at the other end of the line—member of the staff, potential customer, or even your employer —to repeating "Hello? Hello? Hello?" until the speaker gets around to answering. Avoid this discourtesy.

Be ready to speak when you place a call, too. Know exactly what you want to ask or communicate before you touch your telephone.

When the caller must wait. Sometimes you will be able to answer a caller's questions immediately. More often you will have to get additional information from your files, from someone else in your office, or from some other source. If you believe the wait will be a short one, perhaps the caller will be willing to hold the line while you get the information.

When you must keep someone waiting, do not just say, "Hold on." Give the caller a time he can expect to wait. If he will wait, fine. If not, offer to call back immediately—provided your employer permits this procedure (Some employers do not permit "call-backs." Be guided by office policy in all cases.) You might say:

> "If you will please hold the line, Mr. Daniels, I can have that information for you in a minute."

Place your telephone receiver face down on a book or blotter to keep noise and conversation out while you look up the information. If you have a multiple extension telephone with a "hold" button, you can press this button to keep office activities from being transmitted to the waiting caller.

Give the caller a "progress report" if looking up the information takes longer than anticipated. Let him know that you have not forgotten him and that you are still working on his problem.

When you do have the information and come back to the phone, do not rattle off the information at once. People tend to daydream or let their thoughts wander while they wait for you and it is necessary to draw your listener to you by saying, "Thank you for waiting, Mr. Daniels," or perhaps, "I have that information for you now, Mr. Daniels." It is a good idea to call the person by name in a friendly, cooperative spirit.

When it will take you some time to look up the information, tell the caller approximately when you will call back. You can say:

> "It will take me a little while to compile the information you want, Mr. Daniels. May I call you back in half an hour?"

It is important that you do call back within the specified time. Customers have been lost because secretaries have not been courteous enough to call back as promised.

Proper coverage of your telephone. Another form of business know-how and courtesy is to be sure that your telephone will always be answered. No matter how short a time you will be away from your desk, get someone to answer for you. It is certainly to your advantage to get someone who can handle the call.

Personal calls. Most real estate offices have but a single telephone line. You must therefore realize that when you use the phone to make beauty shop appointments or to call friends and family you are tying up the line and possibly preventing an important call from coming through. When it becomes necessary to make a personal call, keep the conversation brief. And don't become a chronic telephoner.

Too many personal calls are a serious problem in any business, but especially in a business which depends on incoming calls for customer contact.

What to Say and What Not to Say

You may feel a little unsure of yourself on the telephone until you become thoroughly familiar with all the aspects of the real estate business and until you know those people who frequently telephone your employer. A knowledge of what to say and what not to say will help you over the rough spots.

Of course you will always use your best English. Although you may feel that colloquialisms or slang enhance your conversation in your personal life, such expressions have no place in a business office and especially should be avoided in telephone conversations. Even the mildest slang, such as "yeah," or "you bet," should never be used in office telephone conversations.

What to say when you answer the telephone. As stated previously, it is very important to answer the telephone on the first ring if at all possible and to be ready to speak as soon as you pick up the receiver. But what do you say? The phrases used in business are well established and you betray your experience or lack of it by how you use them. Learn to use the right phrase automatically and strengthen the impression of friendly competence you give business callers.

In some instances it may not be necessary to give your own name when you answer the telephone. For example, you may answer a departmental phone, and deal with people who want information that is not likely to be followed up and who do not care who gives it to them. However, if it is probable that you will directly handle the call it is better to identify yourself whether you are answering your own telephone, your employer's, or that of someone else. Use phrases similar to these:

When you answer an outside line: "Brown Real Estate, Miss Anderson."

When a switchboard operator has previously answered the call: "Appraisal Department, Miss Anderson speaking."

Your employer's telephone: "Mr. Brown's office, Miss Anderson speaking."

Your own telephone: "Miss Anderson speaking." If there is any possibility that your employer may be receiving a call on your telephone, as is often the case when he is talking on one extension and a second call comes in for him, answer your own extension with the words, "Mr. Brown's office, Miss Anderson speaking," just as you would answer his extension. If the call should be for your employer you have given the correct reply; if the call is for you the person calling will still know he has reached you.

Some authorities object to the word "speaking" and suggest you just announce your name when you answer the telephone. Others point out that the complete phrase, "Miss Anderson speaking," is a little more gracious and does not really take up much time.

Another point worth noticing is that the possessive "s" is not pronounced on names that end with an "s" sound when you answer the telephone. For example, if you work for Mr. Jones, don't say "Mr. Jones'*ses* office." The possessive "s" is retained on names that do not end with an "s" sound.

Answering someone else's phone. When you answer someone else's phone (other than that of your employer) you say, "Mr. Daniel's office." The word "office" is better than "wire" or "line" because it lends prestige to the person whose phone you are answering, even though he may have only a desk in a corner.

It is unlikely that you will be familiar enough with the other person's work to be able to give the caller a complete answer. You do not want to give out information that might be wrong, so all you can do when answering another person's phone is to explain that the person being called is not in and ask if there is any message you can take. Make a note of the call, the time, and any message left, and give it to the person whose phone you are answering when he returns to his desk.

Answering an unlisted number. Your employer may have a separate telephone with an unlisted number. When you answer such a telephone you do not want to identify your office to any chance caller who might have dialed the number by mistake. The best thing to do is simply to state the telephone number or a part of it when answering an unlisted number. For example, if the number is CY press 7–7000, you might answer the phone by saying:

"Seven-seven-thousand"

Answering a second extension. Nowadays most secretaries have more than one extension to answer. What do you do when you are speaking on one extension and you receive a call on the second? At times your first caller will have finished the business of his call and you may be able to end the call politely by saying something similar to the following:

"Please excuse me, I have a call on my other line."

If you still have business with the first caller, you must not interrupt him in the middle of the sentence. Wait for him to finish what he is saying, and then ask him if he would mind holding the line for a minute. Do not answer the second phone until the first caller has acknowledged your request and given you permission. Then, press the hold button on the first line and answer your second call.

Explain the situation briefly to your second caller, and ask if he would please wait until you have finished your first call. You might say:

"Mr. Brown's office. I have a caller on the other line. Will you please hold the line a minute?"

Sometimes your line may ring while your employer is talking on another extension also connected to your phone. Nothing could be more startling to your employer and the person he is talking with than to hear a bright and cheery, "Mr. Brown's office, Miss Anderson speaking" right in the middle of their conversation. Be very sure you are picking up the correct extension. See that the switching device is switched to the extension that is ringing. Then, when you pick up the receiver, do not speak immediately. Listen to make sure your employer is not talking on the line. When you have double-checked that you are answering the right phone, announce yourself.

Guarding confidential information. Of course you know you should not discuss important business transactions or your employer's personal life, but are you aware of the many minor statements that can be considered a betrayal of confidential information? All too often an untrained secretary will inform a caller, when her empoyer is out of town, "Mr. Johnson isn't in today. He's in Chicago at the XYZ Company." This is giving the caller information he should not have. Content yourself with the standard remark, "Mr. Brown is not in the office today. May I take a message?" or "May I help you?"

Avoid general conversations. All business conversations should be brief and to the point. Chatter about irrelevant matters is not only a waste of your time, but often it may be annoying to the person calling. Answer the caller's questions, volunteer information you may feel he needs to know, and listen to what he has to say.

Although you might inquire about a caller's health if you know he has been seriously ill, or ask about his vacation if he has just returned from an extended trip to Europe, in general, matters not related to business should be left out of the conversation altogether. Remember, though, you don't want to be so brief as to sound discourteous. Conciseness and politeness must go hand in hand in a business telephone call.

When your employer won't call back. Your employer may sometimes inadvertently embarrass you by failing to return a call. What do you say when the caller irately demands to know if you have given your employer his message?

This is a situation that demands all your secretarial tact. You must never imply that your employer is unwilling, or too busy, or too uninterested to return the call. If it becomes necessary to take the burden of the caller's displeasure on your shoulders by implying you did not delive. the message, do so. Usually you can model your reply on the following statements:

> "I'm sorry, Mr. Smith. Mr. Brown has been in a meeting all afternoon and probably did not see your message."
> "I'm sorry, Mr. Smith. Mr. Brown has not returned as yet and has not received your message."

If Mr. Smith has called back two or three times and you know Mr. Brown is just avoiding calling back, ask Mr. Brown what you should say the next time Mr. Smith calls.

How to handle unwanted calls. Once in a while you will receive a call from an individual who has no legitimate business with your office but who is for one reason or another making a "nuisance call." You must not be rude to such people. On the other hand, you cannot allow them to take up too much of your time. Explain politely that there is no way in which you can help the caller and end the conversation as quickly as you can. The longer you let a person like this talk, the more involved he gets in his personal problem and the harder it becomes to get rid of him by any means short of actual rudeness.

Say good-bye pleasantly. Sometimes a call that has been otherwise well handled is spoiled by a curt ending and the noisy setting down of the receiver. End your call on a polite note without lingering on the phone any longer than necessary. By a careful use of words you can end a telephone conversation quickly without hurting the feelings of the person calling. Here are some examples of things you might say:

> "I hope I have been of help to you, Mr. Harvey. Thank you for calling."

"I'm sure you will be happy with our service, Mr. Harvey. Thank you for calling."

"If you want any further information, Mr. Harvey, don't hesitate to call again."

Then say "Good-bye, Mr. Harvey," and wait for him to hang up. Don't put your receiver down until you are sure the caller is off the line; you might cut him off while he still has something to say.

Suit what you say to end a call to the particular caller, but never say simply "good-bye," and hang up.

Handling calls in your employer's absence. In handling telephone calls in your employer's absence, find out who the caller is and what he wants and then see if there is any way in which you can handle the problem. Many times you will only be able to take a message until your employer's return, but at other times you may be able to connect the caller with someone else in the office who can help him, or you will be able to settle the matter yourself.

How to Screen Calls

Your duty in screening calls is to decide which you can answer, which someone else in the office can answer, and which ones only the employer himself can answer. Remember that it is just as important to put through those calls which only he can answer as it is to stop those someone else can handle. You are not being efficient if you "protect" out of business!

What to ask. The two questions you must ask in screening calls are "Who's calling?" and "What do you want?", but you cannot use such blunt language. Learn to phrase these questions in a tactful manner so that you will not offend the caller.

Use one of the first three examples below to find out "Who's calling?" and, once you have learned the caller's name, use the last example to answer the equally important question, "What do you want?"

1. "May I tell Mr. Brown who is calling, please?"
2. "Mr. Brown would like to know who is calling, please."
3. "Could you tell me who is calling, please, so that I can announce your call to Mr. Brown."
4. "May I tell Mr. Brown what you are calling about, Mr. Johnson?"

When you use tactful phrases such as these, you are asking for Mr. Brown, not for yourself. Most callers who do not understand why a secretary should want to know who is calling understand that her employer wants to know.

You may work for a very busy man who is bothered by many unwanted calls. In such a case he may want you to say, "He is not in at the moment. May I tell him who called?" at all times. When you give the names and messages to him (either at once or at regular specified intervals during the day) he will then decide whether he wants to call back or not. As mentioned, this procedure is used only for the very busy man who asks you to turn aside all calls. It is not customary in real estate offices where there are few nuisance calls.

When the caller won't identify himself. Most callers will reply politely to your questions. Every now and then, though, you will get someone who will not answer you. He will refuse to give his name or his business. You mut be polite to these people, but if you have been told to screen calls, you cannot connect them with your loss. Keep your voice friendly and make one of the following replies:

> "I'm sorry, sir, but Mr. Brown won't take calls if I can't tell him who's calling."
>
> "I'm sorry, sir, but I can't connect you if I can't announce who is calling."

If the caller does not respond you have no choice except to end the call and let the person call again if he is really anxious to speak with your employer.

When the caller won't state his business. Sometimes an individual will give his name and then refuse to tell you what he is calling about. He may say, "Al Brown knows who I am," or "This is an urgent matter that won't wait; connect me with Mr. Brown at once."

If you have been told to screen calls, don't let such high pressure tactics scare you. The person who insists his business is too important to trust to the secretary is almost always afraid that if he admits what it is he is calling about, he won't be connected. You might tell such a caller:

> "I'm sorry, but Mr. Brown has instructed me to announce what a caller wants to speak to him about before I connect him," or,

"I'm sorry, but Mr. Brown isn't taking any calls just now. If you will leave your number and tell me what you wish to talk to him about, I'll ask him to call you back."

If this does not elicit the information you need, you can suggest that the caller write to Mr. Brown, marking the envelope *Personal*. If he doesn't want to do that, you can only insist that he leave his number and let Mr. Brown call him back. You can then tell Mr. Brown who called and he will use his own judgment about returning the call.

There probably are several people to whom your employer will talk at any time and who should be connected as soon as you hear their names. If you are a new secretary you cannot be expected to know who these people are. You will learn through experience or by having your employer tell you to put calls for certain individuals through immediately.

When others can handle the call. There would be little purpose in screening calls if you were merely to determine who is calling and what his business is and then just put the call through to your employer or a salesman. Very often others in the office could—and should—handle the call. Other times you can take care of the matter yourself.

From what the caller says you may realize that all he wants is an answer to simple questions about your business. For example,

> "Mr. Brown's office. Miss Anderson speaking."
> "Is Mr. Brown there?"
> "May I tell Mr. Brown who's calling?"
> "This is Mr. Harvey."
> "May I tell Mr. Brown what you are calling about, Mr. Harvey?"
> "I wanted to get the average price of new one-family homes in the northeast section of town."
> "That price would be about $30,000, Mr. Harvey. Is there anything else I can help you with?"
> "No. Thank you."

You have handled the call without disturbing others in the office.

When you realize that the caller's problem should be handled by some other department, transfer the call to that department. You might say:

> "Mr. Brown no longer handles listings, Mr. Harvey. May I transfer your call to Mr. Baillie in our Sales Department?"
> "Mr. Richards in our Appraisal Department would be able to answer

your question in more detail than Mr. Brown. Let me transfer your call to him."

Always be sure to explain to the caller what you are about to do and wait until he has acknowledged your explanation.

Keep a Record of Telephone Calls

No matter how good you believe your memory is, there is one essential rule about taking a message over the telephone—WRITE IT DOWN. Messages must be accurate. In addition, you will probably be called upon to check the telephone bill, or at least to account for those calls and charges made over your telephone and that of your employer.

Get names and questions accurately. Keep a pad and pencil next to the telephone, or else use your shorthand notebook to record messages. Although you may feel shy about asking the caller to repeat, remember that your embarrassment will be much greater if you give your employer a garbled or incomplete message.

Ask the caller to spell his name for you if you do not recognize it. Be sure to get his company affiliation if any, and if the company name is unfamiliar or unusual let him spell that, too. Write down the message as he gives it to you and then read it back to him to be sure you have it accurately. Repeat his telephone number so that your employer can call back without difficulty.

A little care and attention to taking messages accurately can save time and embarrassment later.

Toll calls. Keep a record of the long distance toll calls you make. This record will help you in checking the telephone bill, if this is part of your job. In many companies the switchboard operator keeps track of these calls. Even if the company switchboard operator is responsible for keeping track of long distance calls, remember that you must inform her when you place a long distance call yourself instead of placing it through her. It is especially important to let her know when you have initiated a long distance call which was not completed. There is no charge for such calls.

Keep your own telephone list. Your telephone directory can provide a wealth of information both in the listings and in the classified section. However, you should also have your own desk list or small booklet of the numbers you call most frequently. Such numbers should include business numbers your employer calls often; emergency numbers, such as the fire department and police department; your employer's personal numbers, such as his family and doctor; and, in large concerns, it may include the extensions of people in other offices. Having these numbers in a small desk directory will save time you would otherwise spend in looking them up.

Get Proper Service from Your Telephone

You can actually save your company money by using your telephone properly. The yearly telephone bill in many companies amounts to thousands of dollars and a percentage of that bill is caused by inefficient telephone use.

Keep telephone lines clear. Every business must try to keep its telephone lines clear so that incoming business calls can get through, and so that calls can go out. This is especially true in real estate where the telephone is a basic means of communication with clients.

How to place a local call for your employer. The usual procedure when you place a call for your employer is to get the person who is being called on the wire before connecting your employer. For example, suppose you are calling Mr. Rubinstein for your employer, Mr. Brown. After dialing the correct number you will get Mr. Rubinstein's secretary on the wire, and you say, "Is Mr. Rubinstein there, for Mr. Albert Brown of Brown Brothers, Inc.?" Mr. Rubinstein's secretary will put her employer on and trust to your good judgment to see that Mr. Brown comes on the line promptly. When Mr. Rubinstein comes on the line, say to him, "Here is Mr. Brown, Mr. Rubinstein," and establish the connection between the two men at once.

Practice varies from company to company and you may find that your employer prefers to hold the line himself once you have made the initial contact with the other secretary. This latter system wastes your employer's time because there is to no telling how long it may take for Mr. Rubinstein to come on the line. However, a good secretary complies with her employer's wishes.

When the call is being made to a high official or to a close friend or other person to whom your employer wants to show deference, it is appropriate for your employer to wait on the line himself after the initial contact is made.

Be sure that your employer is at hand and ready to take the call as soon as contact is established. It is discourteous to keep the other man waiting.

When another secretary puts through a call to your employer, the procedure is reversed. You put your executive on the line at once and trust to her cooperation and competence to see that he is not kept waiting. When your employer exchanges calls frequently with certain people you will get to know their secretaries and it will be easy for you and the other secretary to connect the two businessmen simultaneously.

How to place long-distance call. In most sections of the country it is possible to place long distance calls by direct dialing. You dial an area code number consisting of three numbers and then dial the desired number. If direct dialing is possible in your locality, you will find in the local directory the code numbers for the various sections in the country and complete directions as to how to use them. All dialing calls are station-to-station. They cannot be person-to-person because there is no way of knowing who will answer the ring any more than there is in a local call.

Where direct dialing is not possible, you must place the call through the long distance operator. Whether you speak directly to the telephone company operator or go through your company switchboard operator, there is certain information the operator must have to place the call.

The first thing to mention when you place a long distance call is the *type* of call—collect call, mobile call, conference call, credit card call, or the like. The operator must record information differently for each of these calls, so this is the first thing she needs to know. Types of call are explained more fully beginning on page 44.

Next, tell the operator

1. The city and state
2. The number in that city
3. The person's name if the call is person-to-person

If you don't know the number of the person you wish to call, the operator will find it for you.

Stay on the line so that you can answer the questions the operator may ask. One of the things she will want to know is the number from which you are calling. After you tell her, if you want the party called to know who is calling, say, "Operator, please tell the party that Albert Brown is calling from Denver."

Save money on long distance calls. Avoid making unnecessary long distance calls. Many times a letter or telegram will serve your purpose, particularly when you know it will take some time for the person you plan to call to compile the information you want. If the call is about an urgent business matter that demands an immediate answer, or if the matter requires discussion with an individual in another city, a long distance call is the best way to handle the situation.

Although a station-to-station call is supposedly cheaper than a person-to-person call, there are times when the opposite is true. When you want to speak to a particular individual and you are not sure that he will be at his desk, do not place a station-to-station call. If it takes much time to locate him, or if he isn't in the office, your call will cost a great deal more than a person-to-person call would have cost.

Person-to-person calls can be made directly to an individual or else to an extension number. Charges begin when the individual or extension number is reached. Although a secretary may answer the phone, the charges would begin only after the individual called is connected. In the meantime you could not carry on a conversation with the secretary. If you agree to talk to the secretary instead of the individual you are trying to reach, the long distance operator must be told and charges then would begin when you were connected with the secretary.

Be brief and to the point on a long distance call since you are being charged by the minute for the service. People calling your office will appreciate it also if you keep this principle in mind when you receive a long distance call.

When you receive a long distance call. Be considerate of the person placing the call. Be as brief and to the point as possible to cut down on charges.

If the call is a person-to-person call to your employer, do not offer to hold the line. Ask the *operator* to hold the line until you locate your employer. She will hold from three to five minutes and charges will not begin until your employer is on the line. Try to find him as quickly as possible in any case because it is impolite to keep the caller waiting any longer than absolutely necessary.

How to transfer a call. You will sometimes receive calls that should be handled by someone else in the company. These suggestions will help you transfer the call properly.

1. Never abruptly transfer a call without telling the caller what you about to do. Say, "Mr. Woods in the Loan Department will be able to help you. If you will hold the line just a moment I'll transfer your call to him."

2. Signal the operator by touching the cradle button of your telephone in a definite 1, 2, 3, release pattern. That is, hold for three counts and release for one and repeat. *Continue the pattern until the operator answers.* If you jiggle the cradle button quickly and impatiently, the operator will not see the switchboard light. If you hold the cradle button down too long, you may be disconnected.

3. Never go to another telephone or another extension and ask the operator to transfer the call on the first telephone. This habit makes the transfer difficult for the switchboard operator, particularly on a large switchboard.

When not to transfer a call. It is usually impossible to transfer a call which has originated within your own company. The person making such a call will have to hang up and dial the proper extension.

A call from the outside should never be transferred just to get rid of it. Unless you know the exact person who can help the caller, offer to take down his questions and have someone call him back. Then immediately find the proper person to help him and see that the callback is made.

Even when you know who should handle the call, there are times when it would be better to take down the problem and have someone call back. An irate customer who has had his call transferred several times before is in no mood to repeat his story again. In such cases you may be able to soothe him by assuring him that someone will call back within a short time with the necessary information.

Telephone Services and Equipment

The telephone is truly a marvelous instrument. There are many types and kinds of service available which enable you to place calls under varying conditions. In addition there are devices and equipment which will make your job as secretary easier. The different kinds of calls and some of the equipment available are described here. If you have a special telephone problem, consult the telephone company. They will recommend those devices that will increase the usefulness of the telephone system within your own company.

Station-to-station and person calls. These two types of long distance calls have already been discussed.

Messenger calls. When you must reach someone who does not have a telephone, you may authorize the operator at the called point to send a messenger for the person with whom you want to talk. You must pay the cost of the messenger's services, which is in addition to the regular person-to-person charge for the call, whether or not the call is completed.

Appointment calls. Your employer may specify a certain time when he will talk with a person. In that case you can place an appointment call and the telephone operator will try to put the call through at the exact time. The charge is the same as for a person-to-person call.

Conference calls. Suppose your employer wants to discuss something with several other people (any number up to ten) who are in different cities. He can place a conference call and he will be connected simultaneously with a number of other stations. He and the others will be able to talk back and forth over long distance just as though they were grouped around a conference table. No special equipment is required.

Perhaps he wants to speak to a gathering of people in different cities instead of to individuals. The telephone company will install loudspeaker equipment, appropriate for the number of listeners. A control dial permits volume adjustment.

When you arrange a conference call, ask to be connected with the Conference Operator and explain to her the setup you want.

Overseas and ship-to-shore calls. It is possible to call almost all important cities in Europe and many points in Africa, Asia, Australia, Central and South America, the Bahamas, Bermuda, Cuba, Haiti, the Dominican Republic, the Hawaiian Islands, Iceland, Jamaica, the Philippines, and Puerto Rico from any telephone in or connected with the Bell System. You can get rates for this service from the long-distance operator.

There is also a ship-to-shore telephone service by means of which your employer can transact business even when he is at sea—provided the ship is equipped for this service and can make effective radio contact with the shore station. Rates for ship-to-shore calls depend upon the location of the ship at the time the call is made. The long-distance operator can give you full information.

Collect calls. It is possible to make a telephone call and have the person called pay for it; he must agree to accept the charges before the call will be put through on that basis. If someone calls you collect, your company policy will determine whether or not you can accept the call. Some firms will accept any collect call; others will accept collect calls only from their own employees or salesmen. If a collect call comes in for your employer and you do not know his wishes, ask him whether or not he will accept the call before you tell the operator to put it through.

Telephone conveniences. Some telephone devices that secretaries have found to be useful are described here. The telephone company will be glad to help you with any telephone problem you may have. Just describe your difficulty and they will recommend the plan best suited to your needs.

The button telephone: Button telephones are furnished in one, four, and six button sets. Some of these lines may be outside lines; others may be inter-communication lines within the company. The buttons can be wired to do various jobs.

When there is more than one line connected to your telephone, you can select the particular line on which you wish to speak by depressing the proper button. An arrangement can be made that will cause the button for any one of your lines to light up intermittently when the line is ringing. These lights can be wired to glow steadily while you are talking so that other persons having the same line connected to their telephones will know that that particular line is in use.

The buttons can also be used to switch calls from one telephone to another when both instruments are connected to the same line. A *hold button* will hold a call on one line while you use the same telephone to place or receive a call on another line. The caller on the first line cannot hear your conversation on the second line after the hold button has been depressed.

A *signal button* can be wired so that when you press it, it signals a person on another phone to pick up the call you have received. Your employer may use this signal button to summon you into his office for dictation, or he may signal you to indicate he wants to talk to you on an inter-office connection.

Signal buttons may also be installed on a separately mounted panel, consisting of either a single button or of four or eight buttons. Signals can be either audible or visible. Visual signals can be obtained in various colors to indicate which line a call is on. Separately mounted signal buttons and signal lamps can be attached to your desk, the wall, or any flat surface.

A *cut-off feature* can be used to exclude other telephones connected to the line on which you are talking. This arrangement assures privacy for important calls.

The call director: In some offices, a six button telephone will not handle all the lines in the office. Call directors are available in eighteen and thirty button models. The buttons on the call director can be wired to do any job that buttons on a button telephone can do.

The speakerphone set: The speakerphone set consists of a microphone and a loud-speaker and enables the telephone user to carry on a telephone conversation without lifting the receiver from its rest. The microphone picks up the individual's voice and the loud-speaker broadcasts it. By sitting in a group around the microphone, several people can engage in a telephone conversation at once.

Automatic answering and recording set: By means of this device messages can still be delivered and received even though both you and your employer are out of the office.

Before you leave the office, let us say for an emergency, you would set the machine on answer and record, and leave a message for anyone who called in your absence. When you return to the office you simply set the machine to hear the messages that have been left.

It is possible also to set the machine so that only your messages are given to the callers but they are unable to record a message of their own. This feature is useful when you wish those who call to know something that does not require a reply.

Chapter 4

Reminder Systems and Practices

Every secretary has the responsibility of seeing that certain things are done at certain times. Therefore, the need for an orderly and infallible system of "reminders" is obvious. Reminders are known by various names: calendars, tickler systems, "bring-up" files, future files, follow-up files. For any reminder system to function properly, the secretary *must* refer to it each day—no system is more perfect than the person handling it.

The practices described in this chapter fall into two parts: (1) how to make and use calendars and (2) follow-up files. Neither is a substitute for the other, although in many instances there is a choice as to which to use. For example, if certain information is to be received by a specific date, you can put a notation on the calendar or a memorandum in the follow-up files.

How to Make and Use Calendars

Calendars that you should keep. Three separate calendars are usually required.

1. *Your own calendar.* Use either a standard desk calendar pad or a yearbook for your calendar, with 15-minute or 30-minute time divisions. Many secretaries prefer desk calendars because the day's activities are then before their eyes constantly.

Enter notations of your own duties and business appointments as well as your employer's appointments and the things that you will have to remind him about. Enter any time-consuming task that must be done by a certain date sufficiently in advance to permit it to be done on time.

2. *Your employer's calendar.* Your employer will use a standard desk calendar pad or a yearbook. Many executives prefer a yearbook because its contents are not visible to callers. The calendar or yearbook must be large enough to enable you to note the caller's affiliation and purpose of the call.

Enter all of your employer's appointments and the important days, such as his wife's birthday, that he should remember. If the important days are not noted on his calendar, he may inadvertently make conflicting engagements. Do not enter items that are merely reminders to you, such as the date certain checks should be written. Although you enter reminders before the actual date on your own calendar, it usually is not necessary to do this on your employer's calendar. Watch his calendar closely for appointments he makes without telling you.

3. *Pocket memo calendar.* Note in a small pocket memo book the engagements that might conflict with future appointments that your employer himself makes. This memo book is for your employer to take with him to meetings, luncheons, on trips, and the like, where questions of future appointments might arise.

When to make up the calendars. Keep a list of events that go on the calendars year after year (see checklist of recurring items). Early in October, enter all of the recurring items, events, and engagements for the forthcoming year in the calendar for the next year. If your employer makes important engagements far in advance, you may have to make up the yearly calendars even earlier. In preparing calendars, work from the list and not from the current year's calendar, because the dates for the events change. For example, if board meetings are held on the first Monday of every month, the actual dates vary from year to year. In making an entry, be certain that the date is not a Sunday or a holiday.

Enter additional appointments or things to do as soon as you learn about them.

Checklist of recurring personal and business items. Here is a list of recurring items that a secretary usually enters on the appropriate calendars for each year. You may not be concerned with some of them and will probably add many others that apply specifically to your position. If dates usually call for presents or cards, enter them about ten days before the date as well as on the date.

Family Dates

Anniversaries

Birthdays of all members of your employer's family and any other birthdays that he likes to remember

Mother's Day

Father's Day

Holidays

Christmas. As the purpose of this item is to bring up the gift and card lists, the entry date depends on the shopping conditions in your locality and on the number of presents. Six weeks is the average time required. Also enter the dates on which presents and cards should be mailed.

Easter

Election Day

Religious holidays

Thanksgiving

St. Valentine's Day

Meetings

Real estate board meetings

Club meetings

Committee meetings (company and outside activities)

Stockholders' annual meeting

Payment Dates

Contributions, under pledges or otherwise, to religious and charitable organizations. If weekly, enter each Friday as the date on which to draw the check.

Insurance premium due dates

Periodic payments, such as salaries to servants, allowances to children, tuition payments, and the like. If the date the check should be sent falls on a day the office is closed, enter it on the preceding day.

Collection Dates

Coupons to be clipped

Dividends to be received

Interest to be collected on mortgages owned and on notes receivable.

Renewal Dates

Real estate and city licenses

Automobile license

Hunting and fishing license

Subscriptions to periodicals

Tax Dates

Federal taxes. Enter the items in your calendar in advance of the due dates to allow ample time for preparation of returns and to note bank balance before the tax payment dates.

State and local taxes.

Use of tickler card file with calendars. The use of a 3″ by 5″ card tickler file will reduce the necessary work in preparing a calendar. A card tickler file has a tabbed guide for each month of the year and 31 tabbed guides, one for each day of the month. The daily guides are placed behind the current month guide. Memoranda are made on cards, and the cards are filed behind the daily guide according to the date on which the matter is to be brought up.

Recurring items can be put on one card, and the card can be moved from week to week, month to month, or year to year. Thus, if a certain check is made out each Friday, you can make one card and move it each week, instead of making 52 entries in the calendar. Furthermore, you can put all necessary information on the card so that you, or anyone else, can make out the check and mail it without referring to any other material.

A card tickler file *does not* take the place of a calendar for noting appointments. All engagements and appointments, even regularly recurring ones, should be entered on the calendar; otherwise, whenever you want to make an appointment for your employer, you will have to look not only at the calendar but also at the tickler cards. Refer to both the calendar and the tickler file each morning.

Indefinite date reminders. An executive might want to be reminded periodically of a particular matter until it has been acted upon. For example, he might want to be reminded to go over a certain file of material. This kind of item should be included from time to time in the typed schedule of appointments and things to do that you place daily on your employer's desk. There are two ways of reminding yourself of the item:

1. Make a notation on *your* calendar at short intervals.

2. If you keep a card tickler file, note the item on a card and move the card from time to time.

Matters to come to the employer's attention in connection with any unscheduled but definite event are best handled by placing a reminder memo in an appropriately labeled folder for the event. For example, if your employer wants to be reminded to call upon a certain person the next time he goes to Chicago and the date of his trip has not been scheduled, make a folder marked "Chicago Trip" and put in it the necessary reminder memo. When the date of the trip is settled, give your employer the entire folder, or include the item in a typewritten schedule of matters pertaining to the trip. If the event is of such rare occurrence that you would need a reminder that there is such a folder, do not use a folder but make the notation on your calendar or in the card tickler file as described above.

How to remind your employer of appointments and things to do. Each morning place on your employer's desk a typed schedule of his appointments, showing the name of the caller, his affiliation, purpose of the call, and any additional pertinent information. See Figure 1 for form in which to type the appointment list. Memorandum paper, about 6" by 9", is desirable for this purpose. At the time of each appointment give your employer any material he will need for it.

To remind your employer of a task that he should do, place the file on his desk. If he has said that he wanted to do a certain thing in connection with the matter, attach a reminder to the file. For example, suppose he told you, "I want to wire Robertson on Friday if we don't hear from him." On Friday you type a memo, "You wanted to wire

---

```
           APPOINTMENTS FOR WEDNESDAY,   JUNE 28, 19 . .

  9:00 A.M.     Mr. Stevens to meet Mr. Harrington at the Simmons property
 10:00 A.M.     Call Mr. Netherland about the closing


  2:00 P.M.     Lunch with Mrs. Harrison about mortgage

  3:00 P.M.     Meet wife at office

  4:00 P.M.     Visit to the doctor
```

Figure 1. Daily Appointment List.

Robertson," and attach it to the Robertson file before placing it on your employer's desk. If possible, draft the wire and give that to him with the file folder.

You may know that a closing is to take place on a certain day and that various papers will have to be checked before then. If you think the time is getting short in which to complete the checking, remind him of the closing date. Similarly, if you know that an appraisal report must be submitted by a certain date, remind him sufficiently in advance to allow time for typing the report.

Some executives make a practice of calling their secretaries into their office daily to discuss pending matters and things to be done. This is the ideal arrangement. For this discussion, you take with you a list of things to do and any material pertaining to them. Your employer will give you his instructions on one matter after another.

Reminders showing appointments for a month. Many executives like to see the month's engagements at a glance. There are

NOVEMBER

	Sunday, 6th	Sunday, 13th	Sunday, 20th	Sunday, 27th
	Monday, 7th	Monday, 14th	Monday, 21st	Monday, 28th
Tuesday, 1st	Tuesday, 8th	Tuesday, 15th	Tuesday, 22nd	Tuesday, 29th
Wednesday, 2nd	Wednesday, 9th	Wednesday, 16th	Wednesday, 23rd	Wednesday, 30th
Thursday, 3rd	Thursday, 10th	Thursday, 17th	Thursday, 24th Thanksgiving Day	
Friday, 4th	Friday, 11th	Friday, 18th	Friday, 25th	
Saturday, 5th	Saturday, 12th	Saturday, 19th	Saturday, 26th	

Figure 2. Appointment Calendar for a Month.

```
                          APPOINTMENTS
Nov.15 Mon. -                    - Sales meeting
             - 12:00 Noon        - Preliminary Meetg. - Cleve. R. C.
             -  3:00 P.M.        - Apex Bd. Meetg.

 "  16 Tue. -  1:30 P.M.         - Internal Revenue Dept.

 "  17 Wed. -  5:30 P.M.         - Cath. Char. - Parlor B - Cleve. Athletic Club
             -  6:00 P.M.        - ? Union Club-Ohio Pub. Expenditure Coun.-WTH

 "  18 Thu. -  6:30 P.M.         - R.E.Board Dinner - Lake Shore Country Club

 "  19 Fri. - 12:15 P.M.         - Amer. Trade Assn. Executives - Public Libr.
             -

Nov.22 Mon. -                    - Sales meeting

 "  23 Tue. -

 "  24 Wed. -  3:00 P.M.         - Closing - Hogan's Office - Hotel sale

 "  25 Thu. -                    - Thanksgiving

 "  26 Fri. -  Evening           - Apex Dance - Lake Shore Ctry. Club

Nov.29 Mon. -                    - Sales meeting
             -                   - Check to W. Shaw

 "  30 Tue. -  1:30 P.M.         - Accompany Mr. Thomas to Corporation Counsel's
                                       Office
Dec.1 Wed. -                     - Sandusky

 "  2 Thu. -                     - Talk at Cincinnati - Wm. Campbell

 "  3 Fri. -                     -

Dec.6 Mon. -                     - Sales meeting

 "  7 Tue. -
             -  6:00 P.M.        - Loyal Service Club - Carter Hotel

 "  8 Wed. -                     - Sandusky

 "  9 Thu. -                     -

 " 10 Fri. - 10:00 A.M.          - VFW Meeting - Hotel Cleveland
```

Figure 3. Four-Week Schedule.

calendars designed for this purpose, usually on cardboard about 9″ by 11″. Figure 2 is an illustration of such a calendar. Note that under the arrangement of dates on this calendar, every Sunday in the month is on the top row, every Monday on the next row, and so on.

Figure 3 is an example of a four-week schedule, which is typed each week. Note that it lists holidays, evening social functions, and things to be done, as well as appointments. If the schedule is to remain on your employer's desk, he might like to have it mounted on cardboard to facilitate handling. Either staple or paste the corners to the cardboard. When your employer is planning to be away from the office for a week or so, he usually likes to know what is on his calendar for that period before he completes his plans. Use the set-up shown in Figure 3 for this purpose.

Special reminders. Some secretaries have found it useful to give an employer a 3″ by 5″ or 4″ by 6″ reminder card each evening when he leaves the office. This contains not only a list of activities for the following day, but aslo reminders of certain things that he should do at home. Figure 4 is a typical reminder card for a man who lives in the suburbs.

Reminder for THURSDAY, MARCH 7, 19--
Tell Mrs. Adams that her draperies will be delivered Mon.
Get exact dimensions of kitchen cabinet
8:30--Parent-Teacher gathering at Westchester High
Pack bag for Dinner at Waldorf (White Tie)

10:30---Mr. John Brown
12:30---Luncheon for Mr. Robert St. John, Pres, Reynolds
            Inv. Assn., at Advertising Club
 2:30---Mr. Smith's office: 250 Broadway, Room 1200
          re: 1 Fifth Avenue project
Evening
7:30--- Reception, Grand Ballroom Waldorf-Astoria
8:30--- Dinner in honor of Mr. Johnson

Figure 4. Special Reminder Card.

Tickler cards for employer's property. If your employer owns various pieces of real property, a separate tickler card file should be kept of all dates on which you must take certain action or check on action to be taken by someone else. The following are the items for which such cards may be made.

1. Interest on mortgages payable. Such a card would show (1) the interest due date, (2) the amount of interest, (3) to whom payable, (4) where to send the check, (5) a brief description of the property mortgaged, and (6) the amount of the mortgage. See Figure 5.

```
Int. due quarterly--15th of Jan., Apr., July, & Oct.

Amt. $200.  Make check to:  Estate of Harvey Adams
            Send check to:  Mr. Ralph Jones
                            Attorney for Estate of
                            Harvey Adams
                            75 Fifth Avenue
                            New York, N.Y.

Mortgage for $20,000 on 71st Street Dwelling
```

Figure 5. Interest Payment Reminder.

2. Payments to be made on the principal of the mortgage. These payments are known as amortization payments (see page 273).

3. Tax payment dates. More will be said about real estate taxes on page 272

4. Insurance premium dates.

The same kinds of date cards will be necessary for mortgages owned by your employer. The interest and amortization payment cards tell you when payments should be received. The tax cards enable you to follow up the mortgagee to be sure that taxes are paid. The insurance cards remind you to see that insurance policies are renewed and the premiums are paid. Your employer, as mortgagee, is vitally interested in seeing that the mortgagor meets all of his obligations on time.

You may use either of the following methods of operating this tickler file

1. File the cards according to dates shown on them, using a tab

for each month. Keep sufficiently ahead of the dates to do whatever is necessary, such as sending out reminder notices to mortgagors.

2. File the cards under the proper monthly tab, and in addition have daily tabs (1–31) for the current monthly. Several days before the beginning of each month, place the cards for the month under the daily guide for the day on which you want to be reminded to take action. For example, on June 20, take out all of the July cards and place them under the daily guides in reminder order. Thus, you might place a card showing interest due from a mortgagor on July 15 under July 5, thus reminding yourself ten days in advance of the due date to send out the notice of interest due. When the interest is paid, the card is put back in its proper place under the tab "July."

Other "date" card files. In most real estate offices, some records are kept of expiration and due dates. For example, the mortgage broker has files of expiration dates of mortgages. The secretary to the building manager may have several date card files—for mortgage payments and interest on mortgages (see page 273), for tax payment dates, and for expirations of insurance policies (see page 273). If the duties connected with these dates files are routine, you do not need a reminder other than the file itself.

Follow-up Files

Matters that ordinarily call for follow-up. There are numerous activities in a real estate office for which a regular follow-up routine must be established. For example, rent collections, expirations of exclusive listings, expirations of protective clauses in exclusive listings, require follow-up, as do prospects who might be interested in new listings, owners who might be interested in listing their properties and others. Follow-ups of this nature may be the responsibility of someone other than the secretary, but in many offices the secretary is responsible for some or all of this work.

Here, however, we are concerned only with the general follow-up files that might be used for reminding the secretary to follow up such matters as:

1. Correspondence or memoranda awaiting answers.

2. Matters that are referred to other executives or departments for information or comment.

3. Orders placed.

4. Items that come up for periodic consideration, such as tax matters, contract renewals, and the like.

5. Promises to be carried out in the future.

For these types of follow-up problems, the systems described below are generally practical.

Follow-up methods. In any tickler or follow-up system one of two methods must be used: (1) The material to come up for action at a certain date must be placed in the tickler or (2) a notation or reminder of that material must be placed in the tickler while the *material itself* remains in its proper place *in the regular files.* The latter method is preferable for the secretary and is the only one described here.

Equipment for follow-up system. Numerous styles of equipment for follow-up purposes are on the market, but many secretaries to busy executives have found the follow-up file system described here, or a variation of it, to be practical, efficient, and time saving.

The only equipment necessary is a file drawer and file folders. Make a set of file folders consisting of (*a*) 12 folders labeled from January through December, (*b*) 31 folders labeled from 1 through 31, and (*c*) 1 folder marked "Future Years." If you have a heavy volume of follow-up material, it is advisable to have two sets of folders labeled by days—one for the current month and one for the succeeding month. In Figure 6 a follow-up file with one set of folders is illustrated.

Tabbed guides marked 1 through 31 and removable separators tabbed with the months will make it easier to locate a particular folder, but these are not necessary to the efficient functioning of the system.

Arrangement of folders for follow-up. Arrange the folders labeled by days in numerical order in the front of the file. Place in these the follow-up material for the current month. The folder labeled for the current month is at the back of the other monthly folders ready to receive any material to be followed up in the same month next year. Immediately following the numerical daily folders is the folder for the forthcoming month, followed by the folder for the succeeding month, and so on. Figure 6 is a diagram of the folders when Friday, April 15, is the current day.

A variation of this plan is to arrange the files labeled by months in

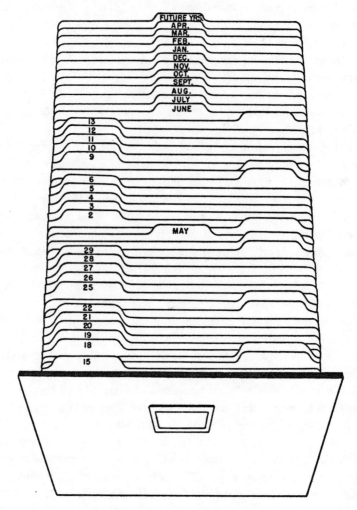

Figure 6. Diagram of Follow-Up Files.

calendar sequence. Thus, January is always the first month-by-month folder. Some secretaries prefer this arrangement because the folders remain in the same position. In this case, as the folder for each day is emptied, it is placed in position for the next month.

Operation of the follow-up system. 1. Make an extra copy of correspondence or memoranda that require a follow-up, preferably on paper of a different color. Mark on the extra carbon the date on which it is to be followed up. When there is no carbon copy of material for follow-up, write a brief memo for the tickler file. For example, if your employer gives you a newspaper clipping and tells you to bring it to his attention on the 30th of the month, prepare a tickler memo for follow-up on the 30th, but file the clipping so that you can put your hands on it if your employer wants it before the 30th. The memo should indicate where the material is filed. File any pertinent papers in the regular files.

2. Place material that is to be followed up in the current month in the proper date folders. Each day transfer the empty daily folder back of the folder for the forthcoming month. Thus, you always have 31 daily folders for follow-ups, part of them for the remaining days in the current month and part of them for the first part of the forthcoming month. Place material that is to be followed up more than 30 or 31 days in the future in the proper month folder, regardless of the day of follow-up. See Figure 6, which is a diagram of the arrangement of folders on April 15. On that day, material to be followed up from April 16 through May 15 is placed in daily folders; material to be followed up after May 15 is placed in the proper month folder.

3. On the first of each month, transfer the material from the folder for that month into the folders labeled by days. To avoid filing material for follow-up on Saturdays (if the office closes), Sundays, or holidays, reverse the folders for those days so that the blank side of the label faces the front of the file. Notice in Figure 6 that the folders for April 16, 17, 23, 24, 30 and 31 (since April has only 30 days), and May 1, 7, 8, and 14 are blank. The empty folder for the current month is then transferred to the rear of the other month-by-month folders—or returned to its proper calendar sequence if that arrangement is used.

How to handle material in the daily follow-up file. Each day when you examine your follow-up file you will find that a large part of the correspondence has been answered without a follow-up. Destroy these carbons or memoranda. If a heavy schedule keeps you from giving attention to all the material in the daily folder, mark the less important items for follow-up at a later date.

Move indefinite follow-ups forward from week to week until a definite date is established or until the matter is completed. This procedure is often referred to as "combing-back."

Follow-ups on a small scale. When you have only a small

amount of correspondence or other matters to follow up, a set of follow-up file folders is not necessary. Mark the carbons with the follow-up date and file them chronologically in one folder, with those marked for the earliest follow-up on top.

Tickler card file or follow-up. A tickler card file is as useful as follow-up file folders for any type of material except correspondence. You can type a notation for yourself on a card and place it in a tickler card file as easily as you can type a memorandum and put it in a file folder. But it is a waste of time to make a card notation of correspondence when you can make an extra carbon at the time of transcription. Therefore, unless you have only a small amount of correspondence to follow up, and handle it as described in the preceding paragraph, use follow-up file folders instead of a card tickler.

Chapter 5

Filing in the Real Estate Office

EVERY REAL ESTATE OFFICE maintains files to house the records of the business. The files and systems vary with the size of the business and the nature of its activities. In a small office, the secretary is likely to have complete charge of all of the files. In a large office, departmentalized into various functions, there may be a file clerk in charge of a centralized filing department. Usually, each of the operating departments maintains its own active files even where a centralized filing department exists. The secretary in a particular department may be responsible for its files. Each executive may also have his own private files that his secretary maintains.

This chapter covers the kinds of files found in a real estate office, whether they are maintained in a central filing department, operating department, or private office. It explains what the secretary should know about filing to carry out filing responsibilities efficiently and in accordance with modern practices. It includes the following sections:

1. Systems of filing
2. Kinds of files
3. Physical setup of files

Systems of Filing

The basic filing systems used for the various kinds of files in a real estate office are alphabetical (name or subject), location, numerical, property classification, and chronological. Each of these will be explained briefly.

Alphabetical system. Under the alphabetical system, the folders or cards are filed alphabetically according to name or subject. A cross-reference index is not necessary with this system of filing. The correspondence file described at page 66 is an example of an alphabetical file. The maintenance file described at page 266 and the appraisal data file described at page 295 are examples of subject files arranged alphabetically.

Guides. Frequent guides make filing and finding easy. Therefore, it is advisable to put guides between every five or six folders.

Alphabetical index guides come in divisions of from 25 to 2,000. The 25 division has a guide for each letter from A to Z, with Mc added and XYZ combined in the last guide. Although in alphabetizing, names beginning with Mc are treated in regular alphabetical sequence, the Mc is included in a 25 division index for convenience where there are more than three or four names beginning with Mc. The Mc guide precedes the M guide. The more extensive divisions contain the first three letters in each division; for example, G may be divided into Gar, Gea, Gei, and so on. In such an index, the Mc guide is in its proper alphabetical position, between, for example, the M and the Me guides.

To determine which division you need, count the number of drawers of filing material. The following table shows the division required for a given number of drawers.

> For 1 drawer ....25 division
> For 2 drawers ....40 division
> For 3 drawers ....80 division
> For 6 drawers ....120 division
> For 8 drawers ....160 division
> For 12 drawers ....240 division
> For 16 drawers ....320 division

Location system. A large part of the files in a real estate office are arranged by location of the properties with which the records deal. The breakdown may be as follows: cities, counties, villages, areas, streets, block and lot, out-of-town property. Within some of the main groups there may be an arrangement by streets. Name streets and avenues are arranged alphabetically; numbered streets are arranged numerically in a separate section. If there are east and west numbered streets, all of the east streets are kept together in numerical order and all of the west streets are kept together. If there are numbered avenues and numbered streets, the numbered avenues may be included among the name streets in alphabetical order. Thus, Fifth Avenue might follow Fenster Street. Within each street, the files are arranged by street numbers. Thus, 30 Fifth Avenue would be followed by 31 Fifth Avenue, and so on.

For some purposes, a location file may be arranged according to numbers of the houses or buildings, with the streets arranged alphabetically where more than one property has the same number. One of the appraisal files in a large firm is arranged in this manner (see page 296). The folders run as follows: 1 Albany Ave., 1 Thompson Blvd., 2 Grant Ave., 2 Hudson St., and so on.

If the location file is by block and lot number, the blocks are arranged numerically and under each block number the lot numbers are arranged numerically.

Guides. Metal tab guides are often used to separate each broad location classification. For example, a metal tab might be used for each city, county, village, east numbered streets, west numbered streets. Alphabetical dividers may be used to separate the named streets, or each street name may have its own guide tab with the name of the street on it.

Numerical system. Under this system numbers are placed on the file folders or records, and they are arranged numerically. This is an indirect method of filing since it must be used in connection with a cross-index that shows what the number stands for. An index card is made for each folder or record and the cards are arranged alphabetically or by location. The advantages of this system are the rapidity and accuracy of filing and the opportunity for indefinite expansion.

A lease file arranged in numerical order is described on page 265, and an appraisal report file arranged in numerical order is described on page 296.

Property classification system. Files and records are often maintained by types of properties. Within each class of property, the file might be kept alphabetically, or by location. The listings file described on page 67, for example, is classified by types of property.

The following classifications may be used as a guide in setting up files to be arranged by types of property:[1]

---

[1] Harry Grant Atkinson and L. E. Frailey, *Fundamentals of Real Estate Practice* (Englewood Cliffs, N.J.: Prentice-Hall, Inc., 1946), p. 303.

1. Residential properties:
   a. Single-family houses
   b. Small multiple-family buildings
   c. Large multiple-family buildings
   d. Residential hotels

2. Commercial properties:
   a. Stores
   b. Office buildings
   c. Commercial hotels
   d. Filling stations
   e. Garages
   f. Warehouses
   g. Markets
   h. Motels

3. Industrial properties:
   a. Loft buildings
   b. Small factories
   c. Large factories
   d. General-purpose buildings
   e. Special purpose buildings

4. Amusement and recreation properties:
   a. Theaters
   b. Motion-picture houses
   c. Bowling alleys
   d. Pool rooms
   e. Taverns
   f. Skating rinks
   g. Dance halls

5. Farm properties:
   a. Truck farms
   b. Chicken farms
   c. Small farms
   d. Large farms
   e. Plantations
   f. Fox farms
   g. Ranches

 h. Fruit farms

6. Civic properties:
 a. Parks
 b. Forest preserves
 c. School buildings
 d. City and county buildings
 e. State and federal buildings
 f. Libraries
 g. Municipal stadiums

7. Vacant land:
 a. Home sites
 b. Commercial lots
 c. Factory sites
 d. Timber—virgin and cut
 e. Hunting reservations
 f. Resort sites

8. Institutional:
 a. Churches
 b. Hospitals

9. Miscellaneous:
 a. Clubs
 b. Golf courses
 c. Camps

Chronological system. A chronological file is one arranged according to years, months and days. It has a tabbed guide for each year, a tabbed guide for each month of the year, and 31 tabbed guides, one for each day of the month. Usually, only the current year has tabbed monthly guides, and only the current month has the 31 tabbed guides. Such a file is ordinarily used as a reminder file of mortgage expiration dates, lease expiration dates, interest payment dates on mortgages, installment payment dates, tax dates, and the like. Such a file has already been described in Chapter 4, in connection with the secretary's reminder duties.

Another example of a chronological file is given at page 296.

Kinds of Files

A great variety of files are maintained in real estate offices. Those most commonly found are:

Correspondence or general
Listings (sold and unsold)
Pending deals and completed sales ·
Deposit receipts
Business opportunities
Prospects
Block and lot
Advertising clippings
Buildings managed
Appraisal
Office personnel and pay roll records
Photographs, scrapbooks, etc.
Brokers' names
Callers' cards
Personal
Forms

Some of these will be explained in detail here; others will be covered in detail in the chapters dealing with special activities.

Correspondence or general file. The correspondence or general file is arranged by names and filed alphabetically. Some material does not lend itself to classification by name and must be arranged by subject. For example, your employer is always interested in rent control; if he manages property, he is interested in labor information. He is a member of various real estate associations and receives correspondence, announcements, and other papers dealing with association activities. For these and other subjects you will have folders labeled with the name of the subject or association. The subject files are combined with the general file, and placed in their alphabetical order.

The following are instructions for maintaining the general file.

Arrangement of material in folders. Make a folder for each correspondent, name or subject, if there is enough material to justify a separate folder. From three to ten papers justify starting a folder. Arrange the papers within the folders by date with the latest date on top.

Miscellaneous folder. Make a miscellaneous folder for each letter of the alphabet and place it behind the last name folder under the particular letter. File any material for which there is no separate name folder in the miscellaneous folder, alphabetically rather than by date. This keeps all papers relating to a particular name together. When they reach the required number, three to ten, make a separate folder.

Voluminous correspondence with the same person. If correspondence with the same person or firm is voluminous, separate it into date periods. You may type the dates on your labels.

Correspondents with the same name. On folders for correspondents with the same name, use a different-colored label. The distinctive color is a signal to use extra precaution in filing or in looking for filed material. Thus, if you use blue labels and you have a folder for *Abernathy, Edgar, Sr.,* with a salmon label, you know immediately that you also have a folder for *Abernathy, Edgar, Jr.,* with a salmon label.

Listing files. When an owner of property authorizes a broker to sell it, he "lists" his property for sale with the broker. When an owner comes to a broker to find tenants for his property, he "lists" it for rental. The broker makes a complete record of the details of the property, as given to him by the owner. He adds to this record any other information that he gathers himself from an inspection of the listed property. The listing records are among the most important in the office. Without listings he has nothing to offer prospects who want to buy or rent. The methods by which the listings are filed are explained in detail in Chapter 13.

Pending deals and completed sales files. The "pending deals" file contains the folders for all properties on which deals are pending at any one time. All correspondence relating to the property, whether with the seller, buyer, or others, and all copies of documents and other papers relating to the deal are kept in a separate folder. A folder is ordinarily made up when a property is sold. However, if one was prepared when the property was listed, that same folder may be taken out of the listings file and placed in the pending file. Each folder remains in the pending file until after the closing, when it is transferred to the "closed sales" file.

The pending and closed sales files are arranged by the names of the sellers or by the address of the property, depending upon the system most suitable for the particular office. A real estate office serving several towns would be likely to have its pending and closed sales files arranged by towns, with the folders under each town arranged by street address. The notation on the tab of the folder, of course, is either the name of the seller or the property address, as required by the method of filing. Ordinarily, each year's sales folders are kept together.

In addition to the folder files there may be a card record of sales. The card would show the address, description of the property, sales price, and date of sale, and would be filed by location. Where such a record is kept it is ordinarily part of a sales record card file used by the firm's appraisers. (See page 294 for a description of this file.)

Deposit receipts file. Some firms keep their files of deposit receipts for sales separate from the folders for pending and completed sales, but in the same drawer, and in front of the sales folders. The deposit receipt file is arranged by years, with folders for each month. The deposit receipts are filed according to the month in which the property was sold.

Business opportunities file. A firm that handles business properties involving the sale of a business might keep the files for this type of transaction separate from its sales files for general real estate such as houses, ranches, lots, apartment houses, and the like. A manila folder is made up for each business opportunity, and the name of the business is placed on the tab of the folder. The folders are arranged alphabetically. All correspondence, deposit receipts, and other papers pertaining to the particular business opportunity are placed in the folder.

This file is divided into an active and inactive file. After the sale or expiration of the business opportunity, the folder is removed from the active file and placed in an inactive business opportunity file.

Prospects file. The prospects files contain the names and addresses of people and organization who want, or might want, to buy property or use the services of the firm. The names may be of (a) people who were interviewed by the salesman as possible buyers of various types of property but who for some reason did not buy; (b) people who wanted to rent, but for some reason did not do so; (c) people who sold their properties through the office; (d) people who bought properties through the office; (e) lawyers who act for investors in real property; (f) real estate operators who buy for resale; (g) people who have answered advertisements; (h) builders who are interested in new sites, and many others. Sources of prospects are given in the discussion of direct mailing advertising, at page 000.

Classification. Prospect files are usually classified files with material in each classification arranged in alphabetical order. There is no one best system; classifications must be devised to suit the needs of the office. Three types of classification, however, are commonly used: (1) Purpose for which real estate is generally bought or sold; that is, by use, speculation, or investment. A prospect's name may appear in more than one file since he may be a possible purchaser of a home for his own use and a possible purchaser of an apartment house for investment. In that case, the record in each file should show that his name also appears in another classification of the same file. (2) Types of property in which the prospect is interested. Some of the classifications mentioned at page 63 are usually used. (3) Source of the name.

Block and lot files. Many cities are laid out in blocks and lots, each block and lot having an official number that appears on the real estate maps of the municipality. A block and lot file is made up of folders for each block and lot number in the territory served by the firm. The folder tab shows the block number and lot number. These folders are arranged by block number, and by lot number under each block number.

Into the folders are placed any information relating to the particular property located on the block and lot numbers indicated. For example, news items reporting sales, mortgage loans, leases, and the like are clipped and placed in the file. A memorandum from the appraisal department showing that an appraisal has been made would be placed in the folder for the designated block and lot number. The block and lot files are used by salesmen, appraisers, and any other people in the office who might have need for the information accumulated.

Advertising clippings. The files of advertising clippings, and other advertising files are described on page 232.

Buildings managed files. These files include all of the correspondence and records relating to buildings managed by the office for property owners. They include such separate files as a management file arranged by owners or address of the property, lease files, lease information files, card records of repair expenditures, maintenance file, rent control information file, and others. They are explained in detail in Chapter 17.

Appraisal files. These files include data that may be helpful in arriving at the value of properties for which appraisals may be made in the future; the working papers that were used in preparing appraisal reports on a particular property for a specified owner or institution; the appraisal reports; and others. How these files and records are made up and maintained is described fully in Chapter 19.

Office personnel and payroll records. Whoever handles the payroll of the office will probably have charge of the personnel and payroll records. More will be said about these records in Chapter 21.

Photographs, scrapbooks, etc. In addition to files of listings and prospects, which are the salesmen's tools, a number of other records that entail filing may be maintained for the use of salesmen. For example, photographs, clippings that may lead to sales, scrapbooks, maps, and the like are filed. The collection and use of these items will be covered in Chapter 13.

Brokers' names file. This file contains the names and addresses of real estate brokers with whom the office has dealt in joint deals, as well as the names of those brokers who might act as co-brokers in the future. The names might come from directories, real estate journals, advertisements, and similar sources.

Callers' card file. The personal cards left by callers can be filed in a small metal file with an alphabetical index. Such a file can be obtained in most stationery stores.

Personal file. The personal file is a confidential file containing matters relating to your employer's personal interests, as distinguished from his business affairs. The personal file is a combination name and subject file and the alphabetical system of filing is used for it. A 25-division alphabetical guide will probably be sufficient.

Make a folder for each letter of the alphabet and for each of the subjects that do not fit into a name file. File the correspondence under the first letter of the correspondent's last name, according to date. Thus, correspondence with Mr. Moss and Mr. Matthews will be in the same folder. If your employer has prolific correspondence with a certain person, make separate folder for that correspondent. Also make a separate folder for each separate outside activity. Should the material for any particular subject become voluminous, withdraw it from the letter folder and file it in a folder of its own.

Forms. Numerous printed forms are used for each of the activities of the business. For example, *brokerage forms,* such as exclusive sales agency contracts, authorizations to sell, listing contracts, buyer's proposition, exchange agreements, deposit receipts, and others; *management forms,* such as management agreements, rent collection authority, application to rent, month-to-month tenancy agreements, leases, notices to tenants, rent receipts, requisitions, purchase orders; collection letters, warning notices, and others; *finance forms,* such as applications for loans on real estate mortgages, land contracts, trust deeds; *title transfer forms,* such as various kinds of deeds; *appraisal forms,* such as application forms, appraisal reports; and many other classes of forms.

A system for the storing of forms is essential (1) to enable those who use them to obtain them readily, (2) to replenish the supply when the stock runs low.

Numbering the forms. Forms that are especially prepared and printed for the firm should carry an identifying number, which should be printed in small type in a corner at the top or bottom of the form. A list of the forms used, arranged by number, is always handy for ordering as well as for assigning new numbers when new forms are devised.

Storage of forms. Supplies of forms are delivered by the printer in packages. When the packages arrive and are checked against the order, write the number of the form, or if it has no number the title of the form, on the package in a position where it will be seen in the storage cabinet or on the shelves. The system used by a large office is readily adaptable to the small office as well: Supplies of forms are kept in a stock room in bins. Each bin is numbered in consecutive order. A list is maintained according to bin number. Under each bin number the forms in the bin are noted by name. If the form has a number, it precedes the name of the form on the list.

File folders for forms. Expansion folders with metal tabs are sometimes used for keeping printed contract forms in current use. The title of the form is inserted in the metal tab, and the folders are arranged alphabetically.

Physical Setup of Files

Types of files used. The following kinds of cabinets and other filing equipment are generally used in a real estate office:

1. Letter-size filing cabinets
2. Legal-size filing cabinets, if the papers include legal documents

3. Cabinets of drawers for filing record cards
4. Books, cabinets, or trays for listing records
5. Post binders for filing clippings that are pasted on sheets
6. Special cabinets for large maps or blueprints.

How to type index tabs and labels. For best results in typing tabs, guides, and folders, observe the following rules:

Use the briefest possible designations. Abbreviate, omitting punctuation whenever possible. Index tabs need to be legible only at normal reading distance. Guide labels should be legible at two or three feet. File drawer labels should be legible at six to ten feet.

Use initial caps whenever needed. Full caps, especially in elite and pica type, do *not* increase the legibility of label designations; they decrease the amount of light background in the vicinity of the letters and make reading more difficult. Do not underline.

Folder labels. The most important part of a folder label is the eighth of an inch immediately below the scoring (the place at which the label is folded when it is pasted on the folder tab). Frequently this space is the only part visible in the file. Therefore, write in the first typing space below the scoring. Typing should begin in the first or second typing space from the left edge of the label, except for one- or two-character designations. If this is done, all folder labels in the file drawer will present an even left margin.

Use initial caps and indent the second and third lines so that the first word of the first line will stand out.

In typing labels for a numbered subject file, leave space between the number and the first word; type the subject in block form. For proper arrangement of various label designations, see Figure 7.

Guide labels. For file guide labels, use the largest type available. Begin the typing as high on the label as the guide tabs will permit. Center one- and two-character designations. Start all other designations in the second typing space from the left edge. Use abbreviations or shortened forms and omit punctuation.

File drawer labels. In preparing labels for file drawers, use the largest type available. Center the typing on the label and leave a double space above and below detailed reference information. It is better to print file drawer labels because type is not legible at a distance.

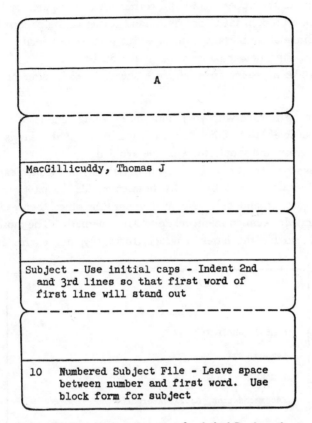

A

MacGillicuddy, Thomas J

Subject - Use initial caps - Indent 2nd
    and 3rd lines so that first word of
    first line will stand out

10   Numbered Subject File - Leave space
      between number and first word. Use
      block form for subject

Figure 7. Proper Arrangement for Label Designations.

Preparation of material for filing. To prepare material for filing, do the following:

1. Segregate papers belonging in different files: general correspondence, clippings, personal, listings (sold and not sold), deposit receipts, etc.

2. Check through all papers that are stapled to see whether they should be filed together.

3. Remove all paper clips.

4. Mend torn papers with scotch tape.

5. Note on the paper where it is to be filed. For a *name file,* underline the name in colored pencil; for a *subject file,* write the name of

the subject in the upper right-hand corner. Place the guide or file number, if one is used, in the upper right-hand corner of the paper.

6. Circle an important word or words in colored pencil to facilitate location of a particular paper when it is wanted.

7. Make necessary cross-reference sheets as each letter or paper is handled.

Keep up to date with your filing by devoting time each day to the task, if possible. Hasty filing the last few minutes of the day is likely to result in errors, and should therefore be avoided.

Cross-reference. Frequently, material may be filed logically under one or more names or subjects. In those cases, file the paper under one name or subject and cross-reference under the other. For example, a letter from Mr. Remsen might relate to Mr. Abernathy. The most reasonable place to file the letter is under *Abernathy*, but a cross-reference

NAME OR SUBJECT:

Remsen, S.J.

REGARDING:

Recommendation, George Abernathy

DATE:

May 11, 19--

(see)

NAME OR SUBJECT:

Abernathy, George

Figure 8. Cross-Reference Sheet.

should be made under *Remsen*. Write the cross-reference on colored cross-reference sheets, about 8½" by 11". They may be purchased in' pads at any stationery store. The cross-reference sheet should contain the information shown in Figure 8. If Mr. Remsen has a regular folder, put the cross-reference sheet in it; if not, put it in the miscellaneous folder under R.

A permanent cross-reference is usually maintained when a name or subject can be filed under more than one designation. For example, a permanent cross-reference should be maintained under *Simon, Franklin, & Company* to *Franklin Simon & Company*. When a permanent cross-reference is desirable, make a guide to serve as a cross-reference signal and insert it in its proper alphabetical position among the regular file folders. The back of an old file folder will serve for this purpose. The cross-reference label should read:

> Simon, Franklin, & Co.
> SEE
> Franklin Simon & Company

Cross-reference labels should be in a color different from the color of the labels on the regular folders. *Use cross-reference sheets freely.*

Control of material taken from the files. To control material taken from your files, use guides the same height as the file folders but of different-colored stock, with the word OUT printed on the tab. The OUT guide provides space on which to make an entry of the material

DATE	MATERIAL	DATE REMOVED	TO BE RETURNED	CHARGE TO WHOM	REMARKS

Figure 9. Out Card.

taken, date removed, who has it, and the date it should be returned. See Figure 9. Place the guide in the files where the removed material was located.

A secretary in a private office does not put an OUT guide in her file every time she withdraws material for her employer. She uses the guide under these circumstances: (1) Someone outside her immediate office wants the material. (2) Her employer expects to take the material out of the office, say, when he goes to a closing. (3) She expects her employer to keep the material a week or so, say, to prepare a report.

Chapter 6

Taking Care of the Mail

A VERY IMPORTANT PART of the real estate business is carried on through correspondence; it is essential that you do a good job taking care of it.

Opening and Sorting the Mail

Preparing incoming mail so that your employer can read it quickly and act upon it at once can save hours of his time each week. Give incoming correspondence your immediate attention. If you have several deliveries during the day, your employer may not want to see the mail immediately after each delivery, but you would nevertheless open and sort it just as soon as it arrives.

Presorting. You can usually tell from the outside of the envelope whether a piece of mail is correspondence, advertising, or a periodical or newspaper. Presort the mail into these three categories before you open it. Placing the envelopes right side up will facilitate opening them later. If there is any doubt in your mind as to whether a certain envelope contains an advertisement or correspondence, place it in the correspondence pile.

You will probably find a number of envelopes marked "personal" or "confidential." Set these aside to be given to your employer unopened. Any envelopes written in longhand that appear to contain personal correspondence should also be left unopened.

Place interoffice mail in a separate pile.

Opening correspondence. Open those envelopes containing correspondence first. Tap the lower edge of the stack of envelopes on your desk so that the contents will drop to the bottom. This step lessens the possibility of your cutting the contents with the letter opener. Now, holding the stack of envelopes with the flaps facing you, slit all the envelopes with a letter opener before removing the contents from any one envelope. The same applies if you have a mechanical opener, which cuts a narrow edge from the envelope.

As you remove the contents from each envelope, check carefully to be sure you have removed any enclosures. Clip enclosures to the correspondence. Glance quickly at the letterhead to be sure the correspondence contains the return address and signature; if it does not, attach the envelope to the letter. Write the postmark date on any letter that is not dated.

Some companies also require that incoming mail be stamped with the "Date Received." Sometimes this is done on the back of the envelope, if there is a mailroom, but more often the secretary will stamp the letter itself after it has been opened.

Put the envelopes to one side until you have completed processing the mail.

Sorting the correspondence. Now read the letters carefully. Interoffice mail may be read at the same time and handled in the same way. As you read, sort the letters into four piles:

1. those your employer must handle
2. those that require attention from someone else in the office
3. those that require your attention
4. bills and statements

While you are reading each letter or interoffice memorandum, keep the following questions in mind:

• Is there previous correspondence in your files which will help your employer handle this letter? If so, attach the file.
• Has some enclosure, mentioned in the letter, been omitted? Make a note on the letter indicating what is missing. (At this time you may want to check the envelope again.) If the letter cannot be handled

without the enclosure, keep the letter in the pile of letters that require your attention. You will have to write to the company to tell them the enclosure was not received. See page 132 for an example of such a letter.

• Should the letter be referred to someone else? Route it to the appropriate person or department head. (See page 80.)

• Does the letter mention something being sent under separate cover? Make a notation on your "mail-expected record" as described below.

As you read each letter, make a notation on it at the top indicating where you will file it when it comes out of your employer's office. This step will save you the trouble of reading the letter again when it is time to file it.

Also note the date and time of any appointments or meetings mentioned in the letters so that you can keep track of them later. Any deadlines for replies, reports, renewals, or the like should be noted in your follow-up system so that you can remind your employer, if necessary.

Mail-expected record. It would be impossible to remember all the items that are being sent to you under separate cover and the dates on which they might be expected to arrive. Therefore, whenever an incoming letter says that further information—a catalog, booklet, or other material—is being sent separately, make a notation in your mail-expected record. This record is simply a sheet of paper ruled into three vertical columns. In the first column write the name of the person or firm sending the material and the date of the letter. In the next column write what material is expected. If you are to forward it to someone other than your employer, write that person's name in this column, too. These two columns are filled in when you receive the original letter. The last column is headed "date received," and in it you write the date when the material is actually received.

This record serves as a guide to remind you to follow up when expected material does not arrive within a reasonable time. You will have to consult it regularly, of course, if it is to help you.

Distributing the Mail

Now that the mail is opened, and all enclosures attached and filing notations made, you are ready to refer it to your employer and others who will take care of it. The mail for your employer takes all precedence, of course.

How to submit mail to your employer. Your employer should receive incoming mail as soon as possible. Try to have it on his desk before he arrives in the morning. If this is impossible, at least bring the mail to him as soon after he arrives as you can. If other people have access to his office, the mail should be in a manila folder. Otherwise put it in a neat pile, with the most important mail on top, and place it on your employer's desk—preferably in the same place each day.

In large companies there may be several mail deliveries, including interoffice mail, each day. Ask your employer whether he wants you to present this mail to him after each delivery, or whether he prefers that you hold the mail until designated times during the day. In the latter case you would make an exception of a special delivery letter or an extremely urgent matter, such as a telegram.

Some executives who have a great deal of social correspondence addressed to them at the office prefer to have these letters separated from business correspondence.

Letters that require someone else's attention. After you have taken care of the correspondence and presented to your employer the letters that are for him, turn to the letters that require the attention of someone else. Some of these letters should just be routed to another department; others your employer will answer once he has additional pertinent information from another department.

Follow the procedure used in your company. In some companies the secretary merely writes at the top of the letter the name of the person to whom it is being referred, together with any comments—for example, "Please reply for Mr. Brown," "May Mr. Brown have your comments so he can reply?" In other companies an interoffice envelope, or "chain envelope" is used. This is a large envelope on which the sender writes the name of the person to whom the correspondence is to be sent. The recipient merely crosses off his name when he receives the material and the envelope can be used over and over again.

Figure 10 illustrates a routing slip. This slip is a quick way of indicating to whom a piece of interoffice mail should go. Any occasional special instructions can be penciled next to the name. If you have a great deal of mail that must be routed to several people, it would save time to have a supply of these routing slips available.

Whenever you attend to part of a letter which you then forward to someone else, make a notation next to the paragraph you have taken care of. Write the date and "done" or "noted" in the margin, and then write your initials. This step will avoid duplication by the next person who receives the letter.

The daily mail record. Both you and your executive hope that mail sent *out* of your department to someone else in the company to handle—either for direct reply or for information so that your executive can reply—will be properly taken care of. Still, you cannot depend on your memory to check on each of these letters to see that the appropriate

Date: 5/5/—

(To be routed in the order numbered)

A. B. Johnson

R. J. Anderson

T. R. Smith

H. T. Hopkins

U. L. Arnold

M. L. Ronson

File

Please initial, date, and forward.

Figure 10. Routing Slip.

action has been taken. The solution is to keep a daily mail record. Here is the way it is done.

• Keep the record either in longhand or use the typewriter, but if you keep it in longhand, use lined paper. Use loose-leaf sheets.

• Have vertical columns headed, "Date," "Description," "To Whom Sent," "Action to Be Taken," and "Follow-Up."

• As you go through the incoming mail and forward certain letters to other individuals or departments, fill in the columns of your daily mail record with the information indicated in the headings: the date on which the material is sent out of your office; a description of the material which includes the date of the letter, subject matter, and name of the sender; the person to whom you are referring the letter; what was to be done about it and the date by which the letter should have been taken care of, in case it is necessary for you to follow up to see that the action has been taken.

• Once the letter has been taken care of, cross off the entry in your daily mail record.

You will be surprised at how helpful this mail record is. Many times the writer of the original letter will send a second letter on the same subject to your employer. You would not always remember who was handling the matter without this record.

Incoming checks and remittances. Various companies handle incoming remittances in different ways, and, of course, you will be guided by the procedure used in your own office. No matter what system is used, you should be sure to check the amount of the check, cash, or money order against the amount given in the letter with which it was enclosed. If there is any discrepancy, make a notation on the letter so that it will be noticed.

Advertisements and circulars. Advertisements and circulars should be examined carefully. Very often they will be of interest to your employer or to some other department within your company. Keep those that might interest your employer and present them to him in a manila folder. Route the others to whichever department might find them useful and throw away any that remain.

Newspapers and periodicals. Unwrap and flatten out, if necessary, the periodicals and newspapers your executive wants to see. Put them in a folder which you can place on his desk, or in his briefcase if he prefers to take them home.

Keep the others in your reference library or forward them to someone else in the organization to whom they are of interest. Ask your employer's permission to cancel subscriptions to any periodicals he does not want and that are not needed by anyone else in the company.

Bills and statements. In most offices, bills and statements are taken care of once a month, and it is only necessary for the secretary to keep any incoming mail of this sort in a folder until that time of the month. The bills must be verified before the remittance is made. After the bill is paid, a record of the payment is made and the receipt filed.

In some large companies all bills are paid by the accounting department. In this case, the bills is approved for payment by the executive and the secretary then forwards it to the accounting department. If this is the procedure in your company, present the bills and statements to your employer once a week, and then forward them to the proper department for payment after his approval.

When the Employer Is Away

Your responsibility with regard to taking care of mail is greater when your employer is away on a trip. The procedures described here are proven and efficient, but your employer may prefer some other good method. When a choice is necessary, always follow his personal preferences.

What to do with the mail. What you do with the mail depends very much on how closely your employer keeps in touch with the office while he is away. These suggestions will help you.

• Your employer may telephone the office each day to check on what has happened. Be prepared for his call by writing the gist of each letter—a phrase such as "wants prices" will do—at the top so that you can tell him about the letter without reading it through again. Jot his instructions right on the letter.

• Telephone or wire him about anything urgent that requires his immediate personal attention, if he does not call you.

• You will have to acknowledge every letter that comes into the office, personal or business, if he is to be away more than a few days.

• Try to dispose of as much mail as possible by taking care of the subject in your acknowledgment or by referring the letter to someone else in the company for reply.

• Make a copy of any mail that requires your employer's personal attention and forward the copies to him.

• If you are to forward mail to him, let him know before he leaves that you will number each packet of mail consecutively. Mark the number on the envelope. This step is particularly important if he is traveling from one place to another; he will know at once if one of your mailings didn't catch up with him.

• What should you do if your employer is on vacation and has told you not to forward any mail? In that case keep the letters that require his personal attention, and in your acknowledgment indicate when the writer might expect a reply.

• Keep the accumulated mail in folders. Mark the folders, "Correspondence to be signed," "Correspondence requiring your attention," "Correspondence to read" (letters that have been answered but in which he will probably be interested), "Reports," and "General reading material" (miscellaneous items of advertising and publications that he might want to read).

Letters to which you can reply. Every letter that comes into your company deserves a reply within 48 hours. Although this is an easy rule to follow when your employer is in the office, you may have a little trouble when he is away on a trip.

You may be able to answer some letters yourself, instead of simply acknowledging them. Certainly this is the best procedure to follow if you can. At other times, you will only be able to acknowledge the letter without really answering it.

You will find help in writing these letters, and many others, in Chapter 8, The Anatomy of a Business Letter.

Mailing Procedures for Outgoing Mail

It will be your responsibility to know how to handle outgoing mail from the time you present it to your employer for his signature until it is in the hands of the United States Postal Service. It is impossible to give all the regulations of the Postal Service here because of lack of space and also because rates are subject to change. The information that is given here will help you to choose the best way to send out the daily mail.

For any problems not solved for you in this section, consult Chapters 1 and 2 of the *Postal Manual* and *The Directory of Post Offices*. These two official documents of the United States Postal Service are kept up to date by supplementary services and are available for a reasonable fee from the Superintendent of Documents, Government Printing Office, Washington 25, D.C.

Make a friend of your postmaster. He can supply you with a number of useful documents to help you with the mail and will also be glad to answer any questions that are puzzling you.

Preparations for mailing. Preparing the mail so that it may be sent out is not difficult. These are the steps:

• Present the mail to your employer for signature. Separate those letters that he dictated from those that you or someone else wrote for his signature.

• After the mail has been signed, bring it to your desk to assemble it for actual mailing. Check these three things:

1. Has the letter been signed?
2. Do you have all the enclosures?
3. Are the inside address and the address on the envelope the same?

• Now fold the letters and insert them in the envelopes. See below for some tips on how to do this correctly.

• Insert any enclosures. The various types are described under the heading *Enclosures* following.

How to fold and insert letters. There is a right and a wrong way to fold letters for insertion into envelopes. This is the right way.

Letters on full-size letterhead to be inserted in long envelopes: One fold from the bottom, with the crease about one-third of the way up; a second fold from the bottom to within one-sixteenth of an inch of the top. Insert in the envelope, top up.

This method of folding applies to "Executive Size" letterhead and to all other sizes of letterhead where 1) the length is noticeably greater than the width and 2) the size of the envelope does not permit a "Half-Size" fold. (See Fig. 11.)

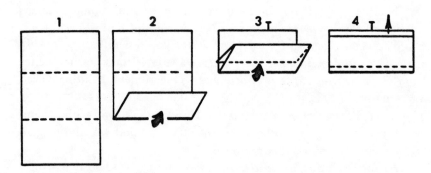

Figure 11. Folding for Long Envelopes.

Letters on full-size letterhead to be inserted in short envelopes: One fold from the bottom to within one-quarter of an inch of the top; a second fold from right to left, about one-third of the way across; a third fold from left to right within one-quarter of an inch of the right edge. Insert with the right edge up. (See Fig. 12.)

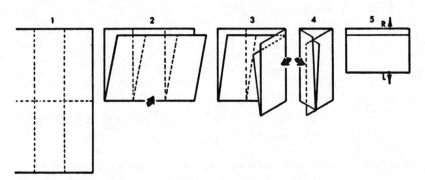

Figure 12. Folding for Short Envelopes.

Letters on half-size letterheads: One fold from right to left, about a third of the way across; a second fold from left to right, leaving about one-sixteenth of an inch between the edges at the right. Insert in a small envelope with the right edge up. (See Fig. 13.)

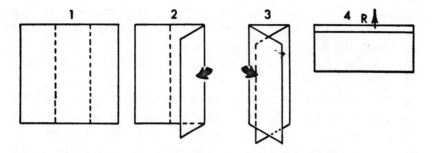

Figure 13. Folding for Half-Size Letterhead.

Enclosures. Never use pins or metal clips to fasten enclosures to letters. When it is necessary to fasten the enclosures, use staples.

Enclosures the size of the letter: If the enclosure consists of two or more sheets, staple them together but do not fasten the enclosed material to the letter. Fold the enclosure, then fold the letter, and slip the enclosure inside the last fold of the letter. The enclosure will then come out with the letter when the letter is removed from the envelope.

Enclosures larger than the letter: Booklets, pamphlets, prospectuses, catalogs, and other printed items too large to fit into a commercial envelope of ordinary size are generally mailed in large manila envelopes. The letter can be inserted with the enclosure in the large *sealed* envelope. In this case first-class postage is charged for both the letter and the enclosure.

Another method of handling enclosures larger than the letter is to use a combination envelope. This is a large envelope that is fastened with a patent fastener of some kind, but *is not sealed,* and comes with a smaller envelope, one that can be sealed, attached to the outside. The letter is placed in the small envelope and the enclosure in the large one. First-class potage is placed on the small envelope and third-class on the large one.

Enclosures smaller than the letter: Staple enclosures that are smaller than the letter to the upper left-hand corner of the letter, on top of it. If two or more small enclosures are being sent, put the smaller ones on top.

Sealing your envelopes. First, second and third class mail is sealed. If your company has a mail room, you probably won't have to seal your envelopes. There are many varieties of postal meter machines that seal, stamp and even address envelopes automatically. If your company doesn't have a mail room and sends out a large volume of mail, it may be wise for you to investigate the different types of mailing machines and present the brochures to your employer.

Save money by choosing the best method of mailing. Although it may seem that the few cents saved by sending a letter in one way rather than another are not worth noticing, it is a fact that you can save your company hundreds of dollars a year by choosing the best method for sending out mail. The cheapest way is not always the best way for a particular purpose and therefore you must learn to distinguish among the various types of mailing services.

You must have this knowledge even if your company has a mailing department. It is still your responsibility to mark the material for mailing; the mailing department merely seals and stamps the envelopes in accordance with your instructions.

Classes of Domestic Mail

Figure 14 on pages 89 and 90 is a chart which will help you to distinguish between various domestic mail services. It contains all the essential information about classes of domestic mail. This information is amplified in the following paragraphs, but if you keep the chart at hand you will have little difficulty in wrapping, sealing, and sending the mail without hesitation about regulations.

There are four classes of mail in domestic service: first, second, third, and fourth. Each class may have some special form of handling, for example, airmail or special delivery. You can check the chart on pages 89 and 90 for more details, but, briefly, the four classes consist of the following:

• *first-class:* sealed matter and certain items the U.S. Postal Service considers first-class matter whether they are sealed or not

• *second-class:* newspapers and periodicals

• *third-class:* matter weighing up to sixteen ounces (although third-class mail may be sealed to avoid loss, it must be marked THIRD CLASS and may be opened for postal inspection. Envelopes with a "gum spot" do not require marking as they are not considered sealed.)

• *fourth-class* (parcel post): packages weighing sixteen ounces or more

	FIRST-CLASS	SECOND-CLASS	THIRD-CLASS	FOURTH-CLASS (Parcel Post)
SPECIAL INSTRUCTIONS	If enclosed with lower rate material, place extra first-class postage on wrapper and mark FIRST-CLASS MAIL ENCLOSED.	To call attention to something in the periodical, use lines or symbols. Write MARKED COPY on the wrapper.	No writing except auto-graphs, inscriptions or legends like DO NOT OPEN UNTIL CHRISTMAS is allowed.	Parcels weighing less than 10 pounds and measuring over 84 inches but not exceeding 100 inches in length and girth combined are subject to a minimum charge equal to that for a 10 pound parcel.
SPECIAL SERVICES RENDERED				
AIRMAIL	YES	YES	YES	YES
REGISTERED	YES	YES 2	YES 2	NO
CERTIFIED	YES	NO	NO	NO
INSURANCE	NO	NO	YES	YES
C.O.D.	YES	NO	YES	YES
SPECIAL DELIVERY	YES	YES	YES	YES
SPECIAL HANDLING	NO	NO	NO	YES

1 The length is the distance from one end of the package to the other, not around it, and the girth is the distance around the package at its thickest part. For example, a package 25 inches in length, 15 inches in width, and 4 inches in thickness, is 63 inches in length and girth combined (25″ plus 15″ plus 15″ plus 4″ plus 4″).

2 Only second- and third-class mail of no intrinsic value may be registered. If matter of this kind is valuable, seal the envelopes and send as first-class registered.

Figure 14. Domestic Mail Service.

	FIRST-CLASS	SECOND-CLASS	THIRD-CLASS	FOURTH-CLASS (Parcel Post)
DEFINITION	All sealed matter and certain items the Post Office Department considers first-class whether sealed or not.	Newspapers and periodicals.	Unsealed matter weighing less than sixteen ounces. Although third-class mail may be sealed to avoid loss, it is assumed that it may be opened for postal inspection.	Packages weighing sixteen ounces or more. No communication except invoices, orders, or sales slips relating directly to the contents may be enclosed without payment of extra postage. See special instructions for first-class mail.
WEIGHT SIZE LIMITS	Maximum is same as fourth-class.	Governed by size of periodical.	Maximum up to but not including sixteen ounces.	Sixteen ounces to twenty pounds (forty if for delivery in the first, second, or local zones) when going from one first-class post office to another. If mailed at other post offices, limit is 70 pounds. Girth and length combined must not exceed 72 inches if mailed from one first-class post office to another. Otherwise, the limit is 100 inches.[1]
WRAPPING AND SEALING INSTRUCTIONS	Seal envelopes. Mark odd-shaped or oversized envelopes FIRST-CLASS. If flap is not gummed, seal with glue or mucilage.	Address an envelope and slit it at the ends, and wrap the piece in it. Write SECOND-CLASS MATTER above the address, TO in front of the address, and FROM before the return address.	Wrap so contents can be examined. Designate contents on wrapper, such as PRINTED MATTER and MERCHANDISE. Although third-class mail may be sealed to avoid loss, it must be marked THIRD-CLASS and "May be opened for postal inspection."	Do not seal unless package bears inscription that it may be opened for postal inspection. Because of likely rough handling, pack carefully and wrap securely.
RATE BASIS	Ounce or fraction thereof.	Minimum of two ounces with increase for each additional ounce.	Minimum of two ounces with increase for each additional ounce.	Weight by pound according to zone of destination. To find zone of destination, consult postmaster or Directory of Post Offices. Rate may then be computed with use of zone key for your city.

Figure 14. Domestic Mail Service (Cont.)

Airmail and air parcel post. Any mailable matter may be sent by airmail except that which might be damaged by freezing or high altitude. Airmail may not exceed 70 pounds or 100 inches in length and girth combined (the Canadian limit is 60 pounds). The rate for matter weighing eight ounces or less is based on the ounce or fraction thereof, without regard to distance. The rate on matter over eight ounces is based on the pound or fraction thereof, according to the distance or zone.

Either regular or airmail stamps may be used, but the use of airmail stamps does help the post office workers identify the letter. Use an airmail envelope or type the words VIA AIRMAIL in the space below the stamp but above the address. Parcels should be stamped AIRMAIL on the top, bottom, and sides.

Save money on airmail. How can you save money on airmail mailings? One way is to be sure you really are receiving the advantages of airmail delivery—fast handling. There is no point in sending airmail late Thursday or Friday. The letter will not reach its destination until late Friday or Saturday. Consequently, within reasonable distances, it would be just as efficient to use regular mail. It can be expected to reach the same destination by Monday, the next business day. At no time should airmail be sent to a destination within 300 miles.

Are you certain your airmail letters will arrive at the post office in time to make the plane? If you miss this shipment, the mail will be held for the next plane, possibly on the following day. Ask the post office what the deadline is.

Did you know that airmail is sent by train when planes are grounded because of bad weather? Keeping this fact in mind will save your company money when you send letters regular mail during snowstorms or other bad weather when planes cannot fly.

Of course the easiest way to effect savings on airmail letters is to be sure they are written on light-weight paper and that any enclosures weigh as little as possible.

Registered mail. Registered mail is an additional safeguard for the transmission of extremely valuable mail. The U.S. Postal Service will pay an indemnity up to $10,000 on registered mail that is lost, rifled, or damaged in transit if no commercial or other insurance is carried; if commercial insurance is carried, the limit that the Post Office will pay is $1,000. Registered mail can be sent by airmail and also C.O.D.

The fee for registering mail is based upon the actual declared value of the goods; however, the U.S. Postal Service will pay only $10,000 at the most in case of loss. Thus, if your package is worth $200,000, you would have to pay the fee on that basis even though you could not receive more than $10,000 indemnity.

For additional fees you can get the following additional services:

• a return receipt card showing to whom and when the article was delivered

• a return receipt showing address where delivered

• you can restrict the registered mail to the addressee only, or to a person designated by the addressee

When you prepare registered mail for mailing, note that all registered mail, except second- and third-class mail valued at not more than $100, must be sealed. Do not use transparent tape or sealing wax; use glue or mucilage.

Write the value on the face of the matter being mailed, near the space for the stamps. Print or stamp your instructions—REGISTERED; REGISTERED, RETURN RECEIPT REQUESTED; or REGISTERED, DELIVER TO ADDRESSEE ONLY—in the space below the stamps, above the address.

Insured mail. Many people are confused concerning the difference between registered mail and insured mail. First- and second-class mail cannot be insured (but you can register it). Third- and fourth-class mail can be insured. The indemnity limit on insured mail is $200 and the insurance fee depends upon the declared value of the mailed matter. Airmail which contains third- or fourth-class matter may also be insured.

Insured mail is sent with the understanding that forwarding or return postage is guaranteed by the sender. Return receipts may be had for an extra fee. Insured mail must be mailed at the post office and not at a mail box.

Insured mail should not be sealed, but it should be wrapped securely. Under the return address write RETURN POSTAGE GUARANTEED.

Certified mail. Certified mail is cheaper than registered mail. The mail is handled like first-class mail and there is no indemnity. Use it for mailing first-class letters with no intrinsic value. A return receipt may be had for an extra fee. Certified mail does not have to be mailed at the post office; you can get the forms to be attached in advance from the registry window of your local post office.

Mail sent C.O.D. By means of C.O.D. mail (collect on delivery), you can send something to a customer and have the mailman collect for it when he delivers it. The post office then sends you a money order for the amount collected. You must pay the postage, plus a fee for the collection service, at the time of mailing, but you can add these expenses to the amount to be collected, if the receiver is supposed to pay for them.

The most the post office will collect on any one item is $200. Any class of domestic mail except second-class can be sent C.O.D. You can also send C.O.D. mail by air, or by special delivery or special handling, if the proper fee is paid. You must guarantee return and forwarding postage on C.O.D. mail.

Special delivery. Special delivery service provides for immediate delivery by the post office of destination, and for expeditious handling between post offices. Any class of mail may be sent special delivery for the payment of a fee.

Use your judgment before sending something special delivery. Quite often, when mail loads are heavy, the special delivery carrier gets to his destination after the regular carrier. It is wasteful to send a letter special delivery if it would ordinarily reach its destination in time to make the first regular mail; nothing would be gained if it were to be delivered earlier because in all probability no one would be in the office to receive it. In many cases "special handling" is preferable to "special delivery" when you are sending something by parcel post.

Special handling. Special handling is a low-cost service that applies to parcel post only. The payment of the special handling fee entitles the package to handling and shipment from one post office to another as if it were first-class mail. It does not provide for special delivery from the post office.

The Zip Code. Remember to include the Zip Code number on all your mail This greatly speeds up the delivery of mail; one glance at the five digits of the Zip Code will tell the postman what postal zone your mail is headed for. It is written after the state, the last thing in both the address and return address.

The International Mails

The postal laws governing the sending of international mail differ from country to country. Although the information following will be of help to you, the best thing for you to do if your office frequently sends mail internationally is to consult your own postmaster when problems arise.

As a general guide, note that there are eight types of international mail:

1. letters and letter packages
2. post cards
3. printed matter
4. samples
5. commercial papers
6. small packets
7. parcel post
8. eight-ounce merchandise packages

Some details on the use of international mail follow.

Letters and letter packages. The rate for letters and letter packages varies with the country of destination and is based on the ounce or fraction thereof. The weight limit is four pounds, six ounces, except on mail to Canada and Newfoundland, where the limit is sixty pounds.

The dimensions in length, breadth, and thickness combined must not excede 36 inches; greatest length, 24 inches. When the material is sent in the form of a roll, the length plus twice the diameter is limited to 40 inches; maximum length, 32 inches. A letter must not be smaller than 4 inches in length and 2¾ inches in width.

Write the words LETTER (LETTRE) on the address side of letters and packages that may be mistaken for other articles by reason of their volume or packing. Typewritten material must be sent as a letter and cannot be sent at the cheaper rate applying to printed matter.

Articles subject to customs duty. Merchandise that is subject to customs duty may be sent at the prepaid letter rate, if the importation of the merchandise is allowed by the country of destination. Form 2976, available at the post office, must be affixed to the address side of each such letter or letter package. This label shows that the article is to be submitted to the customs authorities for examination.

Some countries will not accept merchandise sent at the letter rate of postage. Consult your post office.

Post or postal cards. The maximum dimensions of postal cards (government printed) or post cards (privately printed) cannot exceed 3%16 by 5%16; the minimum dimensions are 3 by 4¼ inches. If the dimensions of your card exceed 3%16 by 5%16 the card is subject to a letter rate of postage.

Printed matter. The rate for printed matter is based on two ounces or fraction thereof, and generally, the weight limit is six pounds, nine ounces. The dimensions for printed matter are the same as for letters or letter packages. Do not seal the envelope. On the wrapper write the words PRINTED MATTER and indicate the specific type, such as SHEET MUSIC or NEWSPAPER.

Samples of merchandise. The weight limit for mailed samples is 18 ounces, and the dimensions are the same for letters and letter packages. The rate is based on each two ounces, with a minimum charge. Articles sent must not have any salable value. However, a note indentifying your company and a price list for the goods may be included. Consult the postal manual to see what goods are admissible at this rate.

Commercial papers. The rate for commercial papers is based on two ounces or a fraction thereof. The weight limit is four pounds, six ounces, and the dimensions are the same as those governing letters and letter packages. Do not seal the envelope. Only reference slips to the material or to correspondence about the material may be enclosed.

Small packets. Some countries will not accept small packets and you should therefore check with your post office or the Postal Manual about the requirements of various countries. The rate for small packets is based on two ounces or fraction thereof, with a minimum charge. The dimensions are the same as those for letters and letter packages. The weight limit is two pounds, three ounces.

Small packets must bear the green label, Form 2976, whether they are subject to customs duty or not. Do not seal the envelope; mark the address side of the packet SMALL PACKET or the equivalent in the language of the counrty of destination.

Parcel post. Packages may be sent to any country in the world, either by direct or indirect service. If they are sent from one country to another through the offices of a third, the intermediate country is entitled to charge for transit.

Consult the postal authorities before attempting to send a parcel to a foreign country because customs restrictions and postal regulations vary greatly from country to country.

Take the packages to the post office. Do not deposit them in a mail box.

Eight-ounce merchandise packages. The eight- ounce merchandise package service is designed for mail which ordinarily would go in letter packets to countries which will not accept them. The rate is based on each two ounces, with a minimum charge. The weight limit is eight ounces. The package must not be sealed or have customs declarations attached. The rates are lower than parcel post rates.

Chapter 7

Improving Your Typing Efficiency

A GREAT VARIETY of typing is done in most real estate offices. All employers value speed and accuracy in their typists, but many of them fail to place a high value on craftsmanship. The reasons are obvious. The real estate man does not deal in a mechanized product; he offers services related to a basic human need—shelter. To him, people and human relationships are far more important than operations achieved by mechanical processes. He fails to see, however, that even the most unbusinesslike housewife is favorably impressed by excellence of performance, whatever the operation.

On the other hand, many real estate firms are more careful. While they regard the personal relationship as the keynote to success, they look upon each written communication as a means of strengthening that relationship. They feel that a carelessly written letter, a smudged correction in a typewritten contract, a sloppily filled out form, may damage a customer relationship, or at least detract from the prestige of the firm. They are convinced that a perfectly written communication may help to gain a customers good will and, at any rate, will add to the firm's reputation for careful work.

The secretarial field embraces typewriting skill. Whether you are in a small office or a large one, whether you have a lenient boss or an exacting one, you should establish for yourself the highest standards of typewriting performance. You are the one who is ultimately responsible for the appearance of every piece of typewriting matter that leaves the office.

In this chapter we shall present a few devices for attaining high standards of typewriting performance under the following main headings:

1. Everyday typing hints
2. How to type tables

In Chapter 12 we shall cover the typing of real estate instruments. In Chapter 20 we shall cover the techniques for typing the document in which eye-appeal is most important—the appraisal report.

Everyday Typing Hints

How to take care of the typewriter. The first essential for delivering an appealing page of typewritten material is a good typewriter. Your typewriter, therefore, must be kept in good repair. You should observe the following instructions to reduce repairs and lengthen the life of the machine:

1. Keep your machine covered when not in use.
2. Move the carriage to extreme right or left when erasing to prevent eraser dust from clogging segment.
3. Oil sparingly—just an occasional drop on the carriage rails is sufficient.
4. Use only light oil—preferably a 3-1 quality that will not gum; never use Dictaphone oil or motor oil.
5. Never oil any other part of the typewriter—wait for the repairman to oil your machine generally.
6. Clean type with a good quality brush and type cleaning fluid.
7. Wipe off entire machine occasionally with soft cloth, slightly dampened with cleaning fluid; never use alcohol, which would destroy the finish on your typewriter.
8. Use properly inked ribbons for the style of typeface.
9. Change typewriter ribbons when necessary.
10. Fasten machines to desks for best typing results.

Standard rules for spacing. Usage has established the following standard rules for spacing:

One space:
    After a comma
    After a semicolon
    After a period following an abbreviation or an initial
    After an exclamation mark used in the body of a sentence
    Before and after " × " meaning "by," for example, 3″ × 5″ card

Two spaces:
    After a colon
    After every sentence
    After a period following a figure or letter at the beginning of
        a line in a list of items

No spacing:
    Before or after a dash, which is two hyphens
    Before or after a hyphen
    Between quotation marks and the matter enclosed
    Between parentheses and the matter enclosed
    Between any word and the punctuation following it
    Between the initials that make up a single abbreviation—for
        example, C.O.D.
    Before or after an apostrophe, unless it begins or ends a word

Never separate punctuation from the word it follows. For example, do not put a dash at the beginning of a line.

How to erase neatly. To erase neatly, use two erasers—a hard one and a soft one. They may be combined into one eraser. Move the carriage as far to the side as possible so that paper and eraser fragments will not fall into the typewriter mechanism. Start with the soft eraser, to remove the excess surface ink. Then change to the hard eraser to remove the imbedded ink. Finally, use the soft eraser again, to smooth off the surface. When erasing, rub with short, light strokes.

A sharp razor blade may be used on a good grade of paper to remove punctuation marks and the tails of letters.

Insert a steel eraser guard between the carbon paper and the copy. The eraser guard is heavy enough to protect the other copies under it and is easy to handle. Or you may use a celluloid eraser shield but *do not use pieces of paper.*

How to make corrections on carbons. Corrections on carbon copies are often much fainter than the rest of the typing. To avoid this, make the correction as follows: After the necessary erasure has been made, adjust the ribbon control indicator to stencil position. Put the carriage in the proper position and strike the proper key. This will leave the impression on the carbon copies, but the original will still be blank. Then switch the control indicator back to the ribbon, place the carriage in position, and again strike the proper key. This permits a perfect match of the typing on the original and will leave the typing on the carbon copies with an equal density of color.

How to erase near the bottom of a page. To erase on a line near the edge of the page, feed the sheet back until the bottom of the paper is free of the platen. Erase, and turn the page back into position for typing.

How to make corrections on bound pages. Corrections can be made on pages that are bound at the top. Insert a blank sheet of paper in the typewriter, as though for typing. When it protrudes about an inch above the platen, insert between it and the platen the unbound edge of the sheet to be corrected. Turn the platen toward you until the typewriter grips the sheet to be corrected. You can then adjust the bound sheet to the proper position for making the correction.

Corrections cannot be made on pages that are bound at the side without separating the sheets.

How to align numerous sheets in the typewriter. When numerous sheets of paper, interleaved with carbon paper, are to be inserted in the typewriter, there is always difficulty in aligning them. You can make a simple device that will enable you to feed a large pack of paper into the typewriter and obtain perfect alignment of the sheets, without jogging. (Figur 15 illustrates the process of making the device; Figure 16 shows it after completion, with paper inserted.) The steps for making the device are:

1. Fold a 5″ × 8½″ strip of flimsy Manila tag (a cheap file folder will do) across the center, lengthwise.

2. Cut three U-shaped slots across the upper half of the folded strip, about one-half inch from the crease.

3. Lift and bend backward the tongues formed by the slots.

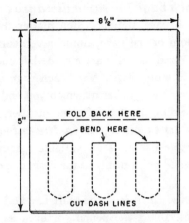

Figure 15. Device for Feeding Paper to Typewriter.

4. Insert the assembled sheets of paper in the folded strip.

5. Feed the tongues from the U-slots into the typewriter. The platen grasps them more readily than it does a thick pack of paper.

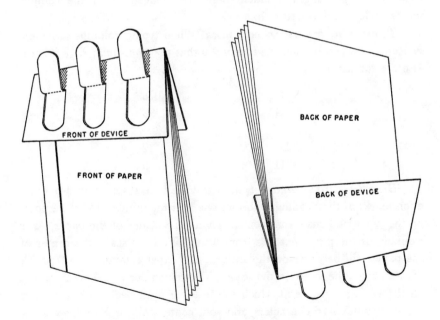

Figure 16. Device for Feeding Paper to Typewriter
(with paper inserted).

How to end each page the same distance from the bottom. To insure ending each page of typewritten matter the same number of spaces from the bottom of the page, number vertically a strip of paper about an inch wide. Wind the strip around the left end of the typewriter platen and fasten with scotch tape. Align each page of manuscript with the number "1." Notice the number at which you end the first page and then finish each succeeding sheet at the same number.

How to draw lines on work in the typewriter. To draw *vertical lines,* release the platen as for variable spacing. Roll the platen up while holding a pencil point firmly at the desired spot, but not through the ribbon.

To draw *horizontal lines,* lock the shift key and release the ribbon as for making stencils. Insert the pencil (or even a pen may be used) in the fork of the ribbon guide. Then move the carriage across the paper until the line is completed.

Tabulator uses. You should use the tabulator for more purposes than tables. Among the uses of the tabulator are (1) placement of the date line, (2) paragraph indentations, (3) placement of the complimentary close and signature line.

Typing numbers in columns. When typing columns of Arabic or Roman numerals, plan the spacing so that the *right-hand edge is even.* Use the tabulator.

VIII	3,078
XI	99°
M	204
XIX	12
II	5

How to center headings. Count the letters, spaces, and punctuation marks in the heading. Subtract one half the number from the point on the typewriter scale that coincides with the center of the paper. (For example, if the paper extends from 0 to 102 on the scale, the center of the paper will be at 51 on the scale; if the paper extends from 0 to 90, the center will be at 45 on the scale.) The remainder will show the point on the typewriter scale at which the heading must begin. Thus, if your heading contains 26 characters, and your center point is 51, your starting point will be 38 (51—½ of 26).

Alternately, the starting point may be determined by beginning at the center point and back spacing once for each two characters in the heading while spelling out the heading. In spelling the heading, include spaces and punctuation marks as though they were letters. This will place the carriage of the machine at the proper starting point.

If part of the left margin is to be used for binding, the starting point will be moved toward the right one half the number of spaces cut off for binding. For example, if 35 is the starting point gauged by the entire width of the paper, and 10 spaces are to be allowed for binding purposes, the starting point will be 40.

Filling in printed office forms. Printed forms are used in real estate offices for all sorts of purposes. Many of these forms have blank lines or leaders in which information is to be inserted. For example, listing forms (see page 207) are full of spaces to be filled in. In some instances, the information is inserted in handwriting; in others it must be typed in.

Be very careful in typing the inserts in a form that is to leave the office. Use the variable line space device and turn the cylinder by hand over the lines in order to place the writing on the line. Adjust the sheet so that the bases of letters with tails that extend below the line of type (*g, p,* and *y*) just touch the ruled lines. If you follow this instruction, your line of typewriting will always be readable and well placed. Follow the same practice when you fill in forms that do not leave the office, in order to acquire the habit.

How to type small cards. It is easier to type a series of small cards if you chain feed them from the front of the platen. After typing the first card, feed backwards until the card has a top margin of about three quarters of an inch. Insert the next card so that the bottom of it will be held in place by the card just completed. Each succeeding card will be held in place by the card preceding it. The cards automatically pile up against the paper table in the order in which they are inserted in the machine.

Perforated strips of 3″ by 5″ cards are available. If such cards are used they are fed into the machine in the usual way.

Move the paper-holding rollers to the edges of the card to hold it pressed against the cylinder.

Chain feeding envelopes. To address numerous envelopes, feed one envelope after another before removing the typed envelope from the machine.

Carbon paper. Select the heaviest carbon paper that will yield a sharp impression. Thin paper is required for making a large number of copies at once, whereas heavy paper, because of its durability, should be used if only one or two copies are needed. Carbon papers are offered on the market today in three general weights: light-weight, which will yield 6 to 12 copies; medium weight, which will yield 2 to 5 copies; billing weight, which will yield 2 copies.

Carbon paper is made in several colors. Black is used generally; blue is the prevailing color for pencil carbon work. Carbon imprint shows up better on white, yellow, or pink second sheets than on blue, green, russet, or cherry.

To avoid curling and wrinkling, keep carbon carefully in the desk, with the coated side down, out of the sunlight, and away from steam pipes.

Cut a small triangle off the upper left corner of the carbon paper so that when you take hold of the upper left corner you take hold of all copy paper but not of the carbon paper. Let the carbons extend slightly beyond the bottom edge of the copy sheets. This makes separating the copy sheets from the carbon paper easier. Carbon paper can be bought with the corner already cut.

Select carbon with a hard finish unless it is for use on a noiseless typewriter. It is more durable than carbon with a soft finish and does not smear.

How to Type a Table

Measurements for typing tables. The following information will be helpful in planning the arrangement of a table:

6 line spaces equal 1 inch, measured vertically

10 spaces of pica type equal 1 inch, measured horizontally

12 spaces of elite type equal 1 inch, measured horizontally

A sheet of paper 8½″ by 11″ has 85 spaces of pica type on a horizontal line

A sheet of paper 8½″ by 11″ has 102 spaces of elite type on a horizontal line

A sheet of paper 8½″ by 11″ has 66 vertical line spaces

Planning the arrangement. Before beginning to type a table, carefully plan the arrangement. Keep these thoughts in mind:

1. Tables usually have three parts: a title, columnar headings, and

a stub (the headings down the left side), which is equivalent to a column in planning the arrangement.

2. Align figures on the right, words on the left (see Figure 17).

3. Center columnar headings, gauging the center by the longest item in the column. Notice how, in Figure 17, the years are centered in relation to the number with the most digits.

PROFIT and LOSS STATEMENT

(Furnished by owner)

	1961	1962	1963	1964	1965
RENTALS	$23,183.36	$19,245.68	$13,134.70	$14,659.28	$18,025.36
Operating Expenses:					
Manager	1,500.00	1,450.00	1,275.00	1,190.00	650.00
Labor	2,748.11	2,633.28	2,070.40	1,582.25	2,316.42
Hse.- Exp.	319.50	258.55	189.33	228.26	165.53
Pub. Utilities ..	2,905.83	3,030.96	3,026.78	3,131.78	2,776.76
Laundry	896.61	1,020.95	450.32	550.97	583.51
Elevator Insp. ..	123.10	96.00	72.00	61.80	54.40
Telephone	1,837.35	1,648.95	1,270.51	1,286.03	354.97
Upkeep Grds.	127.20	135.20	105.00	89.50	83.60
Advertising	181.09	18.18	....	316.21	21.61
Cleaning Ctns. ..	206.65	391.45	126.46	171.11	187.31
Miscellaneous ...	277.06	277.53	257.25	197.15	159.53
Office	858.82	207.45	328.39	74.79	34.63
Linens	155.90	109.36	99.99	136.56	370.13
TOTAL OPERAT-ING	$12,210.58	$11,277.86	$ 9,271.43	$ 9,018.41	$ 7,996.07

Figure 17. Illustration of a Typewritten Table.

Vertical spacing. Allow three line spaces between the title and the subheading, if any, or between the title and columnar headings. Allow two line spaces between the subheading and the columnar headings, and two line spaces between the columnar headings and the items in the column. Therefore, a table with a subheading has ten line spaces in addition to the items in the table (assuming that the title, subheading, and columnar headings take a line each). If the table is short, double space between the items to give the typed page a more balanced appearance.

Headings of tables. Center the headings and subheadings of tables in the same manner as any other headings (see page 102). Remember to make allowance if part of the left margin is to be used for binding.

How to make top and bottom margins even. Here is what

you do to make the top and bottom margins even if a table is to stand by itself on a page.

1. Figure the number of line spaces on the paper that you are using.

2. Count the lines in the table and add the number of lines and spaces to be covered by the title and subheadings.

3. Subtract the total from the number of line spaces on your paper.

4. Divide the difference by two. The result is the number of line spaces in the top and bottom margins.

How to make the side margins even. To make side margins of a table even, follow these directions:

1. Figure the number of spaces across the paper that you are using. If part of the left margin is to be used for binding, subtract those spaces from your count.

2. Count the umber of characters in the longest line in each column, including the stub as a column, and total them.

3. Subtract the total found in Step 2 from the number of spaces found in Step 1. This gives the number of spaces that are available for left and right margins *and* to separate the columns.

4. Decide how many spaces you want between each column. This varies with the amount of available space.

5. Multiply the number of spaces to be put between each column by the number of columns, *not* including the first column.

6. Subtract the result found in Step 5 from the result found in Step 3, and divide by 2. This gives the number of spaces to be allowed for each side margin.

Where to set the tabulators. Before beginning to type a table, set your tabulators as follows:

1. Set the left-hand margin at the point found in Step 6 above. This is the point where the stub or left-hand column begins.

2. Space once for each character in the longest line of the stub, space once for each space that separates the columns (see Step 4 above), and then set the first tabulator key.

3. Beginning at the point where the first tabulator key was set, space once for each character in the longest line of the second column, space once for each space that separates the columns, and then set the second tabulator key.

4. Follow the same procedure until the tabulator key is set for the starting po nt of the last column.

Chapter 8

The Anatomy of a Business Letter

No MATTER HOW skillful your employer is at writing or dictating letters, he must rely on his secretary to type them accurately and neatly. There is more to this than being a good typist; you must also know precisely what the elements of a good business letter are and how they are to be typed on a letterhead.

This chapter explains just what a business letter contains, and describes the slightly different styles of letters that businessmen use. It gives you a step-by-step explanation of the order and arrangement of the elements of a business letter, in each of the various styles.

The Skeleton of a Business Letter

There are fourteen separate elements that can be included in business letters:

1. Date line
2. Reference line
3. Personal notation
4. Inside address
5. Attention line

6. Salutation
7. Subject line
8. Body
9. Complimentary close
10. Signature block
11. Identification line
12. Enclosure mark
13. Copy distribution notation
14. Postscript

The skeleton or framework of any business letter uses varying combinations of these fourteen ingredients. Although you'll probably never use all fourteen in one letter, you will have to be familiar with the proper positioning and the proper form of each element so that you can arrange an appropriate combination for any type of letter. On page 117 you will find a sample letter that includes all fourteen elements for the purpose of demonstration. As each element is discussed, refer to this letter so that you can visualize how it should look and how it relates to the other parts of the letter skeleton.

This sample letter is arranged in Block Style, the letter format that is most widely used in business today. There are other letter formats, however, and in them, the elments are arranged in a slightly different fashion. These arrangements are fully discussed on pages 118–122 of this chapter.

The date line. The first thing to be included in any business letter is the date that the letter was dictated. (You won't have to worry about including your firm's name and address in a heading because business correspondence is usually typed on letterhead stationery.)

The date line is usually placed two to four spaces down from the last line of the letterhead and flush with the right hand margin. Less frequently, the date line is centered two spaces below the heading.

The correct way to write a date line is:

March 7, 196–

Variations like the following are incorrect:

3/7/6–
March 7th, 196–
March seventh, nineteen hundred and sixty–

The reference line. For easy reference you may wish your reader to include a certain file number of yours in reply. If this is the case, or if you are asked to type a reply to a letter that includes a file reference, you will need a reference line.

If you wish your reader to mention your file number in his reply you may indicate this in one of three different ways:

C-382
Our file C-382
In reply please refer to C-382

In reply to a letter with a file reference, you indicate your reader's file number in this fashion:

Your file C-382

If you wish your reader to refer to *your* file number, too, in this *next* reply, then you would write your reference line like this:

Your file C-382
Our file S-301

The reference line is placed on the right side of the page because it is easier to find there; only the date line competes for attention. If your stationery includes a printed reference line such as "IN REPLY PLEASE REFER TO:", then you simply fill it in.

The personal notation. When you are typing a personal or confidential letter for your employer, it is customary to alert the reader by typing *"PERSONAL"* or *"CONFIDENTIAL"* on the letter as well as on the envelope.

The personal notation is positioned about three or four spaces above the position of inside address. It is written in solid capitals and underlined to catch the eye.

The inside address. The inside address looks exactly like the address on the envelope; it contains the name and title of the person you are writing to, the name of his firm, and the address.

The positioning of the inside address depends on the length of the letter. It is placed between two and twelve spaces below the date line, on the left side of the page. You will have to be your own judge about where to place the inside address so that the letter is attractively centered on the page.

It is particularly important to use the correct form for the inside address. The person who receives the letter will notice a mistake; it's *his* name and *his* company! Here is how to avoid mistakes:

1. *The name of the company* must be written exactly as it appears on the company's stationery or its official publications. If "Company" is abbreviated to "Co." on their letterhead, for example, then type "Co." in the inside address; if they use "&" instead of spelling it out "and," do the same.

2. *Use proper forms of address* when you are addressing men in official or honorary positions. (See the practical chart of forms of address on page 112.) Note that Mr. or Mrs. or Miss precedes the individual's name even when the business title is used, except when an academic degree or "Esquire" follows the name.

3. *Don't hyphenate a title,* such as Vice President, unless the title is actually the combination of two offices (Secretary-Treasurer).

4. *If the individual holds several titles,* write down only the title of his highest office, unless he signs his letters differently.

5. *Don't abbreviate business titles and positions.*

6. *Place the business title on the first line,* if it is short. Longer titles should go on the second line. Recently, the trend has been to eliminate the title altogether if it causes the address to run five lines or more.

7. *If the letter is addressed to a department of a company,* the name of the company goes on the first line and the name of the department on the second.

8. *The street number is not preceded by anything.* Don't use No. or # or precede the street number with the room number.

9. *Spell out numbers of twelve or under for streets and avenues;* use figures for all house numbers except "one." When a house number is immediately followed by a numbered street, separate the two numbers by a hyphen with spaces at either end. For example:

99 West Ninth Street
222 East 72 Street
One Park Avenue
13 - 13 Street

Never use *d, nd, st* or *th* after the street numbers.

10. *Don't abbreviate the name of the city.* You can abbreviate the names of the states, territories and possessions, but it is considered better form not to.

11. *If there is no street address,* put the city and state on separate lines.

12. *Use the ZIP Code* if you know it. Put it two spaces after the state, with no punctuation in between.

The attention line. Instead of being addressed directly to a particular individual in a firm, many business letters are addressed to the firm and marked for the attention of a person. This marks your letter as a business communiqué; even if the individual is absent, your letter will be opened without delay. An attention line is written in this fashion:

Attention Mr. Michael R. Weil

It is not necessary to include the word "of," to follow the word "attention" with a colon, or to underscore the line itself.

The attention line is transferred from the envelope to the letter itself without change and is positioned two spaces below the inside address, flush with the left-hand margin.

The salutation. The type of salutation you select for a letter depends entirely on the tone of the letter and the relationship that exists between the two correspondents. Over the years certain styles of salutations have come to suggest precise degrees of formality; the same degrees of formality exist between the various styles of complimentary closes. Consequently, certain salutations can only be used with those complimentary closes that suggest a corresponding degree of formality.

On page 112, is a chart outlining four degrees of formality and the salutations and complimentary closes appropriate to them.

The "less formal" category is the style most popular in business letters today. Refer to the Forms of Address chart on pages 114 and 115 of this chapter if you have occasion to address a letter to government officials. As a rule, titled men are addressed in the salutation with the title first and then the surname: "Dear Doctor Pekarne:" or "Dear Professor Thorp:".

	SALUTATIONS	COMPLIMENTARY CLOSES
VERY FORMAL	My dear Sir: Sir: My dear Madam: Madam:	Respectfully, Yours respectfully, Respectfully yours, Very respectfully yours,
FORMAL	Dear Sir: Gentlemen: My dear Mr. Smith: Dear Madam: My dear Mrs. Smith: Mesdames:	Very truly yours, Yours very truly, Yours truly
LESS FORMAL	Dear Mr. Smith: Dear Mrs. Smith: Dear Miss Smith:	Sincerely, Sincerely yours, Very sincerely,
PERSONAL	Dear Mr. Smith: Dear Mrs. Smith: Dear Miss Smith:	Most sincerely, Cordially yours, Cordially,

Figure 18. Salutations and Complimentary Closes.

This does not apply to business titles, however; designations of position in the business world are never put in the salutation.

Notice particularly in the chart above that the salutations are always punctuated with a colon and the closes with a comma. The only exception is a social letter where salutations are punctuated with a comma, particularly if it is in longhand.

Remember that the salutation must be "Gentlemen:" or "Mesdames:" if you have used an attention line; you are actually adressing the firm or the organization, not the individual.

Salutations are positioned two spaces beneath the inside address, or the attention line if there is one, and flush with the left margin of the letter.

The subject line. For the convenience of the reader and to do away with unnecessarily long first paragraphs that only introduce the subject of the letter, many companies now use subject lines in all their letters. A subject line simply states the subject of the letter. It is much appreciated by the secretary who receives the letter, for it makes subject filing much easier.

Some firms preface the subject line with words like "Subject," "In re," or "Re." If these introductory words are used, they are followed by a colon and no part of the line is underscored. The preferred method of writing a subject line is simply to write out the subject of the letter and to underline it.

Subject lines are centered on the page if the letter uses an indented style of format or typed flush with the left-hand margin if no indentation is used.

The body of the letter. The body of the letter is single-spaced unless the letter is under 100 words long. Even such short letters are single-spaced if they are typed on a small-size letterhead. A letter that is under 100 words long and typed on a regular letter head, however, is double-spaced to avoid a cluttered appearance.

Whether you indent the beginning of each paragraph or not depends on the style or format of your letter [see page 118]. When you do indent, however, set the tab five to ten spaces over from the left margin. Remember to indent if the letter is double-spaced, to set off the beginning of new paragraphs.

If you have a numbered list in your letter, center it so that the margins of the list are at least five spaces in from each letter margin. Single space the material after each number; double space between numbered items. The number is either enclosed in parentheses or followed by a period; the material then begins two spaces to the right of the number.

The complimentary close. We have already discussed the form of the complimentary close on page 111. It is positioned two spaces beneath the body of the letter and slightly to the right of center.

The signature block. The name of the executive who is to sign the letter is typed out underneath his signature exactly as he signs it. Drop down four spaces from the complimentary close to leave room for his signature.

Business titles and degree letters are typed directly beneath the

STATE AND LOCAL GOVERNMENT OFFICIALS

Personage	Envelope and Inside Address	Formal Salutation	Informal Salutation	Formal Close	Informal Close	1. Spoken Address 2. Informal Introduction or Reference
Governor of State [1]	*Formal* The Honorable the Governor of Iowa Des Moines *Informal* The Honorable John R. Blank Governor of Iowa Des Moines	Sir:	My dear Governor:	Respectfully yours.	Sincerely yours,	1. Governor Blank *or* Governor 2. Governor Blank *or* The Governor (Outside his own state: The Governor of Iowa)
Lieutenant Governor	The Honorable John R. Blank Lieutenant Governor of Iowa Des Moines	Sir:	My dear Governor Blank:	Respectfully yours, *or* Very truly yours,	Sincerely yours,	1. Governor Blank 2. The Lieutenant Governor of Iowa, Governor Blank (The Lieutenant Governor *or* Governor Blank)
Attorney General	The Honorable John R. Blank Attorney General of New York Albany, New York	Sir:	My dear Mr. Attorney General:	Very truly yours,	Sincerely yours,	1, 2. Mr. Blank
State Representative or Assembly-man	The Honorable John R. Blank House of Representatives Nashville, Tennessee	Sir:	My dear Mr. Blank:	Very truly yours,	Sincerely yours,	1. Mr. Blank 2. Mr. Blank *or* Representative Blank

[1] The form of addressing Governors varies in the different states. The form given here is that used by the State Department of the United States.

STATE AND LOCAL GOVERNMENT OFFICIALS (Continued)

Personage	Envelope and Inside Address	Formal Salutation	Informal Salutation	Formal Close	Informal Close	1. Spoken Address 2. Informal Introduction or Reference
Mayor of a city	The Honorable John R. Blank Mayor of Memphis Tennessee	Sir:	My dear Mayor Blank:	Very truly yours,	Sincerely yours,	1. Mayor Blank *or* Mr. Mayor 2. Mayor Blank
Commissioners of a city	*Formal* The Commissioners of the City of Buffalo New York	Sirs:	Sirs:	Very truly yours,	Sincerely yours,	1. Gentlemen 2. The Commissioners
President of Board of Commissioners	*Formal or Informal* The Honorable John R. Blank President, Board of Commissioners of the City of Buffalo New York	Sir:	My dear Mr. Blank:	Very truly yours,	Sincerely yours,	1, 2. Mr. Blank
District Attorney	The Honorable John R. Blank District Attorney, Sunflower County County Courthouse Indianola, Mississippi	Dear Sir:	Dear Mr. Blank:	Very truly yours,	Sincerely yours,	1, 2. Mr. Blank
City Attorney City Counsel Corporation Counsel	The Honorable John R. Blank City Attorney (City Counsel, Corporation Counsel) Aliceville, Alabama	Dear Sir:	Dear Mr. Blank:	Very truly yours,	Sincerely yours,	1, 2. Mr. Blank
Alderman	Alderman John R. Blank City Hall Aliceville, Alabama	Dear Sir:	Dear Mr. Blank:	Very truly yours,	Sincerely yours,	1, 2. Mr. Blank

typed name of the writer and flush with the left margin of his name. If you are not using departmental stationery, you may also need to include the name of your department; this is typed on the line directly beneath your employer's title. If the letter is typed on executive letterhead stationery and your employer's name and title are engraved at the top of the page, it is perfectly correct to omit his title and even the typed name from the signature block. Most companies still use the name and the title underneath the signature, however, for the sake of clarity. Follow your company's established policy here.

If you are permitted to sign your employer's name to certain correspondence, never forget to sign your own initials immediately below his signature. When you are signing a letter with your own signature as secretary to your executive the proper form is:

Mary E. Whalen
Secretary to Mr. Smith

The identification line. Usually, it is considered desirable for future reference to include some indication of who dictated the letter and who typed it. Since the signature line shows plainly enough who dictated the letter, the trend in recent years has been to include only the typist's initials in the identification line. Her initials are typed in lower case and only on the second sheet; the original is left blank. Firms that use this system feel that there is no reason to clutter the original letter with reference material that is of no use to the person who receives the letter.

Other methods of writing the identification line are still perfectly correct, however:

NFS:yc (The dictator's initials are first.)
(yc) (Rare—used only when the typist composed the letter.)
NFS/yc (Alternate form)
NFS-yc (Alternate form)

All identification lines are positioned flush with the left-hand margin and on a line with the last line of the signature.

The enclosure mark. If your letter contains enclosures, type the word "Enclosure" or the abbreviation "Enc." flush with the left-hand margin and one or two spaces beneath the identification line. Write the number of enclosures after the word or abbreviation, if there are more than one. Be sure to identify important enclosures.

    Enclosure
    Enclosures 3
    Enc. 3
    Enclosure Cert. ck. $476.50

The copy distribution notation. If you are sending a carbon copy of the letter to another person besides the addressee, include a copy distribution notation. Type the words "Copy to" or the abbreviation "c.c" and the name of the person to whom the copy was sent, flush with the left-hand margin and below all other notations—two spaces below if space permits.

The postscript. If it is necessary to add a postscript, it will be

Figure 19. The Skeleton of a Business Letter.

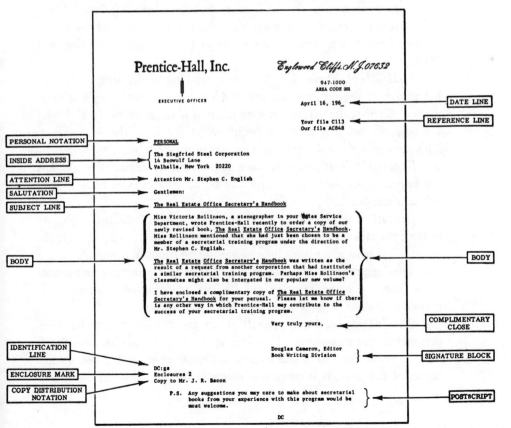

the very last thing that you type. A postscript can be preceded by the initials "P.S." or "P.P.S." for the second postscript; this, again, is a matter of company policy. It is typed two spaces below the identification line or the last notation on the letter. The left margin of the postscript is indented five spaces from the left margin of the letter

Business Letter Formats

We have said that the sample skeleton of a business letter that you have just studied was arranged according to the most widely used format for business letters, "Block Style." The following formats are also correct and are used by many business firms.

Beneath each example of the different formats, you will find a brief explanation of how it differs from the sample business letter skeleton that you have studied. Notice that the fourteen elements remain the same; they are merely arranged in a slightly different fashion. These differences in arrangement are not solely for the appearance of the letter; modern formats are arranged for easier and faster typing, reading and filing.

Full Block style. If you move everything in the sample skeleton letter over to the left margin, you will have "Full Block" style. Notice particularly that the vertical spacing interval is the same as the skeleton; the only difference is that you begin *everything* from the left margin. This modern style is designed to save the secretary time.

Semi-Block style. Look back at the skeleton again. If you indent the beginning of every paragraph five or ten spaces, you have a style called "Semi-Block."

Indented style. Your firm may prefer the "Indented" style. As in the Semi-Block style, you indent five or ten spaces at every paragraph. In addition, you space each line of the inside address five spaces more than the line preceding it and you indent the typed signature four spaces more than the complimentary close. Close punctuation (commas and periods at the end of lines) is used in the inside address.

Official style. Many executives use the "Official" style for their personal letters in business. This format is the same as the Semi-Block format except that the inside address is moved down to the bottom left corner of the page. It is typed two spaces below the signature block and

Prentice-Hall, Inc.

 *Englewood Cliffs, N.J. 07632*

947-1000
AREA CODE 201

EXECUTIVE OFFICES

July 16, 19--

Miss Sheila Jones
The Modern School for Secretaries
12 Harrington Place
Greenpoint, New York

Dear Miss Jones:

You have asked me to send you examples of letter styles being used in offices throughout the country.

This letter is an example of the full block style of letter which has been adopted as a standard at Prentice-Hall. We have reproduced it in our Employee Manual so that everyone will be familiar with the form and the instructions for its use.

Since Prentice-Hall is a leading exponent of modern business methods, we naturally use the most efficient letter form. This style saves time and energy.

As you see, there are no indentations. Everything, including the date and the complimentary close, begins at the extreme left. This uniformity eliminates several mechanical operations in typing letters.

Our dictaphone typists always use this form unless the dictator instructs otherwise. The dictator is at liberty to alter the form if a change is desirable for business reasons.

As the dictator's name is typed in the signature, it is not considered necessary to include his initials in the identification line.

Sincerely,

Martha Scott
Correspondence Chief

cf

Figure 20. Full Block Syle.

Prentice-Hall, Inc.

Englewood Cliffs, N.J. 07632

947-1000
AREA CODE 201

EXECUTIVE OFFICES

July 16, 19--

Miss Sheila Jones
The Modern School for Secretaries
12 Harrington Place
Greenpoint, New York

Dear Miss Jones:

     Most companies have a definite preference as to letter style. Many leading business corporations insist that all letters be typed in semi-block style. This style combines an attractive appearance with utility. Private secretaries, who are not usually concerned with mass production of correspondence, favor it. Here is a sample to add to your correspondence manual.

     This style differs from the block form in only one respect--the first line of each paragraph is indented five or ten spaces. In this example the paragraphs are indented ten spaces. As in all letters, there is a double space between paragraphs.

     The date line is flush with the right margin, two or four spaces below the letterhead. The complimentary close begins slightly to the right of the center of the page. All open punctuation is used in the address.

     No identification line is used in this example. As the dictator's name is typed in the signature, his initials are not necessary. The typist's initials are shown on the carbon copy.

                    Very sincerely yours,

                    Martha Scott
                    Correspondence Chief

Figure 21. Semi-Block Syle.

Prentice-Hall, Inc.

EXECUTIVE OFFICES

Englewood Cliffs. N. J. 07632

947-1000
AREA CODE 201

July 16, 19--

Miss Sheila Jones,
     The Modern School for Secretaries,
          12 Harrington Place,
               Greenpoint, New York.

Dear Miss Jones:

          This is an example of the indented style of letter.
Add this to your correspondence manual along with the other
letters I am enclosing.

          Many conservative organizations still use the in-
dented style in preference to new forms. The indented
style is correct, however, for any type of organization.

          Each line of the address is indented five spaces
more than the preceding line. The beginning of each paragraph is indented the same as the third line of the address,
which is ten spaces. The complimentary close begins a few
spaces to the right of the center of the page. Each line of
the signature is indented three spaces from the beginning of
the complimentary close. Close punctuation is used in the
address but not in the signature.

                                        Sincerely yours,

                                             Martha Scott
                                             Correspondence Chief

Enclosures 5

Figure 22. Indented Style.

flush with the left margin. This format is particularly attractive on an executive letterhead which has only the executive's name and his address engraved across the top of the page.

Simplified Letter style. One of the most modern formats in use today is the "Simplified Letter" style. Like the Full Block style, the simplified letter starts all parts of the letter from the left margin. Unlike the Full Block style, however, it eliminates the salutation and the complimentary close and the "Copy to" preface to the Copy Distribution Notation. As you can see, this format relies heavily on an effective subject line.

Completing the Letter

Additional pages. A long letter that runs more than three lines over the normal length of a letter demands a second page (if you have only one or two lines left over, recenter your original page). Second pages are typed on blank sheets of the same stationery that is used for the first page; only the front page of a long letter is written on letterhead stationery. The top margin and the left margin of the second page should be equal. The name of the person to whom you are writing is then written at the extreme left, the date of the letter at the extreme right and the page number centered on the page:

Mr. Robert Vincent   -2-   April 17, 196-

The page number may also be written Page Two, 2, or (2); whatever form you choose, however, be consistent. Leave a space between the heading and the body of your second page. Set the margins of your second page the same as the margins on the front page.

Addressing the envelope. Copy the inside address exactly as it stands on your letter when you are addressing an envelope. If an address is only three lines long, double space it for greater legibility. If the address is more than three lines long, however, single space it. The address is centered on the envelope, not put off to the right.

Mailing instructions are typed above the address just underneath the stamps where the post office can't fail to see them. The personal notation is typed in capital letters above the address on the left side of

Prentice-Hall, Inc.

EXECUTIVE OFFICES

Englewood Cliffs. N.J.07632

947-1000
AREA CODE 201

July 16, 19--

Dear Miss Jones:

Every correspondence manual should include a sample of
the official style. It is used in many personal letters
written by executives and professional men, and looks un-
usually well on the executive-size letterhead.

The structural parts of the letter differ from the
standard arrangement only in the position of the inside address. The salutation is placed two to five spaces below the
date line, depending upon the length of the letter. It establishes the left margin of the letter. The inside address is
written block form, flush with the left margin, from two to
five spaces below the <u>final</u> line of the signature. Open
punctuation is used in the address.

The identification line, if used, should be placed two
spaces below the last line of the address, and the enclosure
mark two spaces below that. As the dictator's name is typed
in the signature, it is not necessary for the letter to
carry an identification line. The typist's initials are on
the carbon of the letter, but not on the original.

Sincerely yours,

Martha Scott
Correspondence Chief

Miss Sheila Jones
The Modern School for Secretaries
12 Harrington Place
Greenpoint, New York

Figure 23. Official Style

Prentice-Hall, Inc.

EXECUTIVE OFFICES

947-1000
AREA CODE 201

June 16, 19--

Miss Sheila Jones
The Modern School for Secretaries
12 Harrington Place
Greenpoint, New York

THE SIMPLIFIED LETTER

Many modern companies are making increasing use of the
simplified letter style. They feel that this letter style
permits them to come directly to the point in their correspondence without a meaningless salutation and a slow introductory sentence.

Notice that the salutation and the close are missing and
that all the remaining parts of the letter are typed from
the left margin. The subject line is typed in solid capital letters to attract attention and so is the signature
block. Another distinguishing feature about the signature
block is that it is typed on one line beneath the signature.
Finally, notice that the identification line is dropped
along with the words "Copy to" in the copy distribution
notation.

MARTHA SCOTT - CORRESPONDENCE CHIEF

Miss Besse May Limler, Miss Sylvia Scarsdale

Figure 24. The Simplified Letter.

```
PRENTICE-HALL, INC.
  ENGLEWOOD CLIFFS
  NEW JERSEY 07632




            PERSONAL

                    Mr. R. S. Jackson, President
                    Northern Manufacturing Company
                    25 West 79 Street
                    Milwaukee, Wisconsin  00521




8-040HJ
```

Figure 25. Envelope Showing Correct Placement of
Personal Notation.

the envelope. An attention line is positioned two or three spaces up from
the bottom edge of the envelope on the left side exactly as it is on the
letter. Since some other notations can also correctly occupy this position,
it is also considered correct for the attention line as well as the "care
of" line to be typed on the second line of the envelope address. The
sample envelopes on this and the following page will help you visualize
this.

```
PRENTICE-HALL, INC.
  ENGLEWOOD CLIFFS
  NEW JERSEY 07632



                                                    SPECIAL DELIVERY

                    Northern Manufacturing Company

                    25 West 79 Street

                    Milwaukee, Wisconsin  00521


        Attention Mr. R. S. Jackson

8-040HJ
```

Figure 26. Envelope Showing Correct Placement of Attention Line
and Special Delivery Notation.

Proofread your letter. Never forget to proofread a letter before you hand it to your employer for his signature. Don't mistake scanning a letter quickly for proofreading; more than that is involved. To proofread a letter correctly you must read it carefully with separate questions in mind:

- Did I leave anything out?
- Did I transcribe the contents verbatim?
- Is the spelling correct?
- Is the punctuation correct?

Remember, your letter is not complete until it has been proofread.

Chapter 9

Writing Letters Without Dictation

THE REAL ESTATE business is a service business in which the relationship between the real estate man and the people with whom he deals is usually a personal one. The people who write to him about business matters want to feel that he is giving their letter his personal attention. Also, the transactions usually involve considerable sums of money and any misstatement or indiscreet expression might spoil a deal and result in a loss of commission. For these reasons, most letters are dictated by the employer.

However, there are certain letters that the secretary can write without dictation, thus saving her employer's time. For example, letters arranging appointments and letters of acknowledgment are often composed by the secretary. Some of these letters are signed by the secretary with her name; others are composed for her employer's signature. This chapter covers the usual letters written without dictation. They are presented in two sections:

    1. Letters the secretary writes over her own signature

    2. Letters the secretary writes for her employer's signature

Letters the Secretary Writes over Her Own Signature

Letters usually written over the secretary's signature. A letter signed with your name should not be sent to a writer who expects his letter to be answered by your employer. However, there are several kinds of letters that you can write and sign yourself because you are expected to write them or because it is common practice for a secretary to attend to them. These letters include:

Acknowledgments of correspondence received during your employer's absence

Letters arranging appointments

Letters calling attention to omission of enclosures

Travel arrangements

Replies to notices of meetings

Follow-up letters

A pattern and models for each type follow. The signature is the same in each case:

> (*Your name*)
> Secretary to Mr. Moore

Acknowledgment of correspondence received during an employer's absence.

Acknowledgment of a letter received during your employer's absence is a business courtesy. These letters fall into two classes: (1) an acknowledgment without answering the letter, and (2) an acknowledgment that also answers the letter.

Acknowledgment without answer. The pattern for these letters is simple.

1. Say that your employer is out of the city or away from the office.

2. Give the expected date of his return.

3. Assure the writer that his message will receive attention when your employer returns.

Do not refer to your employer's illness when explaining his absence from the office, unless the addressee knows that he is ill. Say, "Because of Mr. Roberts' absence from the office, he will not be able to attend. . . ."

Dear Mr. ————:

In the absence of Mr. Adams I am acknowledging receipt of your letter of July 10. It is being held for his attention upon his return early next week.

Very truly yours,

Dear Mr. ————:

Your letter of August 14 arrived the day after Mr. Tauber left for a short vacation. Since it does not appear to require an immediate reply, I shall hold it for his attention on his return.

Very truly yours,

Acknowledgment that also answers. The important factor in answering, as well as acknowledging, a letter during your employer's absence is to *know the facts.* Here is a suggested pattern:

1. Identify the incoming letter.

2. Say that your employer is away.

3. State the facts that answer the letter.

4. If appropriate, or desirable, say that your employer will write when he returns.

Dear Mr. ————:

Your letter reminding Mr. Smith of the Rotary Club luncheon on October 17 has arrived during his absence from the office on his vacation.

Mr. Smith plans to return to Starkville the 17th and to attend the luncheon. If there are any changes in his plans, I shall let you know.

Very sincerely,

Dear Mr. ————:

Your letter asking Mr. Ainsworth to speak before the ABC Club of your city on January 14 arrived a few days after he left town on a business trip.

Checking Mr. Ainsworth's schedule for January 14, I find that he is to be chairman of a local civic group meeting that evening. It therefore will be impossible for him to address the members of your club.

Mr. Ainsworth will write to you when he returns to Nashville.

Very sincerely,

Dear Mr. ————:

Mr. Smith will be out of town for the next several weeks, but, in any case, he is is not the man in this company with whom you should talk about your service.

Mr. Ernest Jones buys all our building supplies, and he will be glad to talk with you if you will come in any Tuesday or Thursday morning. It might be well for you to telephone in advance just to make sure that he is here.

He will have this correspondence, so please refer to it when you call.

Sincerely yours,

Letters arranging appointments. The letters you write concerning appointments deal with these three situations:

1. Your employer asks for an appointment.

2. You ask someone to come in to see your employer.

3. You reply to a letter asking your employer for an appointment. Here is the general pattern for such letters:

1. Refer to the purpose of the appointment.

2. Suggest, or ask the person to whom you are writing to suggest, the time, the place, and the date.

3. Ask for a confirmation of the appointment or say you will confirm the appointment by telephone.

YOUR EMPLOYER ASKS FOR APPOINTMENT: *You want to fix the time.*

Dear Mr. ————:

Mr. Brown will be in your city for a few hours on Tuesday, March 22. He would like to discuss with you the operating budget for the apartment building at 252 Main Street.

Will it be convenient for Mr. Brown to call at your office at 3 o'clock on March 22?

Very truly yours,

You have to let the other person fix the time.

Dear Mr. ————:

Mr. Brown is returning from Chicago the end of this week. He would like to discuss with you the result of his conference with the owner of the property adjoining yours.

Please ask your secretary to telephone me at Algonquin 4–9200 and let me know when it will be convenient for you to see Mr. Brown.

Very truly yours,

YOU ASK SOMEONE TO COME IN TO SEE YOUR EMPLOYER: *You want to fix the time.*

My dear Mr. ————:

Mr. Brown would like to see you on Monday, February 27, at two o'clock at his office, Room 201, to complete arrangements for the rental of your summer cottage.

Please let me know whether this time is convenient.

Very truly yours

You have to let the other person fix the time.

My dear Mr. ————:

The papers in connection with your rental of Apartment No. 7 C of the Woodstock Apartments are now complete, except for your signature. Mr. Brown would like you to come to his office early next week to sign them. Please telephone me when it will be convenient for you to do this.

Very truly yours,

REPLY TO REQUEST ASKING YOUR EMPLOYER FOR AN APPOINTMENT: *You fix a definite time, but ask for verification.*

My dear Mr. ————:

Mr. Brown will be glad to see you on Monday, December 27, at two o'clock at his office, to discuss with you the program for the annual convention. I suggest that you telephone me before coming in order to be sure that he will be available. Mr. Brown is frequently out of the office and is sometimes unexpectedly detained.

Very truly yours,

You want to let the other person fix the time.

My dear Mr. ————:

Mr. Brown will be glad to see you some time during the week of March 3, to talk over the installation of the elevator in the residence at 20 West 20 Street.

If you will telephone me, we can arrange a time that will be convenient for you and Mr. Brown. The number is Algonquin 4–9200.

Very truly yours,

Your employer signs the letter.

Dear Mr. ————:

I shall be happy to talk with you when you are in Minneapolis next week. Would it be convenient for you to come to my office at ten o'clock Thursday morning, November 5? I believe this hour would give us the best opportunity to discuss your project without interruption.

It will be a pleasure to see you again.

Cordially yours,

You have to postpone fixing a definite time.

My dear Mr. ————:

This is in answer to your letter asking for an appointment with Mr. Brown.

He is away from the office and is not expected back until the end of the month. I shall write to you just as soon as I know when he will be able to see you.

Very truly yours,

You have to say "no" politely.

My dear Mr. ————:

Mr. Brown has considered very carefully all that you said in your letter of December 21. If there were any possibility that a meeting with you would be helpful, he would be glad to see you. However, he does not believe that would be the case and has asked me to write to you to that effect.

Very truly yours,

You fix the time, but say you will verify the appointment.

My dear Mr. ————:

You asked whether you could see Mr. Brown on Monday, March 20. According to his present plans, he will be in the office between 10 and 11 o'clock that day and will be glad to see you then. However, just to be sure that nothing unexpected interferes with this appointment, I shall telephone you early on Monday morning to verify it.

Very truly yours,

Letters calling attention to omission of enclosures. When an enclosure mentioned in an incoming letter is omitted, you should notify the sender. Here is the pattern your letter should follow:

1. Identify the incoming letter and enclosure mentioned in it.
2. State that the enclosure was omitted.
3. Ask that the enclosure, or a copy of it, be sent to you.

Dear Mr. ————:

In your letter of March 3 to Mr. Edwards, you said that you were enclosing the heating guaranty from the Excelsior Heating Co. The guaranty, however, was not enclosed.

As the closing papers will not be complete without this guaranty, Mr. Edwards would like to have it as soon as possible.

Very truly yours,

Letters making plane and train reservations. *Plane.* The points to cover in a letter making a plane reservation are:

1. Name and position of person desiring reservation
2. Flight and date on which space is desired
3. Schedule of flight
4. Air card number (if any)
5. Confirmation

Gentlemen:

Mr. Edward P. Case, president of Case Realty Company, would like to reserve space for Los Angeles on Flight 26 out of Chicago on Saturday, November 24. Our schedule shows this flight leaves at 9.45 A.M., Central Standard Time, and arrives in Los Angeles at 2.55 P.M., Pacific Standard Time.

Please confirm reservation by wire immediately.

Yours very truly,

Train. A letter making a train reservation includes:

1. Name and position of person desiring reservation
2 Accommodation desired
3. Point of departure and destination
4. Date and time
5. Name of train, if known
6. Arrangement for delivery of tickets
7. Confirmation
8. Arrangement for payment

Gentlemen:

Please reserve a drawing room for Mr. Edward P. Case, president of Case Realty Company, on the Rosebowl from Chicago to Los Angeles, leaving Chicago Saturday, November 27, at 3:00 P.M. Mr. Case will call for the tickets at the Chicago station on November 24. Please confirm reservation by wire as soon as possible.

If you will send the invoice for the tickets to this office, we shall remit at once.

Yours very truly,

Letters making hotel reservations. When you write for hotel reservations for your employer include the following information:

1. Accommodations desired
2. Name of person for whom reservation is requested
3. Date and time of arrival

4. Probable date of departure

5. Request for confirmation

Also inquire about checking-out time.

Gentlemen:

Please reserve for Mr. John C. Williams a corner bedroom and bath, preferably a southeastern exposure, beginning Monday, December 14. Mr. Williams will arrive early in the evening of the 14th and plans to leave the morning of December 20.

Please confirm this reservation by wire.

Very truly yours,

Gentlemen:

Please reserve a living room and bedroom suite for Mr. and Mrs. John C. Williams, who will arrive on the morning of Monday, December 14. Mr. and Mrs. Williams plan to leave on Thursday afternoon, December 17.

Please confirm this reservation and also let me know your checking-out time.

Very truly yours,

Reply to notice of meeting. Sometimes the secretary knows whether or not her employer plans to attend a meeting; at other times, she must find out from him what his plans are. Her letter covers the following points:

1. Repeat the time, date, and place of the meeting.

2. Say whether or not the employer plans to attend the meeting.

3. Give a reason if he does not plan to attend.

Dear Mr. ————:

Mr. Mason plans to be present at the meeting of the Executive Committee of the ———— Association of Real Estate Boards to be held on Tuesday, October 26, at 9:30 A.M., in your office.

Yours sincerely,

Dear Mr. ————:

Mr. Mason has the notice of the meeting of the Executive Committee of the ———— Association of Real Estate Boards to be held on Tuesday, October 26, 9:30 A.M., Unfortunately, previous business appointments will prevent him from attending the meeting.

Yours sincerely,

Follow-up letters. If correspondence in your follow-up file (see Chapter 4) is not answered by the follow-up date, trace the letter for ı reply. Your letter should cover the following points:

1. Identify the letter. Identification by date is not sufficient because your correspondent does not know what you are writing to him about.

2. Offer a reason for the recipient's failure to reply, without casting reflection on him.

3. Enclose a copy of your original letter, unless it was very short. If so, simply repeat the contents in your follow-up letter.

Copy of original letter not enclosed.

Gentlemen:
   On February 2 we ordered from you 48, 16 oz., 12 lbs. to a dozen, 16″ long, wet mops at 72 cents each, but we have not yet had an acknowledgment of the order.
   As our first order evidently went astray, please consider this a duplicate.
                                                              Very truly yours,

Copy of original letter enclosed. (If the original letter was signed by your employer, the follow-up usually will also be signed by him.)

Dear Mr. ————:
   In the rush of work you probably have not had time to answer my letter of October 25 asking for additional information about the two pieces of property you own in Fresno. On the chance that this letter did not reach you, I am enclosing a carbon copy of it.
   I shall be grateful for your reply by return mail.
                                                              Very truly yours,

Dear Mr. ————:
   It is possible that my airmail letter of March 6 to you has been laid aside to receive attention a little later. However, on the chance that it went astray, I am enclosing a copy and shall appreciate hearing from you as soon as convenient.
                                                              Very truly yours,

Letters the Secretary Writes for her Employer's Signature

Kinds of letters the secretary composes. The longer a secretary remains with a particular employer and the more familiar she becomes with the business of the firm, the more likely she is to prepare from a few simple instructions letters for her employer's signature. These instructions might be verbal or marked on a letter that requires a reply.

The letters a secretary commonly writes on instructions, for her employer's signature, are of the following types:

1. Letters of transmittal
2. Letters acknowledging receipt of papers
3. Letters asking for additional information
4 Letters transmitting information

The signature. Usually, an employer will permit his secretary to sign *his* name to letters of transmittal and letters acknowledging receipt of papers. In that case the signature should appear as explained at page 116. Letters transmitting information and asking for additional information should ordinarily be placed on your employer's desk for his perusal and signature. Only on specific instructions from your employer should you sign your employer's name to such letters. You must also bear in mind that all *sales* letters should be signed by a licensed broker, if there is a license law in your state. If you write such a letter on instructions from your employer, and indicate in it that you are writing as instructed (see sample at pages 140–141), you will be on safe ground.

Letters of transmittal. In writing a letter to accompany documents, papers, or other important material, follow the pattern given below.

1. Say that you are enclosing the papers.

2. Be specific in identifying the papers. Don't just say that you are enclosing an exclusive listing agreement, lease, contract, or other document. For example, if you are returning a title policy, give the name of the title company, policy number, the property it covers (unless the address is in the reference line), the amount of the policy, and the name of the person to whom issued. By fully describing the paper, you have a permanent record of its disposition.

3. List the papers, if several are enclosed.

4. Be specific about instructions for signing if **any** of the papers require signature. Always put a cross mark (x) lightly in pencil immediately before the line on which the person is to sign, and call attention to it in the letter of transmittal. (In transmitting papers to an attorney the instructions for signing need not be included.) Where the precaution is necessary, call attention to the necessity for signing exactly as the name appears in the document. (See page 199 for explanation of how documents are signed by partnerships and corporations.)

5. Close with an offer to be of further assistance, if that remark is

pertinent, or with some other friendly note. Remember, however, that the closing should add something definite to the letter or it should not be there.

Transmittal letter to purchaser, enclosing a fully executed copy of a contract of sale.

> Park Drive
> Mountainside, N. J.

Dear Mr. ————:

I am happy to enclose your fully executed copy of the contract of sale covering your purchase of the vacant land at the above address.

Will you kindly have your attorney advise us when he will be ready to close title so that we may arrange an appointment for all parties.

> Very truly yours,

Transmittal letter to tenant's attorney, enclosing lease and requesting signature.

> Hopf Lease
> 1083 Louisa Avenue
> Elizabeth, New Jersey

Dear Mr. ————:

I am enclosing three copies of a new lease covering the tenancy at the above address, for the period beginning May 1, 19— and ending April 30, 19—. It provides for a regular monthly rental of $175, payable on the first of each month in advance.

Kindly have your client execute all copies and return them to me with the security deposit of $350. I feel quite certain that Miss Falco will execute this lease. If so, I shall return two copies to your office; the extra one is for Mr. Hopf's files.

> Very truly yours,

Letter to seller reporting the sale of a property and asking seller to sign and return deposit receipt.

Dear Mr. and Mrs. ————:

I am glad to report the sale of your home at 918 Grand Avenue, Fresno, as shown by the enclosed deposit receipt dated February 20, 19—.

Will you please read the deposit receipt carefully, and, if it is all right, sign and return it to me in the enclosed envelope. I have indicated a cross (x) on the lines where each of you is to sign.

The sale has already been escrowed with escrow officer, John Jones, Liberty Title Insurance & Guarantee Company, 1631 Commerce Street.

My warm personal regards to both of you.

Sincerely yours,

Letter returning deposit to co broker, rejecting offer of his client.

623 Westfield Avenue
Elizabeth, New Jersey

My dear Mr. ————:

We regret that we are unable to persuade our seller of the above-noted property to accept your client's offer of $15,500. We are therefore enclosing your check in the amount of $500 posted with us as deposit, together with all copies of the Offer and Acceptance Agreement signed by Mr. and Mrs. Jones.

We feel confident that if you can interest your buyers in submitting an offer of approximately $17,000 we could persuade the Browns to accept it.

Please keep us advised of your progress.

Very truly yours,

Letter transmitting copies of multiple listing agreements, and requesting signature.

Elm Terrace, corner Brookside Road
and
Elm Terrace, adjoining Brookside Road
Rahway, New Jersey

My dear Mr. ————:

Enclosed are triplicate copies of Multiple Listing Agreements covering each of the above-noted properties.

If you will sign two copies of each, on the line marked "Seller," and return them to us, we will immediately enter this listing on our preferred list, re-list it with all of the brokers in the Multiple Listing System, advertise it, and, in short, do everything necessary to effect a quick sale.

Very truly yours,

Transmittal letter covering instructions for signing. (Your employer asks you to send the prospect the regular printed proposition form used in the office. He and the prospect have already agreed upon all the terms.)

Dear Mr. ————:

In accordance with our conversation, I am enclosing two copies of the agreement in which you offer to purchase the property located at 1210 Main Street, Smithtown, Connecticut, from John Jones, the owner. The terms and conditions of the offer have been set forth in full.

Will you please sign the original of the agreement on the line marked with an (x). Your signature should be exactly as your name appears in the agreement. The duplicate of the agreement is to be retained by you.

When you return the signed agreement to us, please enclose your check for $ to cover the deposit called for by the agreement.

Yours very truly,

Letters acknowledging receipt of papers. Important papers received from a client should be acknowledged. Describe the papers sufficiently to identify them.

Letter acknowledging receipt of papers from owner and calling attention to one that was not supplied.

My dear Mr. ————:

We have received the following papers that you sent us on October 15.

1. Receipted tax bill for $80, paid to the Village of Farmingdale, June 12, 19—, covering the period ————.
2. New York Fire Insurance Company Policy No. 444 covering property located at 103 Hemingway Drive, in the amount of $10,000. This policy expires January 1, 19—.

We also asked in our letter of October 10 for the service contract that you have with the Blane Exterminating Co. Will you please send that contract to us by return mail. It is one of the papers that must be examined in connection with the closing of the sale.

Very truly yours,

Letters asking for additional information. This type of letter is ordinarily written on instructions from your employer. He will tell you what to ask for and give you any other points he wants mentioned.

Letter asking for a property description and transmitting information given by your employer.

Dear Mr. ————:

Thank you for your letter of January 31.

You will have to supply an exact legal description of the property, and advise me definitely that you want to sell it.

I do not believe that I can get you $2,000 down on a $2,800 listing.

As much as I would like to help you, I believe I had better not start working on your property until I hear from you. It would be better for you to come to my office. Then we can get together and see what can be done.

Sincerely yours,

Letter asking for several items of information.

Dear Mrs. —————:

Thank you for your letter of February 26.

Will you please show the exact location of your two pieces of property on the map that is enclosed?

I must also have the following additional information:

(1) Are both properties clear? If not, either send passbooks for my information, or tell me the balances, monthly payments, rates of interest, and other details of the loans, and, of course, who made the loans.

(2) What are the exact legal descriptions of the two properties? If you will send me the tax receipts for these two properties, I shall be able to obtain the legal descriptions.

(3) What is the exact legal description of the parcel that is to be sold? Where a seller is dividing a piece of land, an exact legal description must be created for the parcel to be sold.

As soon as I have this additional information, I shall make a careful inspection of the property.

Sincerely yours,

Letter transmitting information. When you transmit information of a selling nature, be sure that the letter is signed by your employer. If you sign it yourself, indicate that you are transmitting the information at the request of your employer.

Dear Mr. and Mrs. —————:

Mr. Woessner instructed me to forward the following information to you about a 1¼ acre piece of lake front property at Bass Lake which our office listed today. There are no buildings. It has approximately 300 feet of lake frontage offering excellent development possibilities for swimming, boating, and fishing. The land backs up to the main Yosemite highway. The slope of the property is fine for cabins. There is an ideal highway spot for a grocery, general merchandise store, and gas station. A full view of the lake and the beautiful back country enhance its value.

Mr. Woessner also stated that property of this kind is hard to find and seldom becomes available for sale. Because of their age, an old pioneer couple have asked Mr. Woessner to put it on the market. The listed price is $21,500 cash. Mr. Woessner said that he was specifically instructed not to accept any offers for lesser amounts.

I was requested by Mr. Woessner to ask you to phone or write him immediately if you are interested.

Sincerely yours,
Hazel Wright
Secretary to Mr. Woessner

Chapter 10

Model Letters for the Real Estate Office

A SECRETARY IN A real estate office may expect to use certain types of letters over and over again. Among these are: (1) letters written without dictation; (2) processed form letters used in carrying out various routines; (3) letters seeking listings; (4) selling letters used in situations that constantly recur or that can be sent out at regular intervals; (5) goodwill letters that are used in recurring situations. This chapter deals with these five kinds of repeat letters.

Model forms for letters written without dictation. Once you have written a good letter to meet situations like those described in the preceding chapter, your letter is a model that you can follow when the situation recurs. It is therefore advisable to make copies of letters you are likely to need and keep them in a form letter file. Analyze your correspondence to see what types of letters, in addition to those given at pages 127–141, you use frequently. In each category select one you have already written to meet the need, improving it if you can. Then place it as a model in your form letter file.

You will also find that model paragraphs can be used in many letters. For example, if you merely acknowledge a letter received in your employer's absence, your opening paragraph could be used again when you write a letter in his absence that is to contain the desired information.

Place the paragraph in your form letter file. In this file you may also place the model letters that you adapt from those given in this chapter.

Processed form letters. A routine processed form letter may be reproduced by multilith, multigraph, photo-offset, printing, or other duplicating process. Whenever the letter is purely routine or when the recipient is interested only in the information it contains, a mechanically processed letter can be used to advantage. A number of examples of processed letters are given in Chapter 18. The fact that anyone can recognize a form letter is not important; you are not trying to fool the reader. If the message is directed to him, the letter will be read. However, it sometimes makes a letter more effective to give it a personal touch. Here are some suggestions for personalizing the appearance and layout of form letters:

1. Use a good quality of paper.

2. Type in the date line, the inside address, the salutation, and the complimentary close.

3. Carefully match the ribbon used for the fill-ins with the type in the letter.

4. Sign the letter with pen and ink.

5. Seal the envelope.

6. Send the letter by first-class mail.

Letters seeking listings. One of the most effective methods of procuring listings is to solicit them with a well-written letter. By this form of direct mail, every property owner in a locality can be reached. The following are examples of listing letters, reproduced through the courtesy of the firms mentioned.

Dear ————:

If you are considering selling your home, call at the offices of Arthur J. Parsons.

Our organization is large enough to give you maximum sales representation, yet small enough to know each owner and his individual problems.

During the many years we have been in business, we have been successful in developing effective plans for selling residential real estate. The effectiveness of these plans can best be proven by the fact that we have succeeded in selling over one hundred properties a year during the past five years.

Just call Boulevard 3–1400 or sign and forward the enclosed card. One of our representatives will call on you and explain our methods.

Unlike most businesses, we in the real estate business have no merchandise to sell. We have only our service to offer you.

We welcome the opportunity of being of service.

Yours very truly,

P.S. If your property is now listed with another broker, we would welcome the opportunity of cooperating with him.

(Courtesy of Arthur J. Parsons, Upper Darby, Pa.)

Dear Sir:

I have a minimum of 250 prospective buyers for your property. Will you let me show it to them?

It is my suggestion that you list this property through me under the Madison Board of Realtors' Multiple Listing Service, the finest established machinery of cooperative real estate selling that has ever been in existence. Not only does it comprise the specialized attention and responsibility of the Listing Agent, but it includes the broad coverage of a vast number of salesmen; and, to top it off, the property owner, desirous of selling, pays NOTHING for this service.

Here are only a few of the services my office will bring you:

DAILY AND SUNDAY NEWSPAPER ADVERTISING IN MADISON

DAILY AND SUNDAY RADIO ADVERTISING OVER WIBA

LONG LIST OF PROSPECTIVE PURCHASERS

EXPERT SALESMANSHIP FROM TOPNOTCH SALESMEN

EXPERT APPRAISAL SERVICE

You have the property for sale; I have the cash purchasers. Call me, and let me serve you.

Sincerely yours,

(Courtesy of Badger Realty Service, Madison, Wisconsin)

Dear ....:

The Home Near You

At ....

Has New Owners

It was sold through our office to some folks we are sure you are going to like as neighbors.

If your home or some neighboring homes you know about might also be for sale, we would appreciate knowing of it. We have some more people who would like to locate in your neighborhood.

Why not give us a ring or drop in and tell us about it.

Yours very truly,

(Courtesy of Hamline Twin City Real Estate Co., St. Paul, Minnesota)

Dear Sir:

While passing through your neighborhood yesterday I saw your beautiful home and admired it very much. It is an outstanding place and extremely well kept. I know you must enjoy living in it.

I have a prospective home owner who I am sure would be delighted to find a place near yours. He wants one of about the same quality and value as yours. If you know of such a place and would like to have another good neighbor, won't you please telephone me or drop me a card giving the name and address of the owner. I will be most grateful to you.

You may be sure that any information given me will be held in strict confidence.

Cordially yours,

(Courtesy of C. C. Walker, Jacksonville, Florida)

Adaptable form letters for increasing sales. Many enterprising real estate offices use the mails constantly in their sales promotion efforts. They have prepared a number of letters that meet specific situations, and they mail these letters to appropriate people. For example, they may have a letter to send to neighboring families of listed properties seeking help in finding buyers. That letter will be used for each new listing. They may have another for all people who have advertised in the "wanted to rent" columns. As advertisements by people who want to rent homes or apartments appear in the local newspapers, the letter is typed and sent to the advertiser. Another prepared-in-advance letter may be a congratulatory note that is sent to people whose betrothal or wedding has been announced, or who have announced the birth of a child. The announcements are clipped from the local newspapers and the appropriate letters are sent out with them.

If your employer already uses such letters, you may be the one who has to take care of sending them out. If your office does not make use of this business-building technique, you may introduce the idea yourself. A number of such letters are given below, through the courtesy of the firms mentioned. You can adapt them to your needs and help to establish the routine for getting them out regularly, if your employer approves of the idea.

A letter to neighboring families to help find buyers.

Dear ————:

Your neighbor, Mr. James Brown, has asked me to sell his home at 1517 Algonquin Street for $25,500.

I am trying to find someone who will be a congenial neighbor for you. It has occurred to me that since you will be greatly interested in this sale you might like to suggest a friend or relative whom you would like to see buy this property.

If you can suggest a buyer, please call Central 7-7700 and give me his name. I will be most grateful for **your** suggestion.

Cordially yours,

(Courtesy of Harry Howes, Clinton, Iowa)

A letter sent to "wanted to rent" advertisers.

Dear ————·

May I bring to your attention an old realty saying:
"Whether you rent, or whether you buy,
You pay for the home that you occupy."

If you are going to pay for the home you occupy, why not own it? Otherwise, you will be buying it for the landlord.

I saw your "wanted to rent" ad in the Sunday paper, and I have a house for sale that fits your needs to perfection. This home, at 6057 Meade Avenue, is like a picture out of *Better Homes and Gardens*.

There is a large living room with unlimited possibilities for furniture arrangement, modern kitchen, breakfast nook that sparkles with inviting charm, and three beautiful bedrooms, including a master bedroom.

I will be pleased to show you this property at your convenience. It can be bought for a small down payment and monthly payments of $60, including $5\frac{1}{2}$ per cent interest.

Sincerely,

(Courtesy of Jolly Jacks, San Diego, California)

A letter congratulating a betrothed person.

Dear ————:

Having noticed the announcement of your engagement to Miss...in the newspapers, we are taking this opportunity to congratulate you and at the same time offer our services in securing desirable living quarters for you. We are in a position to serve you either in the rental or purchase of a single residence, a two-family house, or apartment and should appreciate hearing from you.

We are enclosing a questionnaire upon which you may set forth your requirements.

Cordially,

(Courtesy of Joseph Laronge, Inc., Cleveland, Ohio)

A letter congratulating a married couple.

Hello Happy Couple!
  Congratulations! Best wishes for loads of joy in your married life.
  How about a home or an apartment? Phone or write your require-
ments, and we shall do anything we can to house you.

Cordially,

(Courtesy of V. P. Bradley, the W. M. Dickinson Co., Trenton, New Jersey)

A letter for birth announcements.

Hi "New Comer:"
  Delighted you have arrived. Hope you have a healthy and happy
babyhood, gladdening the hearts of your parents and anyone else who
sees you.
  When you have a moment and can talk, tell Mother and Dad you want
a nicer home now, and that later you will want a safer place to play so you
will grow up to be big and strong. Please tell them to see us about it.
  Wonder if this is the first note you have received. Hope so. Remember
we are very glad you came.

Lovingly,

(Courtesy of V. P. Bradley, the W. M. Dickinson Co., Trenton, New Jersey)

A letter to accompany a brief sent to prospects.

Dear Sir:
  We are pleased to present for your consideration the home located at
287 Blenheim Road
Columbus, Ohio

owned by   Mr. and Mrs. Clarence L. Weaver
  Mr. and Mrs. Weaver and moving out of the city. They expect to be in
their new home by November 1, and possession can be given on the
property at about that time.
  All estimates, statements, and descriptions in the enclosed brief are
correct to the best of our knowledge and, while not guaranteed, were
obtained from sources we deem reliable.
  We shall appreciate your courtesy if, when this brief has served its
purpose, you will return it to us.
  Thank you for interest in this property.

Cordially yours,

(Courtesy of Henry E. Worley, Columbus, Ohio)

A letter to weed out prospect files.

Dear Sir:

Not having heard from you recently, I am naturally led to believe that you have found the home of your choice. If so, I should like to be among the first to congratulate you. Buying a home is one of the most important steps necessary in assuring security and happiness for yourself and for your family.

If, however, you have not yet purchased a home, I am confident that we can locate just what you want—at a price and with a financing setup that will suit your budget.

We are getting new and attractive listings daily, and we are sure that many of them will meet with your approval.

Won't you please let us know if you wish us to keep your name on our prospect list by writing "yes" or "no" on the enclosed self-addressed card. Better still, check the box telling us to drop around to show you our latest listings.

Cordially,

Letter to follow up a property inspection by a prospect.

Dear ————:

From my own observation, and from the information you have given me, I am firmly convinced that the house at 2119 Pine Street is FOR YOU.

This beautiful home meets your requirements in regard to location and commuting distance; it fills the social requirements of a man in your position, and it is within the limits of the price you set.

In plain words, YOU SHOULD BUY THIS PROPERTY. If we do not sell it to you, in all probability we will sell it to the wrong person. The property fits you.

Why don't you sign the enclosed contract and return it with a deposit?

Respectfully yours,

(Courtesy of James A. Rooney, Albany, New York)

A letter announcing a sales call.

Dear ————.

It has been some time since we had the pleasure of talking to you about your personal housing problems.

According to our files, we last saw you at our office when you inquired about the house at 269 Van Buren Street—the one with the large landscaped yard and the outdoor fireplace.

As we recollect, there were a few things about that house that did not quite come up to your family's needs. Since it is our wish to be of service to those who consult us, we are always on the alert to satisfy individual requirements. We now have a listing that will interest you, I am sure.

I would like to drop by your home Thursday evening around 7.30 to tell you about this outstanding home. Please phone me if this time is not convenient and we'll fix a more suitable hour.

(Courtesy of Donald J. Dockry, Green Bay, Wisconsin)

A letter to notify "cold" prospects of new listing.

Dear Dr. and Mrs. ————:

We have found a home that I feel certain will solve your residential problems!

It is conveniently located in a well-established section near the city; transportation, stores, and schools are nearby. It has a library, with connecting bath, that you could use for your office. There are also many features that Mrs. .... would like.

The price is under the figure that you have set. Satisfactory purchase terms can be arranged.

Call us at Main 5–6000 and we will arrange a convenient time to show you this home.

Sincerely yours,

(Courtesy of Joseph Laronge, Inc., Cleveland, Ohio)

Adaptable good will letters. Another type of repeat letter is one designed to build goodwill for the firm. For example, to keep the firm's name before an old customer and to retain his goodwill, a letter might be sent out on the anniversary of the purchase of his home. The following samples, reproduced through the courtesy of the firms mentioned, suggest the situations for which such letters can be used.

Again, you might present the idea to your employer of using such letters because they have been found profitable by the firms that have used them. It would then become your duty to establish the routines for mailing out the goodwill letters. To follow through with the anniversary letter, for example, you would have to get up a record of each closing with the name of the purchaser, his address, and the date of the closing. These cards would be arranged chronologically. You would use them as you do other reminder calendars.

Greetings on the anniversary of purchase of a home.

Dear Mr. and Mrs. ————:
   Birthday Greetings! You bought your home one year ago today.
   We hope that it has given you, during the first year, the service and pleasure you expected when you purchased it.
   It was a real pleasure on our part to have served you.
Cordially yours,

Dear Mr. ————:
   It has been almost a year since you purchased your home at .... Street. By this time you have had extended opportunity to appraise the wisdom of your investment, and we sincerely trust that you continue satisfied with our recommendation.
   We appreciate the confidence you placed in our office. Whenever we can be of further service to you or any of your friends, we shall be pleased to have you call us.
Sincerely yours,

(Courtesy of W. Kelton Evans, Madison, New Jersey)

Goodwill letter to home purchaser.

Dear Mr. & Mrs. ————:
   The following is a list of reminders which we thought would be of value to you now that you are in your new home:
   1. Register it at the Assessor's office.
   2. Notify insurance company which covers your household goods. If you have a fire they might not otherwise be covered.
   3. Notify automobile insurance company. Refund may be in order if you have moved from a higher rate area.
   4. Change address of all drivers' licenses in the family. If you get picked up for a minor violation, and your address is incorrect, you might be liable to a fine or suspension of license.
   5. Your Post Office address is Newton, Massachusetts.
   6. Your nearest railroad station is Newton, Massachusetts.
   7. Your nearest library is Newton Free Library, 414 Centre St., Newton.
   8. Rubbish and ash collection is made every Tuesday. Your next collection will be on December 17th.
   Best wishes to you and your family for health and happiness in your new home.
Very truly yours,

(Courtesy of Carley Realty Co., West Newton, Massachusetts)

"New neighbor" letter upon the sale of a property.

. . . .
will be your neighbor at
. . . .

Dear Friends:

We have recently sold this home near you, and it occurs to us that you will be anxious to know about the newcomers to your neighborhood.

We are very sorry that time does not permit a personal introduction by us, but we feel sure that at the first opportunity you will want to give them a hearty welcome in your own way.

It has been a privilege to handle the sale of this property. Should you at present, or in the future, have need of real estate service, we will welcome the opportunity to represent you.

Cordially yours,

The J. Ashby Miller Company.

By . . . .

The listing, promotion, and sale of this property was handled by

. . . .

. . . .

(Courtesy of J. Ashby Miller, St. Matthews, Kentucky)

Chapter 11

Instruments Used in Real Estate Transactions

A TRANSACTION INVOLVING the purchase, sale, lease, exchange, or other transfer of real estate calls for the preparation of certain agreements, documents, or papers. They are called "instruments" here. The purpose of this chapter is to give you sufficient familiarity with real estate instruments to enable you to recognize the function and importance of each.

The instruments used in real estate transactions vary in different states and even from office to office within a particular state. The forms used in your office may be different from those reproduced in this chapter. You are therefore advised to find out from your employer which of the instruments explained in this chapter apply to his practice. You must also find out what disposition is made of the instruments in your particular office. The discussion that follows will give you a basic understanding of how real estate instruments come into existence, who signs them, and what happens to them generally.

Kinds of papers to be discussed. This discussion must necessarily be limited to the kinds of agreements, instruments, and papers that are used in everyday real estate transactions. It covers:

1. Listing agreements
2. Deposit receipts and memoranda of agreements to sell and purchase

3. Contracts of sale
4. Deeds
5. Mortgages and deeds of trust
6. Leases

Other instruments and terms relating to real estate documents are briefly defined in the glossary in this chapter.

Of the documents to be explained in this chapter, only the listing agreement, deposit receipt, memorandum of agreement to sell and purchase real estate, the contract of sale (in some instances), and lease come into the broker's hands. Deeds and mortgages concern principally the attorneys for the parties involved in the sale or loan, but the broker may be concerned with them at the closing. Later in this chapter the closing will be explained.

Caution to secretary. You are a secretary, not a member of the sales force or a member of the legal department. Agreements such as those to be discussed here have all kinds of legal implications. They entail rights, duties, and liabilities for the broker, the owner of the property, and other parties. Your are not expected to know what these are and if you learn something about them, bear in mind that you will have a mere smattering of knowledge, which may prove a dangerous thing if used unwisely.

You should know, however, that agreements and instruments become highly important when a dispute arises as to whether your employer is entitled to commission. Everything your employer does to try to sell a property may also become important in a disputed case. Treat the signed papers, correspondence with prospects, correspondence with sellers, memoranda of telephone conversations, and all material that is part of the file pertaining to each particular property (see page 67) with the utmost care.

Listing Agreements

What is a listing? When an owner of property wants to sell it, he lists it for sale with a broker and signs a written authorization for the broker to find a buyer. The authorization may be one of the following kinds:

1. *Open listing.* The owner lists his property with one or more brokers at the same price and commission. The first broker to find a buyer

is entitled to the commission. The owner may himself find a buyer, in which case no commission is payable. There may or may not be a time limit, and there may or may not be a requirement that the broker be notified of a sale.

2. *Exclusive listing.* The owner gives the listing to one broker exclusively. In that case the selected broker is given the exclusive right to sell the property within a definite period of time. If the broker does not sell property within that period, the owner may give it to other brokers. Under such an agreement, the broker is entitled to commission if the property is sold within the time limit whether by himself, another broker, or the owner.

3. *Exclusive right with multiple listing.* The owner gives one broker the sole and exclusive right to sell the property within a definite period, but the listing is forwarded by the broker to the Multiple Listing Service or Interchange for distribution to all of its active members for the purpose of cooperative sales. The commission is divided between the broker who secures the listing, the broker who finds the purchaser, and the Multiple Listing Service or Interchange.

You may hear the term "net listing." This means that the commission equals the excess above the net by the owner. This type of listing frequently leads to abuse and is therefore avoided by reputable brokers and discouraged by realty boards.

The secretary's work in handling the records of listings and multiple listings is explained in Chapter 13.

Form of exclusive listing agreement. Some of the real estate boards have adopted standard forms for exclusive listing contracts. The office in which you work may use the board's standard printed form, or it may use a form that the firm has had printed up for its own use. Frequently the board's form is used because it is easier to get the lister to sign it.

An exclusive listing agreement sets forth the terms of the agreement between the owner of the property and the broker. It contains at least a description of the property, the time during which the exclusive listing is to be in effect, the commission that will be paid by the owner if the property is sold, and the broker's agreement to endeavor to procure a purchaser according to the terms of the agreement.

A form of exclusive listing agreement used by members of the Ohio Association of Real Estate Boards is shown in Figure 27. A form of exclusive listing agreement used by members of a Multiple Listing Service is shown in Figure 28. On the reverse side of Figure 27 is a detailed description of the property similar to that shown in Figure 38a on page 207. Notice that in both of these forms provision is made for protecting the

---

In consideration of your agreement to use your efforts in finding a purchaser for my property, I hereby grant you the exclusive right from date hereof up to and including ....
to sell property known as .... and more fully described on the reverse side hereof for the sum of
$...................., payable ....
or at any other price, terms or exchange to which I may consent.

If you are successful in finding a purchaser for my property, or if the same is sold or exchanged during the term of your exclusive agency, or is sold within three months after the period of this agency to anyone with whom you have negotiated with respect to a sale during the period of this agency and of whom I have notice, I agree to pay you commission of .... upon the price at which same may be sold or exchanged.

In the event of such sale I will convey with full covenants of warranty, release of dower and evidence of marketable title.

....
Signature of Owner

....

....
Address

....
Telephone

Agency
Accepted:

.... 19....

NOTE: Both Husband and Wife Should Sign Listing Contract

Figure 27. Exclusive Listing Contract.

STANDARD FORM OF MULTIPLE LISTING
AGREEMENT ADOPTED BY THE UNION COUNTY MULTIPLE
LISTING SERVICE FOR USE BY ITS MEMBERS

Each listing is forwarded to the Union County Multiple Listing Service for distribution to all its active members for the purpose of cooperative sales. Seller will receive verification of the listing within five days from date of this agreement.

Dated:

To   , hereinafter designated as the Realtor.

In consideration of your listing and endeavoring to procure a purchaser for the property described as

the undersigned, as owner, hereinafter designated as the Seller, grants you, hereinafter designated as the Realtor, the sole and exclusive right for a period of _____ months from the date hereof to sell this property for $_____ all cash, or on the terms hereinafter stated, or for any other price or any other terms to which the Seller may consent in writing, or subsequently accept, and the Seller agrees to assist the Realtor and cooperate with him in endeavoring to make such sale.

The Seller agrees to pay the Realtor a commission of _____ per cent of the gross sale price in case this property or any portion is sold or exchanged by the Realtor, the Seller, or any other person during the terms of this contract, or of any extension thereof. If the property is sold or exchanged within _____ months after the termination of this agreement to any person with whom the Realtor had been negotiating, the said commission is to be paid to the Realtor forthwith. The Seller may request a list of any such prospective purchasers at any time following the expiration of this agreement.

The Seller represents that he has the legal right to sell said property, and that he can and will execute a sufficient instrument of conveyance.

The Seller acknowledges that he has read this listing agreement, understands its contents and has received a copy thereof, and that no agreements or conditions exist, other than those contained herein.

WITNESS: _____ L.S.
                                    SELLER

WITNESS: _____ L.S.
                                    SELLER

_____ L.S.
                                    BROKER

Figure 28. Multiple Listing Agreement.

157

broker's commission on a sale made within a specified period after termination of the authorization to a buyer with whom the broker has negotiated. Under the agreement in Figure 27 the seller must have notice of the negotiation. Some exclusive listing agreements specifically describe the notice of negotiation that must be given to the seller. For example, the form of agreement used by members of the Fresno Realty Board requires the broker to notify the seller of the people with whom he has negotiated, either during the term of the agreement or within five days after it has terminated. The work of the secretary in sending out such notices and in watching for sales to such prospects is described at page 215.

Who signs the listing agreement? The listing agreement is dated and signed by the seller and by the real estate broker. If the broker gets both husband and wife to sign the listing agreement, there is little chance for the listing to be cancelled because of disagreement between the husband and wife as to the sale of the property. At the time the listing is taken, the seller is furnished with a duplicate copy of the listing agreement containing the actual signatures of the seller and the broker. The broker keeps the original signed listing agreement.

Disposition of the agreement. The exclusive listing agreement is filed by the real estate broker according to his own system of filing. See page 207 for a description of an exclusive listing agreement file.

Deposit Receipts and Memoranda of Agreements to Sell and Purchase

What is a deposit receipt? As previously indicated, when a broker has found a purchaser, he generally has to get the signature of the seller before there is an actual sale. As evidence of good faith and actual intent to complete the contract of purchase and sale, he obtains a deposit or "earnest money" from the interested buyer. This deposit is usually forfeitable by the buyer if he wilfully fails to complete the contract. A form of deposit receipt is reproduced in Figure 29.

Offer to purchase. When the broker has found a purchaser, he prepares a written offer to purchase, which covers the essential features of the agreement, and has it signed by the buyer. This written offer serves as a record of what was agreed upon and prevents disputes over the terms of the contract. It also meets the legal requirement that sales

Date ...., 19...........
Received from .... of ....
.... the sum of .... Dollars
as deposit on the purchase of ....
.... (City, State) on the following terms
and conditions:

TERMS:
    Price .... Dollars
    Mortgage: ....
    ....
    ....
    ....

REMARKS:
....
....

CONDITIONS:
    Contract to be signed at the office of ....
    Co. at ....M. on .... 19..........
    This deposit is to apply on the amount of ....Dollars
which is to be paid on contract, leaving a balance of ....
Dollars payable on closing of title.
    Taxes, mortgage interest, rents, and insurance premiums to be appor-
tioned.
    Rights of tenants are as follows: ....
....
....
    Title to close at .... on
...., 19..........

REMARKS:
....
....

IMPORTANT:
This deposit is accepted subject to seller's approval. If seller disapproves,
the deposit is to be refunded. If the seller approves and purchaser fails
to sign the contract as above stated, he agrees to pay .... Co.
a sum equivalent to the usual brokerage commission.
I hereby accept the terms and conditions above stated.
Commission due and payable on signing of contracts.

_____
Seller
_____ Co.

_____
Associate Broker

_____
Purchaser
(Please read this receipt and take copy.)

Figure 29. Sales Deposit Receipt, To Be Used as a Memorandum of a Contract of Sale.

(From Benson and North, *Real Estate Principles and Practices.* Englewood Cliffs, N. J.: Prentice-Hall, Inc., 1947)

```
 1                                                          Dated            19
 2
 3
 4                                    and                              his wife, Purchaser
 5   hereby agrees to purchase from
 6
 7
 8                                    and                              his wife, Seller,
 9   through the Realtor named hereon at price and terms as stated below, the premises as follows:
10
11
12
13                               Tax Map          Block          Lot
14   Approximate size of lot:
15
16   Subject to such facts as an accurate survey may disclose
17                                                           Purchase Price $
18                           PAYABLE AS FOLLOWS
19   Cash herewith, for which this is a receipt                               $
20   Additional cash on or before                           19                $
21
22   NONE OF THE FOLLOWING PARAGRAPHS A, B or C IS APPLICABLE UNLESS FILLED IN.
23   A. If purchaser is to assume existing mortgage. By assuming and agreeing to pay the first
24   mortgage lien now on the said premises on which there is presently due approximately    $
25   Interest rate      %, payable monthly, remaining term approximately           years.
26   B. If seller is to take back a mortgage. By purchase money bond and mortgage in the usual
27   form to be drawn by the attorney for the Seller at the expense of the Purchaser           $
28   Interest rate:        %  Term:
29   Amortization and interest payable as follows:
30
31
32   C. If performance by Purchaser is subject to Mortgage contingency. The Purchaser agrees to
33   make immediate application for and to co-operate with the Realtor in securing a mortgage loan,
34   or loans, in the amount of $              through r. e. Scott Mortgage Co. $
35   on what is commonly known as the                year direct reduction plan with
36   interest at       %. If, by         19    , the mortgage loan has not been arranged or
37   this provision waived by the Purchaser, either party may void agreement on ten days written
38   notice sent by registered mail to the other party or his attorney. Pending the outcome of said
39   application, all moneys paid hereunder shall be held in escrow by the Realtor to be paid the
40   seller less brokerage commission if mortgage contingency is met or waived; or returned to the
41   Purchaser if this agreement is voided as herein provided.
42
43   It is expressly agreed that, notwithstanding any other provisions of this contract, the purchaser
44   shall not be obligated to complete the purchase of the property described herein or to incur
45   any penalty by forfeiture of earnest money deposits or otherwise unless the seller has de-
46   livered to the purchaser a written statement issued by the Federal Housing Commissioner set-
47   ting forth the appraised value of the property for mortgage insurance purposes of not less than
48   $                   , which statement the seller hereby agrees to deliver to the pur-
49   chaser promptly after such appraised value statement is made available to the seller.
50       The purchaser shall, however, have the privilege and option of proceeding with the consum-
51   mation of this contract without regard to the amount of appraised valuation made by the Federal
52   Housing Commissioner.
53   Balance of Purchase price by cash or certified check on delivery of deed of bargain and sale,
54   c. v. g.,                            , free from all encumbrances, except as here-
55   in set forth, which deed shall contain a full description of the property, together with the usual
56   affidavit of title, at the office of the Realtor or such other place as may be mutually agreed
57   upon, on or before                    19                                  $
58                                          TOTAL          $
59       The Seller represents that any buildings on the property are within the boundary lines and there are no
60   encroachments, easements or survey defects thereon which would render the title unmarketable.
61       Subject to the following tenancies which the Seller warrants are not in violation of existing Municipal,
62   County, State or Federal rules, regulations or laws.
63
64       Name                    Location                  Rent       Term
65
66
67
68
69
70
71
72
73
74
75
76
77
78
```

Figure 30. Agreement of Sale.

79
80
81
82
83
84
85
86
87
88
89
90
91
92
93
94
95
96   The Purchaser represents that his negotiations for this property have been handled exclusively by
97   r. e. Scott co., Realtors.
98   If the New Jersey Tenement House Act applies to the premises, the Seller represents that the premises com-
99   ply with the requirements of said Act but this representation does not extend to minor repairs or redecoration.
100   The Seller shall have the privilege of paying off any existing encumbrances on the property from the
101   proceeds of this sale at the time of closing title.
102   The Purchaser shall be entitled to possession of the premises and the rents, issues and profits thereof, im-
103   mediately upon closing of title and delivery of deed.
104   This agreement is entered into upon the knowledge of the parties as to the value of the land and what-
105   ever buildings are upon the same and not on any representations made as to character or quality.
106   This agreement shall not be assigned without the written consent of the Seller.
107   If there is a mortgage contingency in this agreement for what is commonly known as a G. I. Loan, the
108   Purchaser represents that the Purchaser is qualified to make said application.
109   Conveyance is to be made subject to telephone and electric utility easements, restrictions of record, if any,
110   and zoning ordinances. The Seller represents that the premises and the use thereof are not in violation of ap-
111   plicable restrictions or zoning ordinances.
112   Rents, water rents, taxes, interest on any mortgage to be assumed, fuel, if any, are to be apportioned
113   to date of passing title.
114   Gas and electric fixtures, cooking ranges and ovens, hot water heaters, linoleum, screens, storm sash,
115   shades, cornices, Venetian blinds, awnings, radiator covers, heating apparatus, television antenna, if any,
116   except where owned by tenants, are included in this sale.
117   Title to said premises has not been derived by adverse or color of title possession, or Martin Act pro-
118   ceedings.
119   The risk of loss or damage to said premises by fire or otherwise, excepting ordinary wear and tear, is on
120   the Seller until title passes.
121   All assessments for public improvements, completed or under construction at date of this agreement, are
122   to be paid in full, or allowed, by the Seller at the time of closing title.
123   The Purchaser authorizes the Realtor to deliver to the Seller all moneys paid under this agreement, ex-
124   cept as otherwise provided herein.
125   The Seller agees to pay the named Realtor, for services rendered in procuring this sale, a commission
126   of   6% on the purchase price, some to be due and payable upon the signing of this agreement unless
127   there be a contingency herein, in which case said commission shall be due and payable when and if said
128   contingency is met or waived. In no event shall the Seller, prior to the date set for closing, be obligated to
129   pay on account of real estate commission any sums in excess of the moneys paid by the Purchaser here-
130   under.
131   The Seller agrees to convey said premises to the Purchaser in accordance with this agreement.
132   This contract contains the entire agreement of the parties and no representations have been made by
133   any of the parties, the Realtor or salesman except as set forth herein.
In the presence of

_____   _____ _____ (L.S.)

_____   _____ _____ (L.S.)

_____   _____ _____ (L.S.)

_____   _____ _____ (L.S.)

_____   _____ _____ (L.S.)

_____   _____ _____ (L.S.)

Purchaser's Address _____ Tel._____

Seller's Address _____ Tel._____

r. e. Scott Company   400 Westfield Ave., Elizabeth, N. J.   Elizabeth 5-8100
_____
Realtor   Address   Tel.

Figure 30. Agreement of Sale (continued).

of real property must be in writing. The written offer is then signed by
the seller. When both the seller and buyer have signed it, it constitutes
an agreement to buy and sell.

This document may not be adequate to consummate the sale because
other people's signatures may be necessary, as we shall see in the discussion of contracts of sale. But the memorandum of sale is very important
from the standpoint of the broker's right to a commission.

A short form of agreement of sale is shown in Figure 30.

Use of deposit receipt as memorandum of sale. Many
brokers use a form of deposit receipt as a contract of sale form. Such
a form may combine a receipt for the deposit with the terms of the
purchase. It shows when and where the contract is to be signed, how
the deposit is to be applied, when title is to close, and that the deposit
is accepted subject to the seller's approval.

Some of the real estate boards have a standard form of deposit
receipt which is separate from, but used in conjunction with, a written
proposition.

*Disposition of deposit receipt and signed offer to pur-
chase.* An original and two copies are made of the deposit receipt. The
broker keeps the original for his record. One duplicate goes to the seller,
and one to the buyer. The broker files the original deposit receipt in
the "deposit receipts" file (see page 68). The seller, buyer, and broker
each keeps a copy of the signed memorandum of agreement to sell. The
broker files his copy in the "pending deals" file (see page 67).

In an escrowed deal (see page 6), the escrow office may want a
copy of the deposit receipt or other memorandum for use in preparing
the escrow instructions. It usually does not retain the deposit receipt in
file.

Contract of Sale

What is a contract of sale? A contract of sale is the agreement between the seller and the buyer in which all of the terms of the
transaction are fully set forth. It gives an exact description of the property
(see page 191), the price, the terms of the sale, the time for closing the
deal, and the time when the buyer will take possession. If the contract
is conditional upon the buyer's being able to negotiate a loan for a certain

𝕿𝖍𝖎𝖘 𝕬𝖌𝖗𝖊𝖊𝖒𝖊𝖓𝖙, *made the*   *day of*

in the year of our Lord, One Thousand Nine Hundred and

    BETWEEN

residing at
in the   *of*   *in the County of*
                            and State of   *part*   *of the first part;*

    AND

residing at
in the   *of*   *in the County of*
                            and State of   *part*   *of the second part:*

    WITNESSETH, *that the said part*   *of the first part, for and in consideration of the sum of*

to be paid and satisfied as hereinafter mentioned, and also in consideration of the covenants and agreements hereinafter mentioned, made and entered into by the said part   *of the second part, doth agree to and with the said part*   *of the second part, that*   *the said part*   *of the first part, will well and sufficiently convey to the said part*   *of the second part,*
                       successors and assigns by Deed of
                       free from all encumbrances, except as hereinafter mentioned,
on or before the   *day of*
                       next ensuing the date hereof,

    ALL
lot *, tract* *, or parcel*   *of land and premises, hereinafter particularly described, situate, lying and being in the*   *of*   *in the County of*
                           and State of New Jersey, and
being more particularly known and designated as

Figure 31. Contract of Sale.

163

AND *the said*

for

successors and assigns, doth covenant, promise and agree to and with the
said part of the first part, heirs, executors, administrators and assigns, that the
said part of the second part, will pay and satisfy, or cause to be paid and satisfied, unto the said part of
the first part, the said sum of

as and for the purchase money of the foregoing described land and premises, in the following manner, that is
to say:

> *On execution of this agreement for which this is also a receipt* $

> *On delivery of the deed in cash,* $

> *By assuming the mortgage at present a lien on the premises and paying*
> *the same according to the terms thereof* $

> *On Bond and Mortgage, same containing usual interest, tax, assessment,*
> *insurance and installment default clauses, and an agreement not to claim credit on*
> *the interest payable on bond and mortgage, by reason of any tax assessed, or to be*
> *assessed against the premises, with interest at % payable*
> *for years* $ _____

> *TOTAL* $

This Contract is entered into upon the knowledge of the parties as to the value of the land and whatever
buildings are upon the same, and not on any representations made as to character or quality.

Figure 31. Contract of Sale (continued).

AND *The said Part* of *the first part hereby agrees to pay to the licensed and authorized agent, r. e. Scott co., Realtors, a commission of 5% on the purchase price aforesaid, said commission to be paid in consideration of services rendered in consummating this sale; said commission to become due and payable upon the execution of this agreement; and the party of the first part hereby directs the closing attorney or attorneys to withhold the same from the closing funds at passing of title if not sooner paid.*

AND IT IS FURTHER AGREED *by the parties to these presents, that the said party of the second part, heirs, executors, administrators, successors and assigns, may enter into and upon the said land and premises immediately following the passing of title and from thence take the rents, issues and profits to* and their use.

AND IT IS FURTHER AGREED *by the parties hereto, that the said deed shall be delivered and received at the office of r. e. Scott co., Realtors, 400 Westfield Avenue, Elizabeth, New Jersey, or at such other places as may be designated by the seller , between the hours of ten o'clock in the forenoon and four o'clock in the afternoon on the said* day of *next ensuing the date hereof.*

The rents of said premises, FHA escrow funds, insurance premiums, electric, gas, fuel, water rents, taxes, and interest on Mortgage, if any, shall be adjusted, apportioned and allowed as of the day of delivery of said deed

Gas and electric fixtures, gas stoves, hot water heaters and chandeliers, carpets, linoleum, mats and matting in halls, screens, shades, awnings, ash cans, heating apparatus, if any, and all other personal property appurtenant to or used in the operation of said premises is represented to be owned by seller and is included in this sale.

The risk of loss or damage to said premises by fire or otherwise until the delivery of said deed is assumed by the party of the first part.

In case the premises shall suffer injury beyond the ordinary wear and tear, the party of the first part, shall repair the damage before the date set for the delivery of said deed or make an appropriate deduction from the purchase price herein stated.

It is understood and agreed that the buildings upon said premises are all within the boundary lines of the property as described in the deed therefor, and that there are no encroachments thereon and that the buildings comply with municipal ordinances and regulations and the provisions of the New Jersey State Tenement House Act as enforced by the State Board of Tenement House Supervision, to be shown by the report of the department or board enforcing the same where such ordinances, regulations and said act apply.

It is expressly understood and agreed that the title to the land and premises hereby agreed to be conveyed is not derived from any proceedings or any Act for the Sale of Land for nonpayment of the municipal taxes or assessments, or adverse or color of title possession.

The premises above described are sold subject to zoning ordinances, restrictions appearing of record, and such state of facts as an accurate survey may disclose.

If at any time before the delivery of the deed the premises or any part thereof shall be or shall have been affected by any assessment or assessments which are or may become payable in annual installments of which the first installment is then due or has been paid, then for the purpose of this contract all the unpaid installments of any such assessment, including those which are to become due and payable after the delivery of the deed, shall be deemed to be due and payable and to be liens upon the premises affected thereby and shall be paid and discharged by the seller thereof, upon the delivery of the deed. Unconfirmed improvements or assessments, if any, shall be paid and allowed by the seller on account of the purchase price, if the improvement or work has been completed on or before the date of this contract.

All sums paid on account of this contract, and the reasonable expenses of the examination of the title to said premises are hereby made liens thereon, but such liens shall not continue after default by the purchaser under this contract.

AND *for the performance of all and singular the covenants and agreements aforesaid, the said parties do bind themselves and their respective heirs, executors, administrators and assigns, and they hereby agree to pay, upon failure to perform the same, the sum of*

which they hereby fix and settle as liquidated damages therefor.

IN WITNESS WHEREOF, *the said parties have hereunto interchangeably set their hands and seals the day and year first above mentioned.*

SIGNED, SEALED AND DELIVERED .... L S.

IN THE PRESENCE OF .... L S.

.... .L S.

.... L S.

In consideration of mutual promises and agreements herein stated, we hereby agree to extend the date for the delivery of the deed and execution of this contract to at same hour and place.

WITNESS, *our hands and seals this* day of A. D., 19

Figure 31. Contract of Sale (continued).

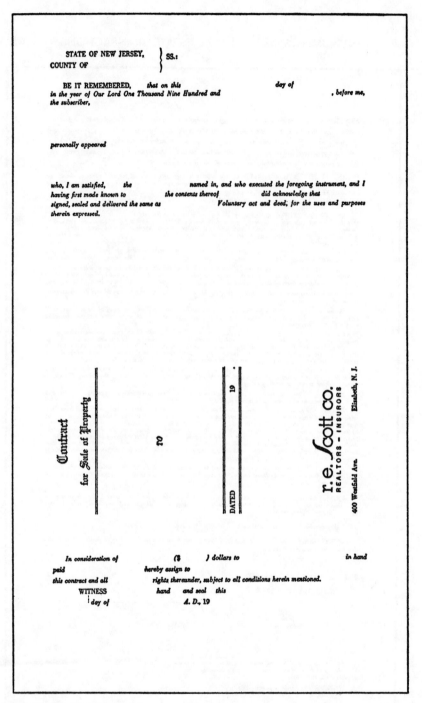

Figure 31. Contract of Sale (back page showing printed panel for names of parties and date).

amount on terms that he can meet, this condition is written into the contract. A form of contract of sale is shown in Figure 31.

The contract is usually drawn up by the attorney for the seller and is reviewed by the attorney for the buyer before it is signed. It may be drawn up by the attorney for the buyer, in which case it would be reviewed by the attorney for the seller. In some cases, the contract is prepared by the broker on a printed form that has been drafted by an attorney.

The contract of sale may be used even though the buyer and seller have previously signed an agreement of sale like the one shown in Figure 30. This might happen, for example, where the broker has had the agreement of sale signed by both parties and the attorney for the buyer or seller insists upon his client having a formal contract of sale.

Who signs the contract of sale? The seller and the buyer sign the contract of sale. Anyone who has an interest in the property that is being sold must sign the contract. For example, the signature of the seller's wife may be required. The careful broker finds out, when he lists the property, in whose name the title rests so that he will know whose signatures will have to be obtained to consummate the sale.

Disposition of the contract of sale. The parties to the contract keep a copy of the signed contract of sale. In an escrowed deal (see page 6) it is held by the escrow office.

Deeds

What is a deed? A deed is a formal written instrument by which title to real property is conveyed from one person to another. A contract of sale is an agreement to convey title, whereas a deed is the conveyance itself.

The parties to a deed are the *grantor* (the person who conveys his interest in the property) and the *grantee* (the person to whom the conveyance is made). The grantor is the seller, and the grantee is usually, though not always, the purchaser, since the purchaser may buy the property for the grantee.

Frequently the grantor makes the deed in a representative capacity, for example, as the guardian of a minor.

Kinds of deeds. There are various kinds, as well as forms, of deeds. The kinds commonly used in a sale of property are the warranty deed, bargain and sale deed, and quitclaim deed.

A *warranty deed* is the most desirable from the standpoint of the purchaser. It not only transfers title in fee simple[1] but also covenants and warrants that the grantor has the right to transfer the title to the property and that the grantee shall enjoy the premises quietly, forever. Should anyone later make a claim against the property, the grantee can sue the grantor for breach of his warranty.

A *bargain and sale* deed (sometimes called a grant, bargain, and sale deed) conveys title as effectively as a warranty deed, but it does not warrant the title against adverse claims, except those made, done, or suffered by the grantor.

A *quitclaim deed* is not used to convey title but to obtain a release from a person who is believed to have some interest in, or claim to, the property, whether the claim is real or not. By this kind of deed, the grantor "quits" any claim he might have, usually for a nominal consideration. These deeds do not obligate the grantor in any way, but if he should have full title the quitclaim deed will operate as a full and complete conveyance of the title.

Forms of deeds. Printed forms of deeds are used almost exclusively. Sometimes, however, a printed form is not adequate for the special clauses and conditions that a deed must contain. In that case, the lawyer will draft a special deed to include his particular requirements and have it typewritten.

Many states provide by statute for a short form of deed, known as a statutory form. By statute, certain covenants and warranties are made part of the deed and, although not set forth in the deed, are binding on the grantor and his heirs. Since the statute is actually part of the deed and a state statute is not effective outside of the state enacting it, a statutory form of deed can be used only in the specific state that makes statutory provision for it.

Who signs the deed? Only the grantor signs the deed, unless the grantee makes special covenants. Whether or not the grantor's

---

[1] Title in fee simple means that the owner is entitled to the entire property, with unconditional power of disposition during his life, and that the property descends to his heirs and legal representatives if he dies without a will.

spouse must join in the deed depends upon the law of the state where the land is situated. Generally speaking, it is necessary for the spouse to join, and for that reason the marital status of the grantor is stated in the deed, as married, spinster, bachelor, widow, widower, or divorced and not married.

Disposition of the deed. The purchaser gets the deed at the closing. He has it recorded for his own protection in the proper public office and pays the recording fee. The usual practice is for the buyer's attorney to attend to the recording. The attorney also sees that the proper revenue stamps, known as documentary stamps, are affixed to the deed. In cases where there is a title insurance company representative at the closing, he may take the deed, attend to the recording of it, and return it to the attorney. Eventually the recorded deed is returned to the owner of the property by his attorney or mailed to him directly by the recorder's office.

Mortgages

What is a mortgage? Very few purchases of real property are made entirely for cash. Usually some kind of financing is necessary to enable the buyer to acquire the property. The real estate broker frequently helps to arrange for the financing of the transaction (see page 8). The most common method of financing is for the buyer to borrow on a mortgage. In some states, California, for example, deeds of trust, which will be explained at page 170, are used almost exclusively in place of mortgages. In Georgia, a _loan deed_ is commonly used in place of a mortgage.

In mortgaging a piece of real estate to secure a loan, the mortgagor gives the mortgagee two instruments, one the mortgage and the other a bond or note. The latter evidences the personal obligation of the debtor to repay the loan. The mortgage evidences the fact that the property is given as security for the repayment of the loan. A mortgage, in other words, is an instrument that pledges real estate as collateral security for the payment of the debt expressed in the bond or note.

A mortgage given in part payment of the purchase price of the property is called a _purchase money mortgage._ For example, if the purchase price is $15,000 and the buyer pays $5,000 cash and gives back a mortgage on the property for $10,000, the mortgage is a purchase money mortgage.

Assuming a mortgage and acquiring property subject to a mortgage. In a sale of property on which there is a mortgage, the purchaser may *assume* the mortgage, or he may acquire the property *subject to* the mortgage. The difference between the two is essentially one of who will be held personally liable for the debt owing the mortgagee.

When the purchaser takes property *assuming* the mortgage, he becomes liable on both the bond and the mortgage. The original owner, however, remains personally liable on the bond unless the mortgagee agrees to the transfer of liability on the bond. If the new owner does not pay the interest or principal when it falls due, the mortgage is foreclosed. Should the foreclosure result in the mortgagee getting less than the full amount of the debt represented by the bond and mortgage, he will look to the person who assumed the mortgage as well as to the original mortgagor to make good the deficiency.

If the purchaser takes the property *subject to* the mortgage, he undertakes to meet all of the obligations of the mortgage, but he does not become personally liable on the bond that was originally given to the mortgagee. If he should fail to meet the mortgage obligations, he may have the property taken from him by foreclosure, but he will have no personal liability for any difference between the full amount of the debt and the value of the property as revealed through the foreclosure. The original mortgagor only would be personally liable for any such deficiency.

Forms of mortgages. In some states the security instrument commonly known as a mortgage is called a *trust deed, deed of trust, mortgage deed, trust indenture,* or *trust mortgage.*

A deed of trust conveys the land to a third party, a trustee, instead of direct to the lender. The third party holds the property in trust for the lender and the trustor until the debt is paid in accordance with the terms of the trust deed. A few states have designated officials, known as public trustees, to whom the estate is conveyed under a deed of trust.

Some states have short statutory forms of mortgages, which save space when recorded. The brief statutory forms are amplified by statute and therefore are not used outside the state of origin.

Printed forms of mortgages and deeds of trust are used extensively. However, they are sometimes inadequate for the special conditions of the transaction. In such cases, a typewritten document will be prepared by the attorney.

Who signs the mortgage? A mortgage is signed by the mortgagor. In the case of a trust deed, it is signed by the trustor (grantor) and in some states by the trustee as well.

Disposition of the mortgage or trust deed. The mortgage (lender) gets the original mortgage instrument. He has it recorded for his own protection in the proper public office and pays the recording fee. His attorney, or a representative of the title company, usually attends to the recording of the mortgage. The attorney also sees that the proper state mortgage registration tax is paid, if required by the laws of the state. Eventually, the recorded mortgage is turned over to the mortgagee by his attorney.

A copy of the mortgage is held by the mortgagor.

In the case of a deed of trust, the original instrument is in the hands of the beneficiary.

Leases

What is a lease? A lease is a contract giving the right of possession of property to a tenant (called the lessee) in exchange for rent to be paid to the landlord (called the lessor). A lease for more than one year, in most states, must be in writing. For obvious reasons, written leases are made even where the term is for less than a year. The written lease contains numerous promises and undertakings by both the landlord and the tenant.

Not all people who are tenants are lessees. To be considered a lessee the occupancy must exist under a lease, whether it is written or oral. A tenant who pays rent monthly and has no lease is usually a month-to-month tenant. There are important differences between a tenant under a lease and a month-to-month tenant with regard to termination of the tenancy and rights and liabilities of the tenant and landlord during the tenancy. They are principally legal differences that need not be brought out here.

Classification of leases. In the real estate business you will hear leases described according to duration, type of property, or kind of rental.

Duration classification. In this classification there are short-term or long-term leases. Although there is no definite duration that takes a lease out of the short-term class, a lease of 10 or more years is generally considered a long-term lease. The fundamental distinctions are in the responsibilities assumed by the lessee and in the bond and security requirements. Under a short-term lease, the lessor usually requires the lessee to deposit with him one, three, or six months rental at the time the lease is executed, whereas under a long-term lease the lessee is required to furnish a bond or collateral in an amount equal to about three-years rental. The most common practice is for the lessee to deposit with a bank or other financial institution negotiable securities of the required amount.

A special type of long-term lease is the 99-year lease, which has been utilized extensively for the purpose of developing business districts in large cities. They are made on parcels of valuable real estate strategically located for business expansion. They contemplate the erection or improvement of buildings upon the property by the lessee.

Types of property classification. Leases may be classified as *commercial* or *residential,* according to the type of property covered by the lease. Short-term leases may be either commercial or residential leases, but long-term leases are almost exclusively commercial leases.

Rental classification. The majority of leases call for the payment of a definite amount of rental, which continues at a uniform rate throughout the term of the lease. The amount is called a *flat rental.* Other leases, especially long-term leases, provide that the rental shall start at a comparatively low figure and gradually increase. A rental provision of this type is called a *graded rental.* Another method of fixing the amount of rental is to require the tenant to pay a specified percentage of the gross income from sales made upon the premises. A lease with this requirement is called a *percentage lease.* These generally cover premises occupied by retail businesses, such as chain stores and department stores. Percentage leases generally run for ten or more years.

Form of lease. The lease instrument is usually prepared by the lessor's attorney and is reviewed by the lessee's attorney before it is signed.

Printed forms of leases covering almost any kind of property are available and are frequently used for short-term leases. The real estate firm may have its own printed form of lease which was prepared originally by an attorney. In large real estate organizations, the leasing department or the building management department does the work of filling in the printed forms (see page 253).

Who signs the lease? A lease of land or commercial property is executed with the formalities of a deed. It may have to be recorded like a deed. The recording, when required, is usually attended to by the attorney of the lessee.

The execution of run-of-the-mill short-term leases, such as a lease on an apartment, is not so formal. Both the lessor and the lessee sign, and usually the signatures are witnessed. Otherwise there are no formal requirements. It is customary to execute leases in duplicate.

Disposition of the lease. The tenant and the landlord retain copies of the lease. Where the real estate broker is acting as the agent for the landlord, the leasing department or the building management department keeps a copy of the lease. The method of keeping leases and records of them is described at page 253.

Assignment and sublease. Technically, if an original lessee transfers his lease for the entire remaining period of the lease to some other party, the instrument by which he does this is an assignment; if he transfers it for only a part of the term, the instrument is a sublease.

Under an assignment of a lease, the assignee is liable to the original lessor for the rent; under a sublease the sublessee is liable to the original lessee for the rent, and the original lessee remains liable to the lessor.

Almost all leases provide that the lessee cannot assign his lease or sublet the premises without the consent of the landlord.

Upon the sale of a property, any existing leases are usually assigned by the landlord to the purchaser of the property.

A lease is surrendered by a tenant when he gives up the leased space and moves out.

Real Estate Closings

What is a closing? A real estate closing is a meeting at which the buyer, seller, their attorneys, a representative of the lender if a mortgage loan is involved, a representative of the title company if title insurance is obtained, and the real estate broker come together and conclude the transaction in accordance with the contract of sale. At this meeting the purchaser makes the required payments, all instruments necessary to transfer the title are signed, and the seller delivers the deed. The broker collects any balance of commission due him at the closing, if it has not been paid to him in full before that time.

The place of the closing is usually set forth in the contract. Generally it is held at the office of the attorney for the seller or at the office of a title insurance company, though the parties may agree to hold the closing somewhere else. In some instances it is held at the broker's office. The time for the closing is usually fixed in the contract of sale, but by agreement between the parties it may sometimes be postponed for a good reason. Postponement frequently occurs because of a delay in completing the examination of title.

The purchaser has with him a certified check drawn to his own order in an amount approximating the sum to be paid at the closing. The balance of the settlement is paid in cash or by regular check.

In the settlement, the adjustments in favor of the seller and those in favor of the buyer, which have been set forth on a closing statement (also called settlement sheet or settlement statement), are reviewed by both parties and their attorneys. Among the adjustments in favor of the seller are such items as prepaid insurance premiums, taxes (if the seller paid them in advance), water, rents from the first of the month to the effective date of the closing (not collected prior to the closing), interest on mortgages that the seller paid in advance, and other items. Among the adjustments in favor of the purchaser there may be advance rents collected by the seller prior to closing, water charged to tenants in advance, interest on existing mortgage, and other items. An explanation of the calculations of adjustments is given at page 177.

Broker's part in the closing. A real estate closing is essentially a matter to be handled by lawyers. The interested real estate broker, however, will see to it that everything is ready for the closing, especially if the parties are not represented by attorneys.

Some brokers use a checklist that has been provided by the Brokers Institute of the National Association of Real Estate Boards in seeing that everything is ready for the closing. This checklist reminds the broker of the numerous items to be attended to, like having the sellers and buyers and/or their attorneys or agents approve the closing statement. It also lists the papers that he should check before the closing, like leases, insurance policies, tax bills, and other necessary papers. The checklist also raises questions such as whether there are any unpaid bills for planting or shrubbery. All in all, there are some sixty odd items on the checklist that might need attention in advance of the closing to avoid omissions, errors, and other misunderstandings.

An alert secretary can be very helpful to her employer in checking to see that everything requiring attention prior to the closing has been attended to.

The closing statement. The closing statement sets forth in detail the amounts due the seller, the credits due the buyer, and the balance that the buyer must pay at the closing. A form of closing statement is shown in Figure 32.

Although the closing statement is usually prepared by the attorneys for the seller and buyer, it is not unusual for the real estate broker to prepare it.

Practice where real estate broker prepares the closing statement. Where the buyer and seller are represented by attorneys, the real estate broker will be careful not to submit directly to the buyer and seller the closing statement he has prepared. Instead, he will send two copies of the statement to each of the attorneys. Then, if the attorneys wish they can forward a copy to their respective clients. Or, they can ignore the broker's closing statement, as some attorneys do, and prepare their own.

The real estate broker will send a copy of the closing statement direct to the buyer and/or seller only if the party is not represented by an attorney.

Preparation of the closing statement. Each broker uses his own form of closing statement. Similarly, attorneys also use their own forms. Consequently, there is no uniformity of arrangement, headings, or listing of items in closing statements.

The form shown in Figure 32 is used by Douglas Van Riper, Manhasset, Long Island. The broker who has made the sale computes the adjustments and inserts all the figures on a copy of the form. (An explanation of the calculation of adjustments is given below.) He then gives the statement to the secretary for checking. To check the computation she must, of course, know how the adjustments were computed. The secretary then types the statement, making the number of copies required for the particular case. One copy is always made for the office

DOUGLAS
VAN RIPER
REALTOR & INSUROR
190
PLANDOME ROAD
MANHASSET
LONG ISLAND

CLOSING STATEMENT

as of_____, 19

Premises:

Conveyed to   By

CREDITS—PURCHASERS	CREDITS—SELLERS
Paid on signing contract	Purchase price
First mortgage held by:	Taxes:
Address	Town: 19........ — $............................ Period
	Jan. 1, 19........... to Dec. 31, 19...........
Interest from to	Prepaid by seller to...........................
@ % mo days	Adjustment .... to...................
Taxes:	School: 19........ — .... — $.................. Period
Town: 19........ — $............................ Period	July 1, 19........... to June 30, 19...........
Jan. 1, 19........... to Dec. 31, 19...........	Prepaid by seller to...........................
Adjustment .... to...................	Adjustment .... to...................
School: 19........ — .... — $.................. Period	Village: 19........ — $.................. Period
July 1, 19........... to June 30, 19...........	.... to ....
Adjustment .... to...................	Prepaid by seller to...........................
Village: 19....... — $..................	Adjustment .... to...................
Period .... to	Insurance:
Adjustment .... to	Fire Policy No._____ of
Water: paid by seller to:	_____ Co.
Adjustment	Coverage: $._____
	Term: _____ to _____
Meter ordered read on...........................	Premium: $_____ prepaid by
Final bill to be rendered and paid by seller.	seller. Adjustment: _____
	to _____
	Oil: _____
	_____
TOTAL CREDIT TO PURCHASERS:	TOTAL CREDIT TO SELLERS
	LESS TOTAL CREDIT TO PURCHASERS
	BALANCE DUE SELLERS
	By certified check $....................
	By plain check $....................
	By check from $....................
Additional Expenses Paid by Purchasers:	
New mortgage cost ....$	Additional Expenses Paid by Sellers:
Title examination ....$	Drawing deed $....................
Recording fee deed...................$	Revenue stamps on deed $....................

Title closed on_____ _at _____M. at the office of

Present were:

Sellers:

Their att'y:

Purchasers:

Their att'y:

representing Douglas Van Riper

Title closer,   of

Figure 32. Closing Statement.

records, one for each of the parties, one for each of the attorneys, and any others that might be required. The broker gives the secretary instructions on this point. Before the closing statement is considered final and sent out, it is checked by the top executive.

Calculation of Adjustments for Closing Statement

How to calculate adjustments. The practice of computing adjustments and the date of adjustment vary with the locality. In many localities, adjustments are made as of the day immediately preceding the day on which title is closed. In other words, the buyer receives the income and is charged with the expenses incurred beginning with and including the day on which title passes to him.

It is much easier to compute interest, taxes, water rates, and insurance by the 360-day method, each month representing 1/12 of the annual charge and each day 1/30 of the monthly charge, than by the 365-day method. This is the practice adopted by many local real estate boards. Rent is usually computed on the basis of the days in the particular month in which title is closed. Even in offices that use the 360-day method of computing interest, taxes, water rates, and insurance, the time is computed by full months and by the actual number of days in excess of such full months where the period for which computation is made is more than one month. For example, the period between March 15 and June 3 is 2 months (April and May) and 20 days (17 days in March, and 3 days in June).

Calculations of taxes, interest, insurance, and rents follow. Other adjustments are calculated in the same manner. For the purpose of the examples, we shall assume that title closes June 8, 1966.

Example of calculation of tax adjustment. Taxes in the locality are payable semi-annually, April 1 and October 1. The seller paid taxes on April 1 for the preceding 6-month period. During the current 6-month period, the seller is responsible for taxes from April 1 to, but not including, June 8, the closing date. He would have to allow the buyer the amount of the taxes for that period—2 months (April and May) and 7 days. Assuming that the taxes for the 6-month period amount to \$1,500, the taxes for one month are \$250 (\$1,500 ÷ 6), for one day, \$8.33$\frac{1}{3}$ (\$250 ÷ 30). An adjustment of \$558.33 is made in favor of the purchasers [2 × \$250 + (7 × \$8.33$\frac{1}{3}$)].

But suppose the seller had paid taxes 6 months in advance. He would be entitled to recover taxes from and including June 8 *through* September 30, or for a period of 3 months (July, August, and September) and 23 days (June 8 through June 30). Allowance of $941.67 would be made in favor of the seller [3 × $250 + (23 × $8.33⅓)]

Example of calculation of interest adjustment. Suppose there is a mortgage of $20,000 on the property, with interest at 6 per cent payable quarterly on 15th of December, March, June, and September. When title closed on June 8, interest had been paid to but not including March 15. The purchaser is entitled to an allowance for interest from and including March 15 through June 7, or for a period of 2 months (April and May) and 24 days (17 days in March, 7 days in June). The interest on $20,000 at 6 per cent per annum is $100 per month, $3.33⅓ per day ($100 ÷ 30). The interest for 2 months, 24 days is $200 (2 × $100) + $80 (24 × $3.33⅓). An adjustment of $280 is made in favor of the purchaser.

Example of calculation of insurance adjustment. Suppose there is a fire policy on the property which had been paid up for three years. The expiration date of the policy is August 1, 1967. The seller is therefore entitled to an adjustment of insurance for 13 months and 23 days (June 8, 1966, the date of the closing, to August 1, 1967). The premium is $10 per month [$360 ÷ (12 × 3)], or 33⅓¢ per day ($10 ÷ 30). An adjustment of $137.67 (13 × $10) + (23 × 33⅓¢) is made in favor of the seller.

Example of calculation of rent adjustment. The seller had collected the rents in advance for the month of June. They amounted to $5,000. The purchaser is entitled to an adjustment for the period from and including June 8 through June 30, or 23 days. Since June has only 30 days, the rent per day is $5,000 ÷ 30, or $166.66⅔ per day. The purchaser is entitled to an adjustment of $3,833.33 (23 × $166.66⅔). If there is more than one tenant, you will have to prorate the rent for each separately, unless the rents had all been collected for the same period.

Glossary of Terms Relating to Real Estate Instruments

Amortization. This term is used in connection with financing the purchase of property. It relates to the method by which payments are to be made on the mortgage or loan. An amortization loan permits the borrower to make payments in periodic amounts. Payments of either principal or interest, or both, may be made at any interval decided upon between the parties.

There are a number of amortization plans. The most popular plan today is the direct reduction monthly payment plan. This plan requires the borrower to make regular simultaneous payments to principal and interest. Most commonly, payments are made monthly, but they may also be arranged on a quarterly or semi-annual basis. There are two variations of this plan. (1) The borrower pays a fixed amount each month during the entire term of the loan. Of this amount, part is applied to principal and part to interest. Inasmuch as the outstanding balance is reduced each month by the payment of the principal, the amount of the monthly payment applicable to interest continually decreases, thereby constantly increasing that part of the fixed payment which is applied to principal. (2) The payments consist of a fixed amortization payment plus the interest payment. Since the amount due as interest decreases with each fixed amortization payment, the total payment constantly decreases. Under this plan, the borrower must either pay for a longer period or make larger payments at the start than under the first variation. The effective interest rate to the borrower under either plan is the same.

Construction loan mortgage. A loan, usually by a lending institution, covering the period of construction of a new building. When the building is completed, a new loan is negotiated for a longer term by the same lender or some other lender, and the construction loan is paid off.

Escrow agreement. An agreement, sometimes called *escrow instructions,* used when a deed is delivered to a third person, who in turn delivers it to the grantee upon the performance of certain conditions. The escrow agreement or instructions specify the conditions to be performed before the deed is delivered to the purchaser of the property. The third person is called the *escrow holder, escrow agent,* or *escrowee.* Banks, title companies, and savings and loan associations act as escrow agents.

Many real estate brokers escrow their real estate deals. The signed agreement to purchase or lease, together with the money the broker has received, is taken to the escrow office where they are deposited with the escrow agent. The parties to the contract both sign the escrow agreement. The broker is entitled to his commission when the parties have signed the escrow agreement. A good broker remains interested in the deal, however, until it is actually completed.

Installment contract. Basically, an installment contract provides: (1) the purchaser must make a down payment; (2) the purchaser must make payments of a stated size upon stated dates thereafter until the purchase price is completely paid; (3) when the purchaser makes the last payment he will be entitled to receive a deed for the property. Sometimes the contract provides that when a certain percentage of the total price has been paid, title will pass subject to a mortgage for the balance due.

After the contract has been executed, the seller may: (1) retain the contract and make collections for himself; or (2) pledge the contract as collateral for a bank loan to obtain funds he may need or desire.

Junior mortgage (second mortgage). A mortgage that is subordinate to a prior mortgage is called a junior mortgage. A buyer who does not have sufficient cash with which to acquire the property after the first mortgage is arranged will ask the seller to take back a second mortgage. The second mortgage is a junior mortgage. For example, the price of a dwelling to be purchased is $20,000. The buyer can borrow $10,000 on a first mortgage and has 6,000 in cash. He gets the seller to take back a second mortgage of $4,000.

Land contract. The buyer makes a small down payment and agrees to pay additional amounts at intervals until the total purchase price is paid. The buyer does not get a deed to the property until a substantial amount, frequently 50%, of the price of the property is paid. At that time the buyer gives the seller a purchase money mortgage for the balance of the purchase price.

Option. An agreement under which an owner of property gives another person, called the optionee, the right to buy the property at a fixed price within a specified time. While the option is in existence, the owner cannot sell the property to anyone else. When the optionee decides to buy the property, he gives the owner notice that he has elected to exercise his option and there is then a contract of sale. Should the owner not exercise the option within the period specified, he forfeits the money he paid for the option.

Package mortgage. A mortgage that permits a home buyer to borrow money from one lender not only on the value of the house and grounds, but also on the value of equipment, such as gas or electric appliances (including stoves, refrigerators, washing machines, and the like), and heating, ventilating, and air conditioning equipment. These items of equipment are considered, under the packaged mortgage, as part of the real estate and as providing security for loans.

Straight term mortgage. Straight or "flat" loans are loans for a definite term of years, payable in full at maturity. During the period of the loan the borrower pays only interest on the principal. At maturity he must (1) pay the loan, (2) refinance the loan for another term, or (3) have the loan carried by the lender as an open or past due debt.

Vendor's lien. An instrument used to secure repayment of a loan on real estate. A vendor's lien is used in lieu of a mortgage in Louisiana and some other states, just as a warranty deed is used in Georgia. Under the vendor's lien, the seller reserves in his deed to the buyer a lien on the land to secure payment of the balance of the purchase price.

Warranty deed. Upon a sale of real property, a warranty deed is the seller's guaranty of the nature and condition of the title to real property. Upon a loan, it is an instrument used to secure payment of the debt. In some states, particularly Georgia, a warranty deed to secure a debt is used in lieu of a mortgage.

(For a more complete glossary of real estate terms see page 334)

Chapter 12

How to Type Real Estate Instruments and Forms

ANY OF THE INSTRUMENTS described in the preceding chapter that come into the hands of the real estate broker—listing agreements, deposit receipts, memoranda of purchase and sale, contracts of sale, leases— might be handed to the secretary to be typewritten. In addition, she may be called upon to typewrite other legal instruments that have been prepared by attorneys and to make copies of legal documents.

The purpose of this chapter is to instruct the secretary in those phases of the setup of real estate instruments that will enable her to do the typing job accurately. The information is presented in the following main sections:

1. The instrument as a whole
2. Typing real property descriptions
3. Setting up the section for execution of the instrument

None of the points made in Chapter 7 about improving typing efficiency generally will be repeated here. The secretary is advised, therefore, to review that chapter.

The Instrument as a Whole

Paper. A legal instrument is typewritten generally on "legal cap" or on a printed legal form. The following explanation relates to typing a legal instrument on legal cap. Instructions for filling in a printed legal form are given on page 188, for copying legal instruments, on page 190.

Legal cap is white paper 8″ or 8½″ by 13″, with a wide ruled margin at the left and a narrow ruled margin at the right.

Margins. Documents typed on legal-size paper are bound at the top.

Top margin. Begin typing either five or six double spaces from the top of the paper, but make a habit of always allowing the same number of spaces on all sheets. By following this practice, you know that every page starts at the same place on the paper and has the same number of typed lines.

Bottom margin. Leave a margin of approximately one inch at the bottom. With a margin of five double spaces at the top and an inch at the bottom, each legal-size page of typing will have 32 lines double spaced.

In a neatly typed legal instrument, the typing on every page ends exactly the same number of spaces from the bottom of the page. Carbon paper with numbered margin or a backing sheet with a numbered margin will insure an even bottom margin. If you do not have carbon paper with a numbered margin or if you are making too many copies to use a backing sheet, mark lightly the place where the typing should end, before inserting the paper in the typewriter.

Left margin. On legal cap, begin typing one space to the right of the colored line that indicates the left margin, except for lines beginning a new paragraph.

Right margin. Allow a leeway of seven spaces between the right margin and the colored line, that is, approximately ⅝″ to the left of the colored line. Avoid excessive hyphenation and a ragged right margin

Under no circumstances should the typing extend beyond the lines that indicate the margins.

Line spacing. As a rule all legal instruments are double spaced. *Quotations* and *land descriptions* may be single spaced.

Triple space before and after all indented material.

It is permissible to single space an acknowledgment (see page 201) in order to get it on the signature page.

Paragraphs. Indent ten spaces for paragraphs. *Never* block paragraph a legal document. The margin of indented material should be ten spaces from the margin of the document itself. Indent five additional spaces for paragraphing the indented material.

Never complete a paragraph at the end of a page. Carry over at least one or two lines.

Marginal and tabular stops. On a typewriter with pica type (pica type is most frequently used in legal instruments), set your marginal and tabular stops as follows:

Paper guide	0
Left marginal stop	15
Right marginal stop	75
First tabular stop	25
Second tabular stop	30
Third tabular stop	35

With the stops set at these points, practically no adjustment of the typewriter will be necessary for margins, paragraph indentations, proper placement of quotations, and the like.

Numbering pages. Number pages on legal cap one-half inch from the bottom of the page; in the center of the line. The number should be preceded and followed by a hyphen, thus: -4-. If the first page is not numbered, the numbering begins with -2-. Be exact in placing the number so that when the pages are collated the numbers will overlie one another.

Space for fill-ins. When a date is to be filled in later, leave a space instead of typing a line for the fill-in.

June   , 1968 (3 spaces)
This   day of June, 1968 (6 spaces)

Do not leave the blank for a subsequent fill-in at the end of a line, because it will not be noticeable.

How to write numbers. In legal instruments, write numbers in words and repeat them in numerals in parentheses, as follows:

One thousand three hundred eight-two (1,382)
Twenty-five and sixty-three one hundredths (25.63) *or* (25 63/100).

Note that when the number is spelled out, *and* is used only for a decimal or fraction.

How to write amounts of money. To insure accuracy, spell out amounts of money and repeat them in parentheses, as follows:

Thirty-eight dollars ($38)
Eight hundred fifty dollars and eighty cents ($850.80)

Note that (1) the figures in parentheses follow the entire amount as spelled out; (2) an amount of dollars without cents is written $1,340, not $1,340.00; (3) *and* is not used unless the amount includes cents.

Dates. Dates may be expressed in figures or spelled out. Even if the day of the month is spelled out, the year may be written in figures. Thus: the twenty-first day of August, 1968.

Ditto marks. Ditto marks are not permissible in a legal instrument. They are used in exhibits and schedules, but not in the instrument to which the exhibits and schedules are annexed.

Erasures and interlineations. If an error is made involving more than a few letters of a word, retype the page. The signer of the document must initial interlineations. Do not insert pages, but retype as many pages of the document as are necessary to work in the additional material.

How to type introductory and closing phrases. Many words and phrases commonly used in legal documents, particularly in introductory and closing paragraphs, are customarily written in full capitals. These words and phrases may be followed by a comma, a colon, or no punctuation, depending upon the sense and preference.

> KNOW ALL MEN BY THESE PRESENTS, That..
> MEMORANDUM OF AGREEMENT made...
> THIS AGREEMENT, made October...
> NOW, THEREFORE, IT IS HEREBY MUTUALLY AGREED, AS FOLLOWS:...
> IN WITNESS WHEREOF, the parties...

Number of copies. In typing a legal instrument, an original, file copy, and various other copies are necessary. Frequently, one or more of the carbon copies is to be a *duplicate original,* which means that it is to be signed and treated in all respects as though it were an original or ribbon copy. The dictator will tell you how many copies to make. Lawyers usually give instructions in this manner: "Two and four," meaning an original, a duplicate original, and four copies; or, "One and five," meaning an original and five copies, no duplicate original being necessary.

Legal backs. Legal documents should be bound with a backing sheet of thick paper, 8½″ or 9″ by 15″, which is endorsed with a brief description of the document. An endorsed mortgage back is shown in Figure 33.

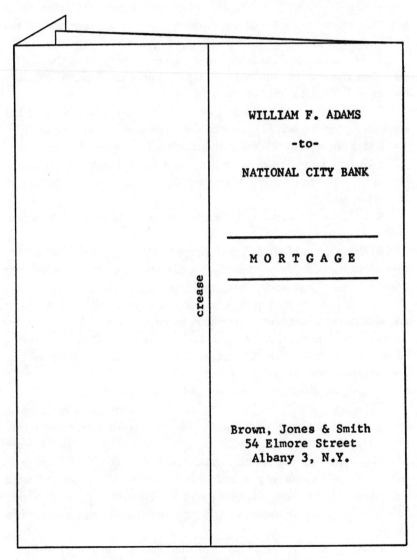

Figure 33. Endorsed Mortgage Back.

To type the endorsement:

1. Lay the backing sheet on the desk as though for reading.

2. Bring the bottom edge up to approximately one inch from the top and crease.

3. Bring the creased end (which is now at the bottom) up to approximately one inch from the top. (You now have a fold with about one inch of the top edge of the backing sheet protruding beyond the fold.)

4. The surface of the folded sheet that is uppermost is the surface on which the endorsement is to be typed. Put a small pencil check in the upper *left*-hand corner of that surface.

5. Partially unfold and insert in typewriter so that the pencil mark is on the upper *right*-hand corner of the surface when you type on it.

6. Do not type to the left of the crease. (See Figure 33.)

7. After typing the endorsement, turn down the top edge of the backing sheet about an inch (see step 3), crease, insert document in the crease, and staple.

8. Fold the document and the backing sheet, creasing the document to fit the creases in the backing sheet.

Filling in printed legal forms. At page 103, instructions were given for filling in printed office forms. Here we are concerned with printed forms of agreements and law blanks.

In the preceding chapter we pointed out that printed law blanks are widely used in drawing up the kinds of instruments that are necessary in real estate transactions. If you are required to fill in such forms, observe the following instructions so that the completed form will be neat and accurate:

Typing on ruled lines. See page 103.

Filling in plurals, "his" or "her," etc. Where the blank form leaves space for completing a word, insert the necessary letter or letters immediately after the printed word to which it is added; that is, leave no space after the incomplete printed word. If a complete word is to be inserted in the space provided, leave space after the printed word and make the insertion. To be sure that these words register, it may be advisable to fill them in on each copy individually and not through carbon.

Filling in surplus space. Some of the blank spaces on printed legal forms are just large enough for insertion of the material, possibly a single word; other spaces are quite large to allow for short or long insertions.

A large space following a land description should be filled in after you have taken the sheet out of the typewriter, as follows: With red ink, first rule a horizontal line from the last word to the right-hand margin; then rule a horizontal line at the end of the allotted space between the left-hand and right-hand marginal lines; then draw a diagonal line between the two horizontal lines connecting them from right to left to form a Z. (Anyone who is not experienced in ruling with red ink should be cautioned against the danger of smudging. A proper pen and ruler will prevent this.)

The same practice may be followed to close up any other large space and thus prevent anyone from inserting something in the document after the instrument has been signed. It is usually not necessary to close up small surplus spaces. In some cases, such as after the insertion of the name of a party, it is advisable to finish the line with dashes to the right-hand margin, just as you would do on a check after you had inserted the name of the person to whom the check is payable.

"Riders" when space is insufficient. Sometimes the space allotted for filling in conditional clauses or other provisions is not large enough for the typewritten material you have to insert. In that case, be careful to leave sufficient space after your last line of type to permit a "rider" with the rest of the typewritten matter to be pasted to the document. For the rider, use legal cap paper, preferably the same width as the printed legal form, and cut off any part of the sheet that is not used. In other words, the piece pasted to the document should be only as large as is necessary to carry the runover plus the initials or signature of the parties who sign the document. Paste the rider securely to the document (after the document and the rider have been examined and found to be correct), using a glue that will stick permanently. DO NOT USE RUBBER CEMENT for this purpose.

In some instances, riders attached as additions or amendments to documents have a heading to show that they are part of the document to which they are attached.

All separate sheets of paper attached to a document should be signed or initialed by the parties who sign the document.

Matching the printed copies. Printed forms bear a printer's mark showing the number of copies printed and the date of the printing. When filling in more than one copy, use forms that were printed at the same time because a change might have been made in the form.

Before attempting to fill in more than one blank form at one time by using carbons, make sure that the printing on all copies registers exactly. To do this, place the edges of the forms together and hold to the light. You can then see whether the printed matter in one copy lies exactly over corresponding material in the other copy.

Fill-ins on both sides of sheet. When making carbon copies of a printed form that has fill-ins on both sides of the sheet, take particular care to avoid having the ribbon copy on one side and the carbon copy on the other, thus rendering the form unfit for execution. Double sheet forms are particularly apt to cause trouble in this respect.

How to copy legal documents. The following instructions relate to the copying of a *signed* document:

1. Copy exactly, even obvious errors, because the copy purports to be a "true and exact" copy.

2. Indicate obvious errors copied from the original as follows: (a) Underline an incorrect letter or figure. (b) Put "sic" in parentheses or brackets after apparently or obviously incorrect words or phrases. (c) Show an omission by a caret.

> agreement entered into the 31th day of April...
> upon reciept...
> as part payment on the principle [sic] of a certain note and mortgage...
> and regulations of the United States, State and ⋀ in which said premises are situate, ...

3. Copy page for page and line for line as far as practicable.

4. If you do not have a paper holder fitted with an adjustable line spacer, place a rule on the line of the original that you are copying, moving the rule down from line to line.

5. When the document is completed, proofread it with some other person. That person reads aloud from the original copy while the typist checks the copy. The reader should indicate paragraphs, punctuation, underlining, full capitals, hyphens, and so on.

How to Type Real Property Descriptions

How land is described. Many real estate instruments that the secretary types contain a description of real property. Such a description constitutes an important part of the instrument. The descriptions are often complicated and difficult to follow when typing. Usually they are copied from some other document or from an abstract of title. An understanding of how these descriptions are evolved will make it easier for you to copy them and will lessen the possibility of error. Accuracy is essential.

Land is identified according to (1) section and township, (2) metes and bounds, (3) lot and block identification. Property is never identified solely by street number (except in a listing agreement or memorandum of sale) because the names and numbers of streets might change.

Section and township description. In the 18th century, when the United States began to sell public lands, it was necessary to adopt some conventional method of describing the tracts that were sold. A rectangular system of surveys was devised by the Government. The survey divided the public lands into rectangular tracts, located with reference to base lines running east and west, and prime or principal meridians running north and south. The prime meridians are numbered, as Third Prime Meridian, or named, as San Bernardino Meridian. The rectangular tracts are divided into six-mile squares, known as townships. A row of townships running north and south is called a range, and the ranges are numbered east and west from the prime meridians. The townships are divided into 36 sections, each one mile square or 640 acres. (See Figure 34.) The sections are numbered 1 to 36, beginning with the section in the northeast corner of the township, proceeding west to the boundary of the township; the next row is numbered from west to east, and so on. (See Figure 35). The sections in turn are divided into half and quarter sections, and the quarters into quarter-quarter sections, designated by their direction from the center as northwest, southwest, northeast, and southeast.

The description of a given five acres of land identified by section and township might read:

The East Half of the Northeast Quarter of the Northeast Quarter

A SECTION OF LAND = 640 ACRES.

A rod is 16½ feet. A chain is 66 feet or 4 rods. A mile is 320 rods, 80 chains or 5,280 ft. A square rod is 272¼ square feet. An acre contains 43,560 square feet. " " " 160 square rods. " " is about 208¾ feet square. " " is 8 rods wide by 20 rods long. or any two numbers (of rods) whose product is 160. 25 X 125 feet equals .0717 of an acre. CENTER OF	80 rods. 80 acres. 20 chains.	10 chains. 20 acres. 660 feet.	330 ft. 5 acres. / 5 acres. 5 ch. / 20 rods. 40 rods. 10 acres. 10 chains. 40 acres. / 80 rods.

SECTION	
Sectional Map of a Township with adjoining sections. 	36	31	32	33	34	35	36	31
1	6	5	4	3	2	1	6
12	7	8	9	10	11	12	7
13	18	17	16	15	14	13	18
24	19	20	21	22	23	24	19
25	30	29	28	27	26	25	30
36	31	32	33	34	35	36	31
1	6	5	4	3	2	1	6		160 acres. 40 chains, 160 rods or 2,640 feet.

Figure 34. A Section of Land.[1]

of the Northeast Quarter of Section One, Township 39 North, Range 12 East of the Third Prime Meridian.

The black box in the diagram in Figure 35 represents the parcel described above, assuming that the diagram is township 39 North, Range 12 East.

---

[1] M. Fred Tidwell, Elizabeth Pelz, and Carol Wells, *Legal Typing* (Englewood Cliffs, N.J.: Prentice-Hall, Inc., 1952), p. 81.

Land identification in the 29 public land states in which section and township descriptions are used is thus precise and orderly.

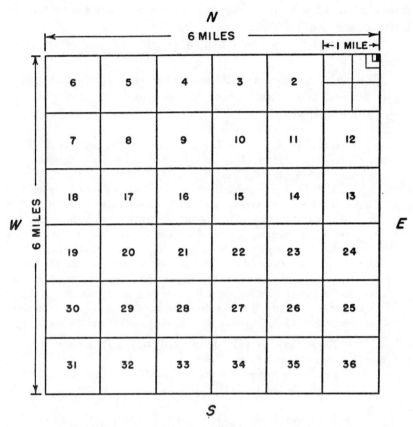

Figure 35. Diagram of Township Divided into Sections.

Metes and bounds description. The land in the area comprising the original thirteen colonies was held under grants from the Crown to the colonists. In the 18 states that grew from the colonies, each parcel of land is different in size and shape and is described by metes and bounds. A metes and bounds description is not correlated to any system of meridians and base lines as in the Government Survey territory; each tract of land is described by the lines that constitute its boundaries. A natural landmark, such as a tree or river, or an artificial landmark, such as a fence, stake, railroad, or street, often marks the corners and angles. These marks are known as *monuments.* A description by courses and distances constitutes part of a metes and bounds description. The direction from the starting point in which the boundary line runs is a course; the length of the line is a distance.

Two examples of a description by metes and bounds are given below.

Examples of metes and bounds description. The following is a metes and bounds description in which the rules given on page 197 are observed.

ALL that lot or parcel of land, situate, lying and being in the Town of Oyster Bay, County of Nassau, State of New York, bounded and described as follows:

BEGINNING at a point in the center line of Buena Vista Avenue distant two hundred sixty-one and thirty one hundredths (261.31) feet southerly from the point of intersection of said line with the center line of Jones Road; running thence along the center line of Buena Vista Avenue South twenty-five (25) degrees thirty-three (33) minutes East four hundred fifty-two and seventy-eight one hundredths (452.78) feet to a point; running thence North sixty-eight (68) degrees thirty-two (32) minutes East three hundred ten and eleven one hundredths (310.11) feet to a point in the center line of a driveway; running thence generally along the center line of said driveway the following courses and distances:

A. North forty-five (45) degrees forty-two (42) minutes West, 50 feet;

B. North thirty-nine (39) degrees two (02) minutes West, 50 feet;

C. North thirty-four (34) degrees sixteen (16) minutes West; 50 feet;

D. North twenty-eight (28) degrees fifty-eight (58) minutes West, 50 feet;

E. North twenty-six (26) degrees seventeen (17) minutes West, 100 feet;

F. North thirty-two (32) degrees six (06) minutes West, 50 feet;

G. North forty-five (45) degrees thirty-four (34) minutes West, 50 feet;

H. North sixty-one (61) degrees thirty-two (32) minutes West, 50 feet;

I. North eighty (80) degrees thirty-three (33) minutes West, 50 feet;

J. South seventy-nine (79) degrees eleven (11) minutes West, 50 feet;

K. South sixty-five (65) degrees thirty-two (32) minutes West, 50 feet; and

L. South sixty-four (64) degrees forty-seven (47) minutes West, 77 feet, to a point in the center line of Buena Vista Avenue, the point or place of beginning;

Containing, in area, approximately two and seven hundred seventy-four thousandths (2.774) acres;

Being and intended to be all of Plot No. 5, as shown on a map entitled "Plot Plan, Property of John Doe Estate, Town of Oyster Bay, Nassau County, New York, made by James Brown, Surveyor, November 1, 1960, as revised January 13, 1962, and December 31, 1965.

The legal description by metes and bounds of the irregular shaped plot shown in Figure 36 will be as indicated below the illustration.

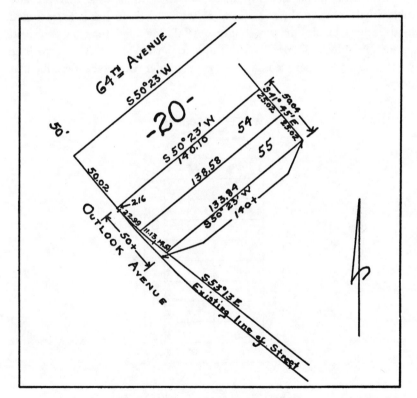

Figure 36. Map of Irregular Plot.[2]

2 M. Fred Tidwell, Elizabeth Pelz, and Carol Wells, *Legal Typing* (Englewood Cliffs, N.J.: Prentice-Hall, Inc., 1952), p. 82.

Beginning at the intersection of the northeastern line of Outlook Avenue with the northwestern line of said Lot 54; and running thence along said line of Outlook Avenue, southeasterly 2.16 feet; thence southeasterly along the arc of a curve to the left, tangent to the last said course, having a radius of 671.51 feet, an arc distance of 50 feet, more or less, to the direct production southwesterly of the southeastern line of said Lot 55; thence along said line produced and along the southeastern line of said Lot 55, northeasterly 140 feet, more or less, to the northeastern line of said Lot 55; thence along the last named line and along the northeastern line of said Lot 54, northwesterly 50.04 feet to the northwestern line of said Lot 54; thence along the last named line southwesterly 140.10 feet to the point of beginning.

Lot and block description. Where land has been surveyed and subdivided into parcels, and a map of the subdivision has been recorded in the office of the proper county official, the land may be described by lot and block. Figure 37 illustrates a portion of such a map. The parcel of land designated in the heavy border would be described as follows:

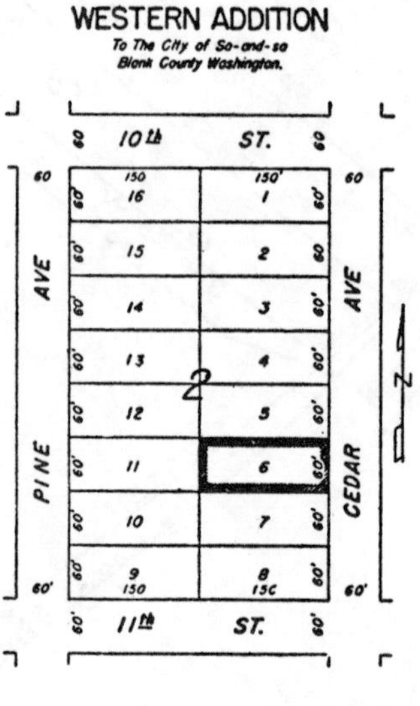

Figure 37. Map of Subdivision.[3]

---

[3] M. Fred Tidwell, Elizabeth Pelz, and Carol Wells, *Legal Typing* (Engleood Cliffs, N.J.: Prentice-Hall, Inc., 1952), p. 80.

Lot 6, Block 2, Western Addition to the City of ....as recorded in Volume 7 of Plats, page 48, records of ....County, State of ....

How to type real property descriptions. Unless otherwise instructed, observe the following style in preparing descriptions of real property for real estate instruments:

1. Single space, with double space between paragraphs.

2. Do not abbreviate Street, Avenue, Road, Boulevard, in the text.

3. Write the words *North, Northeast, South, West, Southwest,* and the like with initial capitals, but do not capitalize the words *northerly, northeasterly,* and the like.

4. Capitalize *Quarter, Township, Section,* and *Range,* and the name or number of a *Prime Meridian.*

5. Write courses as follows: "South twenty (20) degrees, thirty-three (33) minutes, forty-five (45) seconds West."

6. Write distances as follow: "One hundred thirty-three and twenty-nine one hundredths (133.29) feet."

7. When several courses and distances are given in succession, introduced by a phrase such as "...the following three courses and distances..." each of the courses and distances is written separately, indented and single spaced, separated one from the other by a double space, and each course and distance is ended with a semicolon. The sentence after the last course and distance is flush with the left-hand margin of the text preceding the itemized courses and distances.

8. It is preferable not to use figures, symbols, and abbreviations, but many law offices use them because of the limited space on a printed form. A description would then be written: "South 20°, 33', 45" West, 30 ft.".

How to check land descriptions. A typographical error in the description of land in a deed can cause considerable trouble and even result in a law suit. The importance of checking the description cannot be overemphasized. It is easy to make a copying error that is not always discernible from merely reading the description. For example, the section and township description on pp. 191–2 contains the phrase "of the Northeast Quarter" three times. It would be easy to omit the phrase once, but difficult to realize the omission in reading over the description; yet the omission would quadruple the amount of land conveyed by the deed.

Nor is it advisable for one person to compare the description line by line. The safest method of checking the typographical accuracy of a land description is to have someone read aloud to you the original copy, slowly enough to permit you to follow your typed copy carefully.

Setting up the Section for Execution of the Instrument

Meaning of " execution " of an instrument. Technically, execution of an instrument includes signing and delivery. In office parlance, execution frequently refers merely to the signing of an instrument by the party or parties described in it.

You will understand how to set up the section for execution of the instrument from the following explanation of (1) the testimonium clause, (2) attestation, (3) signatures, (4) sealing, and (5) acknowledgment.

Testimonium clause. The testimonium clause is the clause with which the instrument closes. It immediately precedes the signatures and usually begins, "IN WITNESS WHEREOF,...," typed in solid caps. It is a declaration by the parties to the instrument that their signatures are attached in testimony of the preceding part of the instrument. The testimonium clause is not to be confused with the "witness" or "attestation clause" (see below). The testimonium clause relates to the parties themselves, whereas the witness or attestation clause relate to those who sign the paper as witnesses, not as parties to the instrument.

Quite often, the testimonium clause will guide you in setting up the signature lines. It will indicate (1) what parties are to sign the instrument; (2) what officer of a corporation is to sign; (3) whether the instrument is to be sealed; and (4) whether a corporate seal is to be attached. For example, from the following clause, which is a form commonly used, you know that the president of the corporation is to sign, that the seal is to be affixed, and that the secretary of the corporation is to attest the seal:

IN WITNESS WHEREOF, Alvin Corporation has caused its corporate seal to be hereto affixed, and attested by its secretary, and these presents to be signed by its president, this 26th day of October, 196–.

On the other hand, from the following clause, also commonly used, you know that the instrument is not to be sealed:

IN WITNESS WHEREOF, the parties hereto have hereunto set their hands the day and year first above written.

The introductory words to the testimonium clause, *in witness whereof, in testimony whereof,* and the like, are usually typed in solid caps. The following word begins with lower case unless it is a proper name.

Attestation clause. Frequently the signatures to an instrument must be witnessed in order to make the instrument legal. The act of witnessing the signature to a written instrument at the request of the party signing the instrument is attestation. The witness is called a subscribing witness, because he signs his name as a witness. A legend or clause that recites the circumstances surrounding the signing of the instrument often precedes the signature of the attesting witnesses and is called the *attestation clause.* The wording of the attestation clause may be simply "In the presence of."

The legend and the lines on which witnesses sign are written opposite the lines for the signatures of persons who will execute the instrument.

Signatures. The parties signing an instrument vary with the instrument. Thus, all parties to a contract sign, but usually only the grantor signs a deed and only the mortgagor signs a mortgage. As a general practice, lines are typed for signatures. Type the first signature line below the body of the instrument, beginning it slightly to the right of the center of the page. Type a line for the signature of each person who must sign the instrument. There are no special requirements for the spacing of signature lines, except that sufficient space should be allowed for average handwriting and the lines should be evenly spaced. Three or four spaces between lines are sufficient.

When a corporation is a party to an instrument, the instrument is signed in the name of the corporation by the officer or officers authorized to execute it. Type the name of the corporation in solid caps, leave sufficient space beneath it for a signature, and type "By" and a line for signature. Under the signature line, type the title of the corporate officer who is going to sign the instrument, as shown below. The testimonium clause (page 198) usually recites the title of the officer who is supposed to sign the instrument.

BLANK CORPORATION

By——————————————

(Title)

When a partnership is a party to an instrument, type the name in solid caps, leave sufficient space beneath it for a signature, and type "By" and a line for signature. Since partnerships do not have officers, there will be no title under the signature line.

How to fit the signatures on the page. Arrange the body, or text, of the instrument so that at least two lines appear on the page with the signatures. The signatures must all be on the same page unless there are so many that they require more than a full page. To comply with these requirements you must gauge carefully the length of the material to be typed. This is not difficult if you are copying from a draft; otherwise, you might have to make a test copy and adjust your spacing accordingly. Here are methods by which you may lengthen or shorten the available typing space in order to fit the signatures on the page:

1. Leave wider or narrower top and bottom margins.

2. If you are using paper without ruled margins, leave wider or narrower left and right margins.

3. If the last line of a paragraph is full-length, adjust the right margin of that paragraph so that at least one word carries over to another line, thereby taking up an extra line of space. Or, if a paragraph ends with one word on a line, adjust the margin so that it is not necessary to carry over the one word, thereby saving a line of space.

4. Triple space between paragraphs.

5. Leave less space between the text of the instrument and the signatures.

6. Leave less space between the signatures.

Sealing an instrument. If an instrument is to be sealed, the testimonium clause will so indicate.

An individual's seal. At the end of the signature lines on an instrument that must be sealed, type (SEAL) or (L.S.) in solid caps. Thus:

———————————————(L.S.)

L.S. stands for *locus sigilli,* which means place of the seal.

A corporation's seal. Almost all corporations adopt a formal seal. It is engraved on a metal plate and impressed by this means upon the paper. An officer of the corporation impresses the seal on the instrument when it is signed. In many cases the corporate secretary must bear witness, or "attest," to the fact that the imprint on the paper is the seal of the corporation. Whenever the testimonium clause recites that the seal is to be attested, type the following on the left side of the page, opposite the signature line:

ATTEST

_____

Secretary

The seal will ordinarily be placed in the margin immediately above or below the "attest" line.

*Acknowledgment.*Technically, an acknowledgment is the act by which a person who executes a legal instrument declares to an officer designated by statute (usually judges, clerks of courts, and notaries public) that he is the person who executed the instrument. In common parlance, the term signifies both the declaration of execution and the officer's written certificate of the declaration.

It is common practice for a legal instrument to carry a certificate of acknowledgment because almost all states require the acknowledgment of an instrument before it can be recorded or filed. Furthermore, when an instrument is introduced in court as evidence, the certificate of acknowledgement is usually sufficient proof of the authenticity of the instrument.

Many states have adopted the Uniform Acknowledgment Act governing the use of acknowledgments and the form of the certificate. Otherwise, the law varies with the state. Some of the statutes are very precise in their requirements, and they must be adhered to strictly.

How and where to type the acknowledgment. Acknowledgments are usually double-spaced. They follow the signatures. Although there is no rule of law governing the placement of an acknowledgment on the page, it is desirable that the entire acknowledgment be placed on the signature page of the instrument, even if single-spacing is necessary to accomplish this. If the entire acknowledgment cannot be placed on the signature page it is preferable to type it all on another page. In the case of some instruments—for example, a power of attorney that authorizes the conveyance of any interest in real estate—it is practically mandatory to type the acknowledgment on the same page as the signatures.

Forms of acknowledgments to be signed by a notary public. The acknowledgments illustrated in the forms below are for the purpose of showing you how acknowledgments are set up when typed and to give you a general idea of the wording of the acknowledgment. They are not supposed to be copied word for word:

(Individual)
STATE OF ....
COUNTY OF ....

SS.:

On the .... day of ...., 19.., before me came ...., to me known to be the individual described in and who executed the foregoing instrument and acknowledged that he executed the same.

....
Notary Public
(Affix stamp and seal)

(Corporate)
STATE OF ....
COUNTY OF ....

SS.:

On the .... day of ...., 19.., before me personally came ...., to me known, who, being by me duly sworn, did depose and say that he resides at ....; that he is .... *(title)* of .... Company, the corporation described in and which executed the foregoing instrument; that he knows the seal of said corporation; that the seal affixed to said instrument is such corporate seal; that it was so affixed by order of the .... of said corporation, and that he signed his name thereto by like order.

....
Notary Public
(Affix stamp and seal)

(Partnership)
STATE OF ....
COUNTY OF ....

SS.:

On this .... day of ...., 19.., before me personally came ...., to me known and known to me to be a members of ...., and the person described in and who executed the foregoing instrument in the firm name of .... and he duly acknowledged to me that he executed the same as and for the act and deed of said firm of ....

....
Notary Public
(Affix stamp and seal)

Chapter 13

Helping the Salesman

A REAL ESTATE SALESMAN is employed by a broker to perform certain duties. These duties may include obtaining listings, selling or offering property for sale, leasing, and performing any other duties the broker himself might perform. The term includes both men and women, and both sexes are referred to whenever the word salesman is used here.

Whether a real estate office has only one or two salesmen or a staff of salesmen with or without a sales manager in charge, the opportunities available to the secretary to help them toward success in their daily work are unlimited. The way in which you perform those duties that touch the actual work of the salesman obviously affects his efficiency. Equally important, however, is your treatment of him as an individual.

It is extremely important that you do not show partiality where there are a number of salesmen in the office. Each man must be given an equal amount of your secretarial service.

What you do for the salesmen. Th. way in which you meet the public, how you answer the telephone, the efficiency with which you maintain the files, the care with which you write the salesman's letters, your skill in preparing the real estate instruments he dictates for you to type, the way in which you help with the advertising—all are important in helping to make the salesman's job easier. These and other subjects are treated fully in separate chapters.

There are some duties, however, that are more closely connected with the salesman's primary function of selling property. They fall into the following categories:

1. Handling listings for routine office processing
2. Helping with other sales office routine
3. Taking care of signs and windows
4. Eliminating sales distractions

Handling Listings

Work involved in handling listings. A listing is an authorization to sell real property, given by the owner of the property to the real estate man who will act as agent for the seller. The term also refers to the record of the property to be sold and to the property itself. Nothing is more important to the real estate man than that he have a good supply of salable listings. Equally important is the efficiency with which all listings are handled in the office. Forms of listing agreements and a full explanation of them are given in Chapter 11.

Each real estate office has its own listing system, but fundamentally all systems provide for the following operations: (1) obtaining listings, (2) recording them, (3) keeping the records up to date, and (4) filing the records of all listings, sold and not sold. In each of these operations the closest cooperation between the secretary and the salesman is necessary. The four operations are explained fully in this section.

Obtaining listings. There are two basic ways of obtaining listings: (1) through the efforts of the broker and his salesmen and the cooperation of the secretary and the office staff; (2) through a Multiple Listing Service. The work of handling multiple listings will be explained at page 211, after the four listing operations mentioned above have been discussed.

Sources of listings. Listings are completed in numerous ways, each of which involves work on the part of the broker, salesmen, and secretary. The most common sources of listings are:

1. *Observations by the salesmen.* A good salesman will do a lot of walking around instead of hurried auto riding. In his walking, he will notice "for sale" signs that owners have themselves put on their homes. He will try to convince the owner to list with his firm. He will find some houses that look as though the owner might want to sell. For example, he will observe properties that are no longer functionally efficient. In this class are large residences occupied by elderly people whose children have

married and moved away; small houses occupied by families that have grown in size; stores no longer adequate for an expanding business. The observant salesman will find listings in changing neighborhoods. For example, when a residential neighborhood is being encroached upon by business property, the owners of the homes are likely to be good listing prospects. This is especially true if the area has been changed by the zoning ordinances from residential to business.

2. *House-to-house canvassing.* This is a common method of securing listings.

3. *Telephone canvassing.* A systematic plan must be developed for covering an area thoroughly by telephone, and a record must be kept of the people who have been called.

4. *Classified and display advertising.* A real estate wanted ad for the type of listing desired will produce inquiries from prospective sellers. The salesman must follow up the inquiries.

5. *Direct mail advertising.* A letter or card prepared for the specific purpose of obtaining listings is sent to owners of property in the community or to former buyers of property. A city directory is the best source of property owners. A symbol usually identifies the property owners. See Chapter 14 for other sources of names and examples of such advertising.

6. *Stuffers.* A self-addressed, stamped post card inviting the reader to send in information about properties for sale is stuffed into outgoing mail, such as rent notices and insurance bills.

7. *Owners' ads in the classified columns.* An owner who advertises his property for sale in the classified ads hopes, of course, to save the broker's commission by selling the property himself. But if his ad does not bring satisfactory results he will soon be in the mood to discuss the possibility of letting a broker sell it for him. Such ads must be watched and followed up at once by the salesmen. (See page 216.)

8. *Newspaper stories.* Opportunities for real estate sales are found in many news stories. Local news items must be scanned for them. This is a job often done by the secretary.

9. *Sold signs.* The firm's "sold" sign on a property attracts to the office owners who have property to sell. The secretary's part in taking care of signs is discussed starting on page 217.

10. *Owners of properties in the same block adjacent to those sold.* A sale of a property frequently makes the owners of neighboring properties think of doing likewise. The firm, therefore, may send every family within

a block or two of a recently sold residence a notice of the sale. (See letter on page 152.)

11. *Friends and acquaintances.* The broker's wide circle of friends and acquaintances constitutes a rich source of information about listings.

12. *Attorneys.* Attorneys who have a real estate law practice have a great fund of information about prospective listings.

13. *Builders.* The speculative builder who does not handle his own sales has many prospective listings. He also frequently knows someone who has property to sell. Building permits reported in some newspapers give the names and addresses of builders. Among them may be private parties who are speculative builders.

14. *Doctors and dentists.* These professional men are in intimate touch with many families in the community. If the broker wins the confidence of these men, he may be able to get the names of patients who want to sell property.

15. *Ministers.* Ministers frequently know the personal problems of their parishioners. They may be able to tell the real estate man the names of owners who for one reason or another are finding it necessary to dispose of their property.

16. *Officers of banks, insurance companies, and building and loan associations.* Officers of such institutions are in a position to know of people who want to sell their property. The real estate man should make friends of such officers.

17. *Out-of-town owners.* Every property in the community owned by someone in a distant place is a potential listing. The names of absentee owners can be gotten by examining public records.

18. *Public records.* Each public record of a transfer, trust deed, mortgage, tax sale, or foreclosure points to the possibility that one or more of the parties involved may have property to sell. A periodic inspection of such public records may yield many potential listings. Public records of leases will disclose lease expiration dates, which furnish a lead to possible rental listings.

Open and exclusive listings. A listing may be an open one which, as explained on page 154, means that the property is listed with a number of brokers; or it may be an exclusive one, which means that for a definite period of time the broker has the sole right to sell the property. In the case of an exclusive listing, the owner and the broker sign an exclusive listing agreement. A brief explanation of the agreement, with illustrations, is given starting on page 155. The broker and the seller are bound by the agreement which they have signed. Therefore, no notations should be made on this agreement by anyone. This is a rule that the secretary should clearly understand. Any additional notations about the property should be made on the record of the listings.

File of exclusive listing agreements. The signed exclusive listing agreements are generally kept in a filing cabinet in folders arranged alphabetically by towns. Since there are not usually many such agreements, all of the agreements for a particular town may be kept together in one folder. The tab on the folder shows the name of the town.

Records of listings. Each real estate office supplies itself with printed forms of cards, sheets, or slips on which it records certain information. The items on the form are a checklist of facts about the property needed by the broker. A different form of card is provided for each type of property. Illustrations of a card for one-family, multi-family, and commercial property are shown in Figures 38a, 38b, and 38c.

The records are made up by the secretary from information supplied by the salesman or whoever brings in the listing. Some brokers use a

FORM 81			ONE FAMILY		R. E. SCOTT CO. REALTORS	
Town		Section		PRICE		
Street				TERMS	Cash; $	Mo.
Design		Construction		BUILT		
Heat		Fuel		CONDITION		
Radiation		Insulation		POSSESSION		
Rooms		Baths		RENTAL		
Roof		Showers		Lavs.		
Basement				Type H. W.		
1st floor						
2nd floor						
3rd floor						
Kitchen		Bkft. nook		Plumbing		
Floors		Porch		Size of lot		
Storm sash		Venetian blinds		Weather stripping		
Fireplace		Awnings		Garage		
Ass't Land	Bldg.		Garage	Total	Taxes	
1st Mortgage	@	%	for	years payable $		Month inc. taxes
Multiple Listing				Mtgee,-		
Remarks:						

TOWN	STREET NO.	TYPE	HEAT	ROOMS	BATHS	GAR.	PRICE

Figure 38a. Listing Card for One-Family Houses.

MULTI FAMILY

Town	Section	PRICE
Street		TERMS Cash; $ Mo.
Families	Construction	BUILT
Heat	Fuel	CONDITION
Radiation	Insulation	POSSESSION
Rooms	Roof	RENTALS: 1st. Fl.
Baths	Showers	2nd. Fl.
Basement		3rd. Fl.
1st Floor		4th Fl.
2nd Floor		Garages
3rd Floor		Monthly Gross
4th Floor		Annual Gross
Kitchen	Bkft. Nook	Plumbing
Floors	Porch	Size of Lot
Fireplace	Awnings	Garage
Ass't Land	Bldg. Garage	Total Taxes
1st Mortgage	at % for	years payable $ Month inc. taxes
Remarks:		Mtgee.-

TOWN	STREET NO.	FAM	HEAT	ROOMS	BATHS	GAR	PRICE

FORM 33

Figure 38b. Listing Card for Multi-Family Houses.

FORM 37

r. e. Scott co., 400 Westfield Ave., Elizabeth, N. J.

COMMERCIAL PROPERTY

Town		PRICE
Street No.		TERMS
Type	Construction	BUILT
Size of Plot	Elevators	CONDITION
Heat	Fuel	LEASED TO
Floors	Refrig.	GROSS INCOME
Insulation	Type Baths	NET INCOME
STORES	Type Tenancy	
Rentals		Gross
LOFTS	Type Tenancy	
Rentals		Gross
APTS 1 Rm.	; 2 Rm. ; 3 Rm.	; 4 Rm. ; 5 Rm.
Rentals		Gross
GARAGES @	Month	Gross
First Mortgage $	@ % for	years, held by
Second Mortgage $	@ % for	years, held by

TOWN	STREET NO.	TYPE	PLOT	GROSS	PRICE

Figure 38c. Listing Card for Commercial Property.

combination listing card and agreement. One side of the form contains the property data and the other side the listing agreement. The secretary makes up the master file card, sheet, or slip from the data given in the listing agreement form.

Different colored cards may be used to identify different types of property. A card for an exclusive listing may have a special symbol, such as a star, or a special color, to identify it as an exclusive.

Preparing the salesmen's listing records. Each salesman usually has his own listing book. This book is made up of sheets that contain forms exactly like the record cards just described. The sheets, however, may be a different size and may have room for pasting on a small photograph of the property. The sheets fit into a loose-leaf binder which is divided into categories such as residential property—one-family and multiple family—industrial, and business property, businesses for sale, residential lots, and others.

After the secretary has typed up the record for the master file, she prepares the sheets for the salesmen's books and delivers them to the men. They place them into their own books and attach the photographs.

The salesmen keep their books up to date from the information which the secretary supplies to them periodically, as shown below.

Keeping master listings file and salesmen's books-up-to-date. Both the master file and the salesmen's listing books must be kept up-to-date by adding records of new listings as they are received, removing the records of sold properties or those that have been taken off the market, and by making changes in price and other data as they occur. The salesmen report the sales, removals, and changes in price and terms to the secretary, who then conforms the master records. The secretary may also have to check daily sales records that are published in various places like real estate magazines, newspapers, city court bulletins, and the like. The listing record for sold properties or those taken off the market is withdrawn from the master active file and placed in an inactive file.

Periodically the secretary prepares a statement of all changes made in the master listing file, including properties sold or taken off the market and changes made in prices. A sufficient number of copies is made to supply each salesman with a copy. The salesmen keep their own books up to date from these statements. They return to the secretary the sheets that they remove from their books, and the secretary removes the photographs and pastes them on the back of the master record.

The master file of listings. The master file of the listings records may consist of a loose-leaf record book, a card file, a Kardex tray file, or any other type of container. The cards or sheets are classified for easy filing and selection under a system of classification designed to meet the needs of the office. Although there is no one best classification, a system that meets the needs of most offices is described here.

Two active files are maintained—one of "property for sale" and the other of "rentals." A property that has been listed for sale or rental would appear in both files, with a cross-reference on the record in each to the record in the other.

Each file is arranged according to location of the property. The principal breakdown is the towns in which the broker operates, each town having its own guide card. The towns are arranged in alphabetical order. Within each town, the cards or sheets are further broken down into smaller areas, such as communities or streets.

Within each location division, the cards are arranged by type of property, such as "one-family," "multiple-family," farms," "lots," "commercial," and so on. The commercial property cards are further subdivided by classification into types, such as "stores," "office buildings," and so on. Each type of similar property is then filed according to price classification, beginning with the lowest.

In systems where different colored cards are used to identify particular kinds of property, there may not be this type of subdivision of the location file. The color of the card is sufficient to reveal the type of property listed.

Inactive listings file. When listings are removed from the active file they are placed in the inactive file, which is arranged in the same manner as the active file. The file of discards is never "dead" because properties once listed may again come on the market.

Control of the master file. Since the salesmen are supplied with their own listings books, there is little occasion to remove a listing record from the master file. When a record has to be taken temporarily from the master file for office use, it is advisable to insert an OUT dummy card or sheet in the place of the removed record. The OUT card or sheet should contain sufficient information to identify the listing and should show to whom it is charged. In large offices it might be well to have the borrower sign the OUT card or sheet.

Listings folder files. In addition to the master listings file, many offices maintain a supplementary listings file in letter-size filing cabinets for the papers relating to listings. For example, some listings of commercial and other types of property arrive in the form of mimeographed sheets which are distributed to various brokers. After the information on the sheet is entered in the master listing record, the sheet is filed in a folder with the address of the property noted on the tab. The folder is used for all other information concerning the listed property—memoranda dictated by members of the broker's staff, carbon copies of letters, financial data, pictures, and many other items. The folders are arranged by location.

Where such a file is maintained, each type of property is kept separate in different drawers, or in the same drawer subdivided by guides with tabs to indicate the type of property.

In some offices, a file folder is prepared in the name of the owner when a property is listed for sale. This folder is eventually transferred to the sales folder when the property is sold. (See sales file, page 67.)

Multiple listing of exclusives. Although a broker may have an exclusive listing agreement with an owner, other brokers may still have an opportunity to find a buyer for the property. This will happen if the broker with the exclusive is a member of a real estate board that conducts a Multiple Listing Service. Many real estate boards offer such a membership.

Multiple listing is a system under which multiple members are given an opportunity to try to sell properties that any other member may have listed. All listings that are to be interchanged must be exclusives, according to the rules of the Service. Each listing is forwarded to the central office of the Multiple Listing Service on a form provided by the Service for the purpose. When the central office receives these forms, the listing is copied, given a number, and sent to the multiple members in a bulletin or other form of communication. The system makes it possible for a multiple broker to give an owner the active services of many offices, including their representative salesmen.

When a sale of one of the multiple listed properties is made, it is reported to the broker with whom the property was originally listed. The sale is also reported to the Multiple Listing Service, and brokers are advised by the Service that the listed property has been sold and is to be removed from the files.

The commission on sales of properties that are multiple listed is divided between the listing broker and the selling broker on a prearranged basis. The Multiple Listing Service is paid a small percentage of the commission for its services.

In escrowed deals, the escrow office may deduct the amount due the Service from the broker's commission and forward the payment to the Service.

The Multiple Listing Service furnishes its members with a standard form of exclusive multiple listing agreement. An example is given on page 157. It indicates that the listing will be distributed to all of the Multiple Listing Service members for the purpose of cooperative sales.

Duties relating to multiple listing. If your broker participates in a Multiple Listing Service, your duties in handling listings may include the following operations:

1. Checking the daily Multiple Listing Service bulletins.

2. Notifying the Multiple Listing Service of items to be included in the bulletins. This is usually done by mail.

3. Keeping track of payments due other brokers.

Checking the Multiple Listing Service bulletins. The material received regularly from the Multiple Listing Service contains three types of information that must be entered on the master listings records and transmitted to the salesmen: (1) new listings with complete information about the property listed; (2) listings that were sold or cancelled; (3) changes in prices in previously listed properties, and other changes.

The manner in which these items are presented varies with the particular service. Some interchange services send their information about new listings in the form of mimeographed bulletins; others submit the new listings in the form of a completed listing card with a photograph of the property on the reverse side.

The secretary must carefully check the material, make up the new listing record for the master listings file, remove the sold or cancelled listings, and note on the records any changes in prices or terms of previously listed properties. She must make copies of the new listings for the salesmen's books, and get information to them of listings to be removed or changed (see page 209).

In some offices, a sufficient number of copies of the Multiple Listing Service bulletins or sheets are obtained to supply each salesman with a copy. The salesmen then keep their listing books up to date from the sheets.

Notifying the Multiple Listing Service of bulletin items. A form similar to that shown in Figure 39 may be supplied by the interchange service for reporting new listings and other items to the central office of the Multiple Listing Service. The secretary fills out this form from the exclusive listing agreements submitted by the salesmen and places it on the salesman's desk for final checking and signature. She then forwards it to the Multiple Listing Service office.

Keeping track of payments due other brokers. Whoever keeps the records of real estate transactions or the books of account has the responsibility of seeing that the commissions due other brokers on sales of multiple listed properties are paid. The manner in which this is done is described in Chapter 21 (see page 319).

Keeping track of expirations and activity. The listing period for exclusives generally expires ninety days from the date of the listing. The expiration dates must be watched carefully. The reminder may be made in the manner described in Chapter 4.

Some agreements contain a clause in which the property owner agrees to pay the agent a commission if the sale is made within six months after the termination of the authorization to sell. The sale must be made to someone to whom the agent or his salesmen had previously shown the property.

You must keep track of the termination date through your reminder system.

To remind the owner of this six-months protection clause, the broker should send a letter to the owner within five days of the close of the 90-day period, if the property has not been sold or if the listing has not been cancelled, reminding him of the protection. An example of such a letter, used by Charles Woessner, Realtor of Fresno, California, is reproduced below.

DEAR MR. AND MRS. ————:
   In line with the written authorization to sell, which you gave me

Fresno Realty Board Interchange
2123 Amador St., Phone 006-2447

PLEASE use this form for submitting
Listings to the ....
Fresno Realty Board Interchange

Date....................

Location: ....

....

Legal: ....

....

....

Write up for Bulletin:

Price $ ....

Down
Payment ....
Monthly
Payment ....

Loans: ....

....

....

Interest ....

Held by: ....

....

No. Rooms ....

No. Bedrooms ....

Square Feet ....

Lot Size ....

The information contained hereon is submitted for publication in the Interchange Bulletin. This information is taken from a listing signed exclusively with this Office. This listing expires on the following date:

....

I understand that this listing must be exclusive with the office submitting said listing and must have at least 30 days remaining before expiration to be eligible for publication.

MUST BE SIGNED BY BROKER..................................

Phone..................................

Figure 39. Form Used in Submitting Information to Multiple Listing Service

October 30, 19. ., covering the property at 4780 Grand Ave., I am glad to advise that during the 90-day listing period I submitted the property to the following prospects:

Mr. A. Brown	Mr. & Mrs. S. Smythe
Mrs. M. Johnson	Mr. & Mrs. B. Bird
Mrs. T. A. Jones	Mr. & Mrs. H. Wright

As to those prospects I am protected for six months after the termination of the listing; in other words, until July 28, 19. .. If you again put your place up for sale or if you have any new ideas as to procedure, feel free to call me because I am always at your service.

Sincerely,
CHARLES WOESSNER

CW:hw

Where this practice is followed, the secretary is responsible for preparing the letters and for including the names of the prospects to whom the property was submitted. She keeps careful records of the submissions of the exclusive listings. She also checks the names on recorded deeds in the *Daily Real Estate Report and Abstract of Records* (see page 293), or similar publication, to discover whether any sale has been made to people to whom the property was shown.

The checking of sales is useful whether or not the listing is an exclusive. A nonexclusive listing might have been sold to a prospect who was shown the property by the broker, and he may be entitled to a commission.

Helping with Sales Office Routine

Sales management and the secretary. Each salesman represents a considerable investment on the part of the broker. To make that investment yield sales and profits, the broker organizes his sales force for maximum selling results and uses various devices to keep his salesmen stimulated and active. The practices, of course, vary from office to office. Just a few are mentioned here to illustrate how the secretary can cooperate to achieve the main objective of the sales manager—greater sales.

Assisting at sales staff meetings. Among the devices used to arouse enthusiasm of the salesmen and to promote a clearer understanding of current sales programs are sales contests; tours for inspection of property; sales meetings for which quizzes, outside speakers, and other events are programmed; "morning value meetings" at which each sales-man presents special information about a selected listing; and other sales training devices. The secretary does everything she can to make the program operate smoothly, from getting the meeting room ready for the salesmen and supplying the salesmen with paper and pencils to keeping track of accomplishments.

Suppose it is the practice at each sales meeting for someone to discuss the week's events that touch upon real estate. The items reported may be new laws, court decisions, trends, and forecasts. The alert secretary will call the attention of the person responsible for this feature of the program to pertinent items she may have clipped from newspapers, periodicals, bulletins from the Multiple Listing Service and the real estate board, and other places.

Carrying out routines for equalizing salesmen's opportunities. The office may have installed a system that gives all sales-men an equal opportunity to participate in leads that come directly to the office. For example, each salesman may have the "floor" for a day. All inquiries from prospective purchasers and sellers are automatically turned over to this salesman; the telephone operator gives him all such telephone calls; clients coming into the office are directed to his desk; and all mail inquiries are given to him. If the salesman leaves the office with a prospect, all calls are referred to the man who will have the "floor" the next day.

The secretary must know the rotation with which the system works and see that the equalization plan is administered fairly. As indicated at page 16, you sometimes act as the arbitrator.

Salesman's report. The firm may require each salesman to fill out at the end of each day a work sheet or some other prescribed form from which the sales manager can determine the strengths and weaknesses of each of his men. It may be the secretary's duty to see that the reports are submitted regularly.

Clipping items for sales and other purposes. A great deal of clipping is done in the real estate office for various purposes that directly or indirectly lead to commissions and fees. The secretary should keep on hand a list of all of the kinds of clippings that are used in the office and what disposition is made of them. Such a list will enable you to pass the clipping duty along to an assistant or substitute when you are absent or on vacation. It should also be part of any office manual in which the procedures of the office are written up. The following checklist can be used for preparing the clipping list.

1. Ads placed by the firm or salesmen (see page 232)
2. The firm's publicity releases (see page 244).
3. Local news items that might lead to listings or sales:
    a. Announcements of sales by other brokers
    b. Engagements and marriages
    c. Death notices
    d. Changes of residences or places of business
    e. Legal notices of tax sales, foreclosures, probates of wills, etc.
    f. Divorces.
4. Owners' ads in classified columns.
5. News items that may be used at sales meetings.
6. Sales and other historical data reported in newspapers and other publications (see page 293).
7. Appraisals by other brokers and by the valuation committee of the local real estate board.

Some of these clippings should be pasted into books maintained for the particular kind of clippings (see page 244).

In some offices, each day's clippings of items of interest to salesmen are pasted on a sheet of paper and placed on the sales manager's desk.

Watching the appointment calendar. If you know that a salesman is not going to be able to keep an appointment with a customer, it is your duty to call that customer and arrange for another meeting, giving the reason for the cancellation. See page 30 for handling telephone calls, and page 130 for letters making appointments.

Keeping track of salesmen's whereabouts. Upon leaving the office, each salesman should indicate to the telephone operator, receptionist, or the secretary where he will be and when he expects to return. Such a rule is usually established in any well-run office, and the secretary sees that it is enforced.

Taking Care of Signs, Windows, and Displays

Sign duties. A sign says that property is for sale, or rent, or lease and John Doe is the agent for it. Not all real estate men agree on the value of signs, and you must therefore know what the policy of your firm is in using them.

It is part of the secretary's duty to keep track of signs placed on properties and to see that they are returned after the sale has been closed or the rental accomplished. If the practice is to add the word "Sold" to the sign when the sale occurs, it is the secretary's responsibility to see that this addition is made. Another duty is to keep tabs of the supply of signs on hand and to place the order for replenishing the supply before it runs out.

Window duties. Unless the firm uses professional help in arranging its windows, it may be part of the secretary's job to look after the window displays. Here are a few pointers and ideas that will help you:[1]

1. Cut down the space in a large window with screens or curtains so that your exhibit holds together.

2. Use a plain background for more effective displays.

3. Use spotlights, if possible, to highlight the display.

4. Put few items in the window; the less you use, the better.

5. Use only large objects or pictures. Photographs should be "blown up" to a large size.

6. Use as few statistics as possible. Most people cannot digest them in large doses.

7. Use posters and printed matter as sparingly as possible; be sure to use an oversized type when using any sort of printed matter.

8. Arrange your displays so they will stop the passerby. You can appeal to the passerby with the design of your display or through the story that the window tells. Mechanical devices, like lights going on and off, may be used to attract the eye.

9. For small displays, use cardboard as a background. Corrugated cardboard can be used effectively for making pedestals and covering bases or backgrounds. Use wallpaper for covering cheap base material for a decorative background.

10. Have a window board constructed as a base for all window displays.

11. Place photographs in cellophane envelopes to protect them against curling and fasten them to the board with scotch tape.

12. Change displays regularly, say every two weeks. When a property on display is sold, write the word "Sold" over the description.

13. Your window can display not only some of the listings you have, but a placard asking for the kind of listings you want.

---

[1] Acknowledgment for some of these points is made to *Planning Your Exhibit*, by Janet Lane and Beatrice K. Tolleris, The National Publicity Council, New York, N.Y.

14. Don't use a whole blackboard to list numerous properties. They make messy displays and cannot be clearly read at a distance.

15. Make a collection of old photographs of sold houses and then have someone arrange them attractively into a permanent background for the window.

Maps and photographs as selling tools. Maps may be used as a selling tool. For example, a large wall map may be used to show clearly each section of the firm's territory. On this map you can locate every listing, using different colored pinheads to signify the type of property and whether it is for sale, rent, or exchange. (See page 309 for further information about maps.)

The display of photographs in the office also helps the salesmen. The secretary must frequently assume the responsibility of seeing that the pictures of sold properties are removed and that those of new listings are mounted.

Eliminating Selling Distractions

Keeping children occupied. When a prospect arrives at the office with one or more children, the secretary must realize that she may have to stop what she is doing to keep the children occupied. No salesman can concentrate properly upon finding out what the customer wants, and no parent can relax sufficiently to give full attention to the salesman's remarks, if some child is squirming about, creating a racket, or generally interfering with the purpose of the call. It is especially important that distractions be eliminated when the salesman is trying to close a deal.

To prepare for the emergency of children's interference with a conference, have on hand a number of picture books and inexpensive toys for children of all ages. Tell the child that if he is good he can take the book or toy home. Have some lollypops on hand, without wooden sticks. Remove the wrapping before giving one to a child so that he can "go to work" on it immediately. In selecting toys, be careful not to purchase any nat might cause accidents. Don't get anything that a child can swallow or that can cut or hurt him in any way.

Keeping track of keys. If the key to a listed property is not where it should be, the prospect must be kept waiting while the key is located. That is a distraction from selling to be avoided by establishing and enforcing some simple rules for the use of keys. You should make a record each time the key is taken for the purpose of showing a listing.

Even though a prospect has been to a property with a salesman, it is generally not advisable to give him the key and let him go unaccompanied to the property. If there is no salesman present who can be sent with the prospect, it may be necessary to give the prospect the key. This should not be done, however, without getting the prospect's full name, address, and telephone number, and without reminding him that all doors must be left locked and all windows closed. Occupied or furnished homes must *always* be shown with a member of the firm present, unless the lady of the house or the owner is at home. This rule is a protection against pilferage.

Chapter 14

How You Can Help with the Firm's Advertising

ALMOST EVERY REAL ESTATE office does some advertising to attract buyers for properties they have for sale. Some firms advertise extensively, others occasionally.

A large firm not only inserts advertisements in the classified columns of metropolitan and local newspapers regularly, but also uses all other available media to reach prospects for specific offerings. It might spend money on newspaper display ads, on ads in trade journals, periodicals, and local programs, and on direct mail advertising; it might even use billboards. It tries to make the firm name familiar to the public by repeatedly advertising and by getting publicity in the real estate news columns.

In a small office, the real estate man who believes strongly in advertising is usually one who has himself mastered the art of writing classified ads. His ads usually bring good results.

The secretary's part in advertising. How you help with the advertising depends generally upon what the firm's advertising policy and practices are and how familiar you are with advertising techniques and procedures.

A heavy advertiser may have an experienced advertising man or woman handle the firm's advertising. This person may be the owner of the business or a trained employee. In such an organization the secretary to the advertising man works closely with him, following specific instructions and performing details assigned to her.

Many large real estate firms use an advertising agency. At page 235 we shall show you how to smooth the way between the agency and your employer.

In a small office that uses only classified ads, a capable secretary may have to prepare the ads for selected home properties and do all the work that the firm's advertising entails. In the next chapter we shall give you the rudiments of writing effective classified ads.

If you are with a firm that is publicity-minded, you can be very helpful in recognizing happenings in the office that make acceptable news stories. You can collect the facts and assist in preparing the news releases. How you do this is explained in the next chapter.

Many secretaries have the responsibility of checking all advertising bills and preparing the checks for payment. For points on checking the classified ads, see page 224. For drawing of checks, see page 322.

Getting acquainted with the local newspaper's advertising work. Since the secretary does most of the talking with the local newspaper concerning the ads to be placed, some brokers take their secretaries over to the newspaper office and introduce them to the heads of the classified and display departments. They arrange for the secretary to go through the photoengraving department and to see generally how the advertisements are handled from the time they are delivered.

Kinds of advertising undertaken. The advertising man generally works on two kinds of advertising—institutional and specific property advertising. Institutional advertising aims at (1) selling the standing and stability of the concern to the public, (2) creating a reputation for the advertiser, and (3) making the public familiar, by the force of repetition, with the name and the services offered. No particular property is offered for sale or rent. Although there is no way of checking the results of institutional advertising, its value in creating good will and prestige is not questioned by firms that have used it.

All advertising other than institutional advertising is undertaken with the object of (1) selling homes, home sites, business or industrial property, apartment houses, or farms, (2) renting homes, apartments, office space, lofts, showrooms, factories, or stores, or (3) obtaining listings.

An advertisement of the sale or rental of particular properties may include institutional copy. For example, statements about the experience of the firm, its leadership in the field, the kinds of organizations that use the services of the firm, are added. Such items are institutional in nature. They help to create confidence in the firm.

Advertising media. Any vehicle that carries an advertisement is called a medium. The advertising media used by the real estate profession include:

(1) Publications
    (a) Newspapers
        1. Classified
        2. Display
        3. Free publicity
    (b) Magazines
        1. General
        2. Trade

(2) Direct mail
    (a) Letters
    (b) Leaflets
    (c) Folders
    (d) Circulars
    (e) Booklets

(f) Mailing cards
(g) House organs
(h) Miscellaneous advertising pieces

(3) Out-of-door advertising
    (a) Billboards
    (b) Signs
    (c) Car and bus signs
    (d) Window displays

(4) Miscellaneous
    (a) Radio
    (b) T.V.
    (c) Novelties

Since newspapers and direct mail are the media used most often, we shall limit this explanation to those vehicles.

Newspaper Advertising

Kinds of newspaper advertising. Newspaper advertising is divided into "classified" and "display."

Any advertisement that appears in the columns set aside in newspapers for classified advertisers is a *classified* advertisement. The ads appear in uniform typography under fixed headings like "Houses for Sale," "Farms, Estates, Acreage," "Business Properties." In large city papers, the ads are subclassified by counties, by communities within the county, and by state. No illustrations are used. By effective use of white space, varying line widths, varied spacing between lines, and other devices, an ad may be made attractive. However, as the ads are closely read by those who turn to them, their appearance is not so important as what is written in them—that is, the copy.

Display advertising is advertising matter that is not included in the classified section. It has an attention-getting quality obtained through the skilful use of display type, art work, and space. Display type is a large-size type (more than 14 points). In display ads different sizes and styles of type are used, as well as varying line widths and various leading between them.

Uses of classified and display ads. Classified advertising is used for properties that appeal to the mass audience. Thus, the sale of small homes, renting of residential properties, and sales or renting of farm properties are advertised in the classified columns.

Properties that require the seeking out of the prospect and that appeal to a limited number of people are generally advertised through display space. Thus, high-priced homes, expensive commercial properties, investment opportunities, and large real estate projects such as subdivision properties are ordinarily brought to the attention of readers through display advertising.

What the secretary should know about classified advertising. In firms that have an advertising man, the secretary has little to do with the actual writing of the classified ads. Elsewhere the secretary may have to write ads, and we shall explain in the next chapter how to do so effectively. Here we shall cover the aspects of classified advertising that relate to the secretary's duties in assisting the advertising man. They are:

1. Obtaining essential data from the newspapers
2. The importance of timing
3. Typing the classified ad
4. Getting the classified ad to the newspaper
5. Checking the classified ads

Obtaining essential data from the newspaper. The secretary should obtain the following data from the advertising departments of the various newspapers to be used, and keep them readily available:

1. The advertising rates. These are usually set forth on a rate card furnished by the publication.

2. The closing date (for weekly newspapers) and the closing hour (for daily newspapers), that is, the latest time at which copy will be accepted. This information is on the rate card.

3. Type styles used for the classified ads. Newspapers frequently set up rules as to the manner in which classified advertisements will be printed. Some permit the use of diverse type sizes, while others insist upon

solid 5½ point agate type. Some newspapers also permit not more than 10-point boldface caps for the body type; others tolerate 14 point and even larger. This information may also be on the rate card.

The classified departments of some newspapers will furnish you with a style sheet containing typical advertisements set in every form permitted in the makeup of the classified section of the paper and numbered for identification. The copy (any piece of writing that is sent to a printer) is "marked" with instructions to the printer on how to set it. A style sheet simplifies the marking of the copy for type setup other than straight composition.

If no style sheet is supplied by the newspaper, make up your own for each newspaper to be used. Clip and paste on a sheet of paper examples of the various type sizes and styles that have appeared in the classified ads in the particular newspaper. Then ask the advertising department of the newspaper to indicate next to each sample how it is to be identified. When the copy is marked, the appropriate identification is used.

The importance of timing. The time for inserting a classified ad is given careful consideration by the advertiser, as a badly timed ad may bring meager or no results. Again, if you understand the importance of timing you will be able to carry out instructions intelligently.

In determining what day of the week would be best for running an advertisement in a daily newspaper, the advertiser takes into consideration the particular type of property, the habits of the readers, and his experience with similar classified advertisements. The best day of the week for classified ads in one part of the country may not be best in another. The selection depends upon experience in the particular community.

The Sunday newspapers are the best medium for the sale of homes and the renting of residential property. Suburban properties that appeal to the family with an automobile are best advertised for week-end attention.

Typing the classified ad. Typewrite the copy of the advertisement given to you by your employer on an 8½″ × 11″ sheet of paper. Make carbon copies for reference purposes, but send the original to the newspaper. In typing the ad, observe the following rules:

1. Measure off on the sheet a ruled column that will hold the maximum number of characters that appear in one line in the classified column in which your ad is to appear. To do this, select a full line of type

from one of the ads printed in the newspaper, and typewrite it on your own machine. That gives you the measure of your typewritten line. Draw vertical lines to the left and right of the typewritten line. That gives you the space in which your copy should be typewritten. Once you have that measurement, you can use it in typewriting all advertisements for the particular newspaper.

2. Typewrite the heading in the position in which it is to appear in the advertisement; for example, in the center, if that is where you want it.

3. Typewrite the body of the ad, in single space, within the ruled column. If you reach the right-hand line in the middle of a word that cannot be divided, you can run over the line or start the word on the next line. Your typed copy is merely a guide to the printer; it is not intended to be exactly the same as the ad will be when set in printer's type.

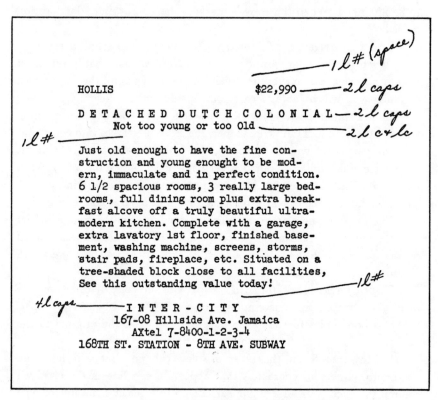

Figure 40. Marked Copy of Classified Ad.

4. Indicate paragraph indentions clearly, if the ad has more than one paragraph. If the newspaper type is indented two characters at a new paragraph, indent two spaces on your typewriter.

5. Capitalize the words that are to appear in capitals.

6. Indicate white space between lines by double-spacing on the typewriter. Indicate other spacing by writing varying line widths about the length you want them to appear, in the position in which they are to appear; for example, at the right, at the left, in the center, etc.

Your employer will mark the copy to tell the printer clearly and concisely what he wants, if the typewritten sheet does not itself indicate it. Figure 40 illustrates a marked, typewritten copy for a simple, classified ad. Figure 41 illustrates the ad as set by the printer.

Figure 41. Classified Ad Set According to Marked Copy.

Getting the classified ad to the newspaper. The advertisement must be in the newspaper office before the closing date or closing hour for the given issue. The original marked copy of the ad is usually delivered in person to the office of the newspaper; the ad should not be phoned in. Errors are likely to occur if you phone in the ad, and the newspapers do not like to make credit adjustments for mistakes.

It is advisable to deliver the copy well in advance of the closing time in order to give the composing room sufficient time to set the copy carefully. Instructions are given as to when the ad is to appear If it is to be run until orders are given to discontinue it, the instructions should indicate that it is a *till-forbid* (abbreviated t.f.) order. When such an order is placed, the secretary should make careful note of it in her tickler file (see page 50), and keep her employer reminded of it.

If any corrections are to be made in the copy, get in touch promptly with the newspaper's advertising department by telephone.

Some local newspapers have "ad" collectors who make their rounds, picking up the ads. Treat the ad collector with consideration; have the copy ready for him.

Checking the classified ads. You check the ad to see that it appeared correctly. If there is a printer's error in it like an incorrect telephone number, wrong addess, terms, price, or some other inaccuracy that reduces the effectiveness of the ad, the newspaper will usually make an adjustment. In a large city daily, you should call the adjustment department; in a local newspaper, the advertising department should be informed.

You will also have to check the results of the advertisements. Such checking is done for the following reasons: (1) to show the advertiser the comparative pulling power of the newspapers he is using; (2) to guide him in directing new advertising efforts; (3) to determine the types of property for which classified advertising is suitable; (4) to determine the type of appeal that is most effective for readers of a particular newspaper or readers interested in a particular type of property.

Various methods can be used for checking the results. The simplest method is to clip the advertisement, paste it in a book or on a separate sheet, and enter the following information relative to it:

1. The date and place in which the advertisement appeared
2. The cost of the advertisement
3. The number of prospects who called
4. The name of the salesman to whom the property is assigned
5. Any other data, such as the type of prospects, and reasons why the prospects were not interested after seeing the property. This file of clippings is arranged by dates.

The file of clippings is useful for reruns. Also, you might have to keep track of lineage runs and be able to show how much advertising each member of the firm ran with each of his listings and what the cost was.

What the secretary should know about display advertising. Knowledge of the following aspects of display advertising will be helpful to the secretary to an advertising man who prepares his own display advertising:

1. How the layout is marked for the printer
2. How art work is handled

3. How to typewrite the copy for a layout

4. How space is purchased

How the layout is marked for the printer. A display ad makes use of illustrations, good typography, suitable copy, and emphasis devices. The advertising man determines the size of the advertisement, writes the headline and copy, and makes a rough layout for the purpose of obtaining the best arrangement of the material. A "layout" is the working of a display ad. An example of a layout is given in Figure 42.

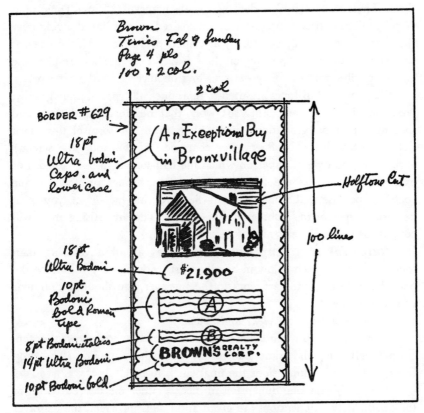

Figure 42. Layout of a Display Ad.

The layout must show the exact dimensions of the ad. Notice in the illustration that the width is indicated by the column space and the depth by the number of lines. The size appears not only at the top of the sheet but on the layout itself. Exact instructions must be given about the size and style of type for each line of copy to be used by the compositor who sets the type. In the illustration, Bodoni and Ultra Bodoni are the styles of type to be used. The layout must also indicate the type of plate to be used to reproduce the art work.

How art work is handled. Two types of plates are generally used to reproduce art work: line cuts and half-tones.

Line cuts. Line cuts are used to print black and white drawings without any gray tones. Pen drawings are in this category. It is possible to produce shading in line cuts through the use of transparent cellulose sheets that have various coarse patterns and shading effects printed on them. These sheets (sold under such trade names as "Zip-a-Tone" and "Crafttint" at artists' supply stores) are placed on the line drawing over the area to be shaded, cut to fit, and then pressed on. This process is commonly known as "putting on Ben Day." For the best results, the engraver will apply Ben Day patterns or tints directly to the art work.

Half-tones. Half-tones are used to reproduce all types of photography, wash drawings, and any other art work that has tonal gradations and shading. The tonal gradations on the plate are in the form of tiny black dots close together. The fineness or coarseness of the dots (the screen) varies with the type of paper on which the half-tone is to be printed. For example, newspapers use a 65-line screen; magazines printed on fine coated paper use a 133-line screen. When ordering half-tones, you must be sure to specify the number of the screen. The advertising man will consult his printer or engraver if he is in doubt.

Rules for handling art work. The careful advertising man follows the rules given below in handling art work. Since you may be the one who will deliver the art work to the engraver, you should be familiar with these rules.

1. *Make instructions clear and explicit.*

a. A photograph must have four crop marks, to show the top, bottom, left side, and right side of the cut being ordered. (The crop marks indicate the dimensions the final cut is to be.)

b. Specify only one dimension in inches, either the desired width or the depth. If two dimensions are given and one is incorrect, the engraver will be confused as to which dimension to follow.

c. Do not give directions such as "double in size," or "reduce one third," which always leave doubt as to whether linear or area measurements are intended.

d. Be sure any special instructions accompanying the art work are conspicuously marked in the margins or on the overlay sheet which protects the art work. Remember, engraving corrections are expensive.

2. *Prepare the art work so that it is protected from damage in all stages of processing.*

a. Rubber cement or library paste may be used for paste-up work. Rubber cement avoids wrinkling or shriveling of the paper. However, unless it is applied correctly, the pasted piece will later fall off. Also, the pasted portion will discolor in time. Library paste will wrinkle the paper if it is not used sparingly. Slight wrinkling and shriveling, however, will do no harm.

b. Do not write on the back of photographs. The impression of the pen or pencil will show through.

c. Do not write on the face of photographs as that may ruin them for future use.

d. Never use clips on photographs as that may mar their surface. If it is necessary to attach special instructions, use an overlay sheet.

e. Always pack all art work between stiff cardboards to eliminate any danger of cracking the photographs or drawings.

How to type the copy for a layout. You will notice on the layout illustrated in Figure 42 that the places where copy is to appear are marked "A" and "B." This material will probably be handed to you in rough manuscript form for you to type. Type each insert on a separate sheet of paper, and mark it Insert "A," Insert "B," and so on. Use double space in typing the inserts.

How display space is purchased. Most newspapers sell space by the agate line. An agate line is 1/14 of one inch deep and one column wide. A 14-line advertisement, therefore, is one inch deep and one column wide. Space for display advertising is ordered according to the exact size of the advertisement. A 10-inch advertisement to appear in one column would be indicated as 140 × 1 (read "140 on 1," or "140 by 1"), meaning a space of 140 agate lines deep by one column. Some newspapers sell space by the column inch. In such cases space would be ordered by column-inches, for example, 10 inches × 1 column. The depth of the column, its width, and the number of columns to the page vary with the newspaper and must be ascertained from the particular publication.

Space rates. Information about rates is given on the rate card supplied by the newspaper (see page 224). It is advisable to find out whether "quantity" discounts or "time" discounts are allowed.

Quantity discounts. A "quantity" discount refers to the decrease in rate allowed to advertisers who use more than a certain number of lines during the year.

Time discounts. The "time" discount refers to the decreasing scale of rates charged as the number of insertions increases.

"Short rate" and "long rate." When the amount of space contracted for is not used, there is a "short rate" adjustment. If a better rate is earned because more than the contracted space has been consumed, a "long rate" adjustment is made. The advertising man contracting for space is informed about short rates and long rates.

Preferred position. The advertising rates quoted by the newspaper apply to "run-of-paper" position. This means that under the normal rates the publisher decides the position of the advertisement. If some choice position is desired, the advertiser can purchase "preferred position" by paying an extra rate.

In forwarding newspaper advertisements under "run-of-paper" contracts, it may help to indicate that a certain position is requested; it is not advisable to say that the advertisement must appear in that position.

One way to try to get a good "run-of-paper" position is to get the advertisement in well in advance of the closing time.

Clipping and filing display ads. Keep the file of clippings of display ads separate from the clippings of classified ads. Paste them in a book or on a sheet of paper, and note above the clipping the date and place in which the advertisement appeared. Arrange the sheets in chronological order.

File of cuts and mats. Maintain a file of mats and cuts used in display ads, as well as printer's proofs of all cuts. Some real estate offices have at least twelve glossy proofs run off of each new cut. These copies are pasted on new ad layouts as needed.

Direct Mail Advertising

What the secretary should know about direct mail advertising. Direct mail advertising is any advertising matter sent through the mail to lists of individuals or firms. As shown on page 223, the forms most commonly used are letters, leaflets, folders, circulars, property briefs, booklets, brochures, house organs, and other advertising pieces. Firms specializing in farm properties may send out a catalogue each year to selected lists of brokers and other prospects. Similarly, firms specializing in industrial properties may mail catalogues of listings. Postal information for direct mail advertising is given in Chapter 6.

In the preparation of the material to be mailed, the secretary assists the advertising man just as she does in the preparation of display ads. In addition, she may be the one who runs the letters or announcements on the duplicating machine, if the firm has such equipment. If not, she may have to deliver the letter to the processor and see that the ordered copies are returned in time for use in the mailing. Her most important duty, however, is usually in building and maintaining the mailing lists.

Building and maintaining mailing lists. Without good mailing lists, the advertiser cannot use direct mail successfully. The secretary can be extremely helpful by exercising care in the physical maintenance of the lists, by adding names from various sources, by classifying the lists, and by keeping the lists "clean."

The physical care of mailing lists. Some lists will be kept on 3″ × 5″ cards, with the names and addresses of prospects and any other specific information that will show the types of properties in which they are interested. Check the spelling of the name and the correctness of the address when you make up the card to be sure that there are no mistakes. A letter sent to a wrong address is a waste of time and money; a letter with an addressee's name misspelled annoys the recipient. Other lists may be kept in the form of directories, typewritten sheets, or in the style in which they are received from various sources. The lists of cards should be arranged alphabetically to facilitate the weeding out of "undeliverables." Devise a system for locating the lists as they are needed. File boxes, drawers, and books are generally used for housing them. '

Classification of mailing lists. A real estate advertiser must determine who his prospects are and what types of persons he wants to reach in advertising by mail. The mailing lists should therefore be broken down into various classifications comprising those who are in a position to act on the offers made in the advertisements.

The classification depends upon the business needs of the firm. A suggested breakdown might include:

1. Persons who have bought and sold property through the real estate office and who might again buy or sell. This group can be further broken down by (a) types of realty in which they are interested, (b) sections of the city in which they are interested, (c) locality in which the prospect lives, (d) financial resources of the prospects

2. Operators who buy property for resale at a profit

3. Lawyers who represent investors in real estate

4. Brokers with whom the firm might associate in a joint deal

5. Builders who are interested in new sites or who will have homes and other properties for sale when their developments are completed.

If only one master list of all names is maintained, some scheme must be used for identifying the names belonging to each classification. The scheme may consist of using a differently colored card for each classification or of using tab cards with a key-number on the tab to mark the classification. The master list should be maintained in strictly alphabetical order.

Another plan is to maintain a master file in alphabetical order and separate files for each of the classifications. In that event, the list may be kept on cards or in a loose-leaf notebook. The alphabetical card or entry should show, by symbols, the classifications to which the prospect has been assigned. The classification files should each be identified by a symbol, color, or other mark. When this method is used, care must be exercised to avoid duplication. If a mailing piece is to go to two of the classified lists, and John Jones' name appears in both, there will be duplication, with its unnecessary waste and annoyance to the prospect, unless steps are taken to pull out the duplicates.

Cleaning out the mailing list. Lists grow stale with time, and unless they are kept up to date diminish in value. From time to time it is necessary to remove the names of persons not receiving the mail. To accomplish this step the statement "Return Postage Guaranteed" is included on the envelope under the sender's return address, in the upper left-hand corner of the envelope. All undeliverable envelopes carrying this statement are returned to the sender with the reasons for nondelivery. The pieces returned by the post office as "unclaimed" should be checked against the list and the inaccurate records thrown out.

When a list is very old, it is usually worth while to obtain forwarding addresses of prospects. The post office will provide known addresses on postal form 3547. To secure this information there must be printed or rubberstamped on the lower left-hand portion of the envelope or wrapper used to send third- or fourth-class mail: "Form 3547 Requested."

Checking the results of mailings. The advertising manager will usually test every extensive direct-mail campaign by sending it first to a portion of the list, selected at random. He generally insert a return card and the number he gets back will show whether the material used is bringing sufficient results to justify a complete mailing.

As assistant to the advertising manager you will usually keep the records of test mailing results as well as the results of the complete mailings after the tests have proved satisfactory. A special form may be supplied to you for this purpose. If not, make your own record, showing the following:

1. The list used and the quantity
2. The first and last names addressed (so that you will not duplicate any part of the list)
3. The letter, card, or circular used
4. The postage and envelope used
5. The type of return card or slip
6. The inquiries received day by day or week by week

In addition to this record, keep a permanent file of the *complete* mailing. Extra copies of the mailing should also be available for at least several months, in case it is decided to repeat the mailing.

If direct mail is undertaken only occasionally, you can keep your record and the complete mailing in the same file. Clip together all of the material that went out in the mailing—the letter, folder, return card, and other enclosures—and place a record sheet on top. Note on this record the items mentioned above.

Mailing list typed on gummed paper. When only three or four mailings to persons on a mailing list are contemplated, much effort and time may be saved by typing the list in triplicate, or quadruplicate, on gummed paper interleaved with carbon paper. When this is done, the names and addresses on the carbon copies can be cut out and pasted on envelopes for use in future mailings. Or you can buy gummed paper cut to $8\frac{1}{2}'' \times 11''$ and type the names and addresses in three columns, cutting the names later. Gummed paper labels in perforated sheets may be used instead, but the cost is slightly higher.

Working with an Advertising Agency

The secretary's duties in dealing with an agency. The secretary smooths the way for the agency and the advertising man. She attends to routine details like relaying messages from her employer to the agency executive, and vice versa. She arranges the appointments for conferences between the agency executive and the real estate man, and, when necessary, with the owner whose property is being advertised. The agency representative might drop in with material while the employer is away and discuss with the secretary questions that need clarification. She will pass along the information to her employer and perhaps relay the answers to the agency. She might examine proof, and if she is alert to the details that always concern her employer, she will watch them carefully. For example, if the firm name must always appear in a certain style of type, the secretary watches this detail and gives instructions for corrections when necessary.

If you are secretary to a person who handles the advertising under an agency arrangement, it will generally be part of your job to keep the records of ads placed and the advertising files. Records and files of ads placed are kept for the following reasons: (1) to check the agency's bills, (2) to facilitate replying to inquiries resulting from the ad, (3) to provide inspiration in preparing future ads, (4) to be available for the property owner's information. How you keep the records depends upon the established methods of the office and your own initiative in improving them. Some practices will be described that may help to expedite your work.

Advertising files. You will invariably have a file for the agency that handles the firm's work. In it you keep correspondence, copies of proofs of advertising, and perhaps even the clippings from the publications in which they appear. In some large offices that advertise heavily, the clipping is done by a file clerk and pasted on sheets as described on page 232. You may also have to file copies of the ads of managed properties in the buildings managed file (see page 264).

When the agency sends its bill, it may have copies of the itemized ads attached to it. This practice, of course, simplifies the checking. At any rate, the items can be checked against the material that has been put into the advertising file since the last previous checking was made.

Records of classified ads placed with agency. One large real estate firm uses a simple system that serves all of the record-keeping purposes mentioned above. The advertising man writes out the classified ad and gives it to his secretary. She types the copy on a special form making four carbons. She sends the original to the agency. Copy one is sent to the accounting department to be used by them in checking the agency's bills and statements. Copy two is given to the salesman who is to handle the inquiries resulting from the ad. Copy three is given to the file clerk. It furnishes her with notice of the ads she is to clip when the publications arrive. Copy four is sent to the telephone operator to enable her to route the call to the interested salesman.

Chapter 15

Helping to Prepare Classified Ads and Publicity Releases

IF YOU ARE CALLED upon to help your employer write classified ads, or if you are handed the responsibility of writing them yourself, you should have some basic information at your fingertips. This chapter is designed to give you this information.

Preparatory steps. Your employer or a salesman will probably select the properties that are to be advertised. If he uses good judgment, he will select only the choicest listings. It is a mistake to advertise a property that will disappoint the prospect who answers the ad. If you write a splendid ad about a poor property you will antagonize the prospect. He will look at the property, decide that he has been deceived by the ad, and will show little interest in looking at the firm's other listings. He might even tell his friends that your ads are attractive but not your properties. Without misleading the public, you can write exciting ads even about ordinary properties, if they have some merit. Here are the steps:

1. Get as much information as you can about the property selected for advertising.

2. Imagine the families that have enjoyed living in similar houses.

3. Write the copy with such families in mind.

The importance of detailed information. The listing card will give you many facts about the house, but only by knowing all you can about the property will you be able to write a compelling ad. Talk to the salesman. Try to get a feeling about the property. Make notes of the good points and the bad ones. Find out about the other houses in the block, the kind of people who live in the community, the nearness to transportation, the closeness to the shopping district, and similar items. Consider the condition of the property, the attractiveness of the style, the landscaping, the backyard possibilities, the garage.

Find out about the interior of the house from basement to attic, and note, on each floor, the size of the rooms and the attractive and unattractive features. Note especially such special features as breakfast nooks, closet space, built-in bookcases, and standard-make equipment.

Using your imagination about the prospects. People buy homes for a number of reasons—they take pride in ownership; they have a spirit of independence; they want security; they value comfort; they are thinking of the benefits to their children; they expect to obtain social distinction; they want to save money now spent in rent; they think home ownership will develop their personality. By envisioning a family that will enjoy owning the home you are to advertise, you will hit on the right note of appeal. The selection of the appeal determines the features that you will emphasize in the copy.

Writing the ad. The best way to write a classified ad is to sit down with your notes and think of the families you imagined enjoying the property. If you have had no experience in writing ads or if you find them hard to do, make up your mind that you are going to write several for the same property—practice ads, in a sense. A successful real estate woman has suggested that you do it this way:[1] "Pretend you are addressing each one to a different person. Make one flowery, one factual, one absurd, one extremely brief, one dignified, and one complete. Read the first five ads with an open mind. Certain ideas will come out of the assortment. Then write a sixth ad. It will probably be a good one. Do this over and over again on different houses. Before too long, the right kind of language and the right choice of words will spring to your mind the moment you begin."

Attract attention. A striking heading attracts attention. To be effective, it should be concise, specific, interesting, and colorful. You hit on the heading by thinking of the people who might consider the property,

---

[1] Mary Warren Geer, *Selling Home Property* (Englewood Cliffs, N.J.: Prentice-Hall, Inc., 1951).

the selling points of the property, the positive aspects of a weakness in the property. The heading is the keynote to the ad. It is followed by the features that make the heading true. A few examples are given to demonstrate the qualities of a "punch" headline.

Bargain properties
    NORTH PARK—MUCH LESS THAN COST
    QUICK SALE VALUE
    MUST LIQUIDATE
Economy is the appeal
    A WORD TO THE WIVES IS SUFFICIENT. Women usually know value.
    WHAT A LIFE! Less rent than we used to pay—more conveniences.
Location
    COMMUTER'S SPECIAL
    PICTURESQUE AS AN ETCHING
Sound construction
    NOT A CRACKER-BOX but a well-built solid brick home.
    BUILT FOR KEEPS. Nothing flimsy about this building.
Emphasizing space
    EXTRA SPACE! Extra space for the things you want to do, but nothing added to your rent.
    "ROOM-ATTICS" SUFFERER? Are your rooms as small as attics?
Reasons for selling
    OUT-OF-TOWN OWNER MUST SELL
    SHE LIVES IN CALIFORNIA
A feature of the property
    ONE ACRE AND A HOME
    MODERNIZATION JUST COMPLETED
A negative aspect made positive
    I'M HUNG BY A SKY-HOOK ON THE SIDE OF A HILL
    NEEDS PAINT AND PAPER—BUT
A colorful phrase for the imagination
    OUT WHERE IT IS COOL
    NEIGHBORLY HOME
Urge to action
    OWNER GONE THIS WEEK—YOU CAN GET AS "NOSEY" AS YOU LIKE
    YOU HAVE A DATE with us today to see how much real living you'll get in owning this charming brick colonial
Selection of audience
    TOO BIG FOR TWO PEOPLE
    IDEAL FOR THE LARGE FAMILY

Arouse interest in the ad. A certain degree of interest can be assumed from the fact that readers of classified ads generally have a definite need to be satisfied and therefore are interested in the advertisements. Headlines serve partly to attract attention and arouse interest. Beyond that, the interest is created principally through the manner in which the property is described, the selling points presented, and the price indicated. No rules can be laid down as to the order in which the property should be described. It is generally conducive to interest to have the leading sentence short and the words as simple as possible.

Create desire. The desire to see the advertised property is created by the description of its merits. The most attractive features should be emphasized, and the copy should be complete enough to convey a picture of the offering. This does not mean that every detail from cellar to roof must be mentioned. Arouse the reader's curiosity and leave room for him to raise some questions. You might even omit a favorable detail that will come as a pleasant surprise when the prospect examines the property.

Convince the reader. Make your copy convincing by using simple, direct, and understandable language. Keep the copy concise, but use enough words to kindle interest. Be specific. Do not use *large* or *big* in reference to room size, because what one person considers large another may consider small. Exact dimensions do not convey the size of a room as well as such phrases as "living room accommodates a concert grand piano." "Brass plumbing" is more convincing than "excellent plumbing." Eliminate superlatives, and thus avoid exaggeration. Understatement is preferable to overstatement. Give the reader a valid reason why the price is low. Admit the faults of the property.

Notice how the copy below is strengthened by conciseness and elimination of superlatives.

BARGAIN

Here is an opportunity to buy a fine, charming residence located in the very best neighborhood of the South Side, near the Montclair center. Nine rooms, 3 baths, large living room, sleeping porch or lounge. One-half acre beautifully landscaped and planted with formal flower garden. Has large shade trees, pool, 2-car garage. This house cost $60,000 and is

EXTRAORDINARY SACRIFICE: ESTATE MUST SELL

Colonial residence located in the best neighborhood of the South Side, near the Montclair center. Nine rooms, 3 baths, living room 30 x 20 ft., sleeping porch. Half-acre beautifully landscaped with formal flower garden, pool shrubbery; shaded with full-grown maple, beech, and pine trees. Actual cost, $60,000; priced for immediate to be sold for the very low price of $45,000. We think this property represents the greatest bargain ever offered. Your immediate inspection invited.

sale at $45,000. An opportunity of a lifetime. Prompt action and inspection invited.

Precipitate action. Copy should contain a suggestion for action. This may be a strong direct command or an invitation to investigate. Sometimes the heading will urge the reader to act immediately, but generally the close of the advertisement is the better place at which to impel action. Some ideas for closings which suggest action follow:

1. *Show the consequences of delay.* Will be snapped up quickly.

2. *Give the reader a reason for acting promptly.* Hy Elliott will be there this afternoon, so why not give it an inspection? See it before the spring market starts.

3. *Invite the reader to inquire further.* Shown by appointment only. Phone BK6–1234. Let us tell you about it.

4. *Use a direct command.* Write for appointment today. Ask us for particulars—better still, come and see it today! Let us show it to you.

5. *Name the person to ask for.* Call Mr. Jones. Ask for Mr. Brown.

Use colorful words and phrases. A description reading—6 rooms, 2 baths, garage, oil burner, porch, etc.—can apply to any number of American homes. The words are cold and colorless and do not awaken desire for the house. Give the property individuality and stimulate the imagination of the reader by using vivid words and phrases. A few examples will demonstrate the technique.

Rooms and layout: well-proportioned rooms; wealth of closets; gay, sparkling decorations; deeply recessed windows.

Physical environment: rolling hillside; quiet, rustic neighborhood; peaceful heart-warming beauty; secluded without isolation.

Building design, construction, etc.: rough hewn stone; sturdily built; soundly constructed; a rambling country home with the warmth and cheer of an old-fashioned Christmas card.

Exposures: breeze swept; morning sunshine; sun seems brighter.

Assisting a Publicity-Minded Employer

Recognizing a news item. A publicity-minded employer wants to get the name of his firm into the real estate news columns as frequently as possible because such publicity is free and adds prestige to the firm.

Some large firms leave it to their advertising agencies to write news releases about the company; others engage professional publicity men. Here we shall show you how to help the real estate man who handles his own publicity.

The publicity-minded real estate man generally knows what will make a story that the newspaper will accept. But if you are going to help him, you too must be able to recognize a news item. Then when you note an event that he will probably want to write up, you will collect the facts for him in advance.

A story to be acceptable must contain the pertinent facts and must have authentic real estate news of interest to the readers of the paper. The simplest way to acquire an aptitude for sensing an event that will make a story is to read regularly the real estate news columns in the papers that circulate in your community and to note their headlines. After a while you will acquire the ability to recognize news story items that arise in the office. The following items culled from a number of newspapers will get you started:

Real estate firm enlarges its office

President of real estate firm makes rental vacancy study; finds fewer vacancies

Real estate firm takes over management of building and begins modernization

Real estate firm reports the volume of total sales for a particular period

Broker's client begins to build unusual houses

Dozen dwellings to be ready in May; two exhibit homes now open for inspection

Managers appointed for three buildings

Broker rents apartment to prominent person

Mortgage broker arranges for refinancing of property

Appraiser's opinion aids court in reducing assessment

Historical site, held by one family for many years, changes hands

1,000 trees planted in a housing project

Store building scheduled for prominent street

Apartment house changes hands three times in three months

High-speed elevators installed in apartment building

News items from employer's public relations activities.
Election of your employer to the local real estate board, local civic

organization, and the like makes a news story. Anything else he does in connection with his public relations activities that is of interest to the community might be suitable for a release to the newspapers.

How to prepare the news release to insure publication. All of the rules that should be observed in preparing a press release are given below.[2] Some of them concern the person who actually writes the story; others deal with the mechanics of typewriting and forwarding the release. They are given in full in case you eventually take over the writing to some of the news stories.

1. Always tell *who,.what, when, where,* and *why* as briefly and as soon as possible in your story, preferably in the first sentence or the first paragraph. The first paragraph should be so complete that it would tell the reader all the essentials if it were printed by itself. After this opening statement, subsequent paragraphs of the story can be devoted to further details, explanations, and additional information about the story.

2. Begin to type your story halfway down the page. This leaves room for the editor to write instructions to the copy desk (where headlines are written and corrections made) and to the typesetter.

3. Always type your stories, double or triple space, using one side of the paper only; 8½″ by 11″ white paper.

4. Make your story easy to identify by writing your employer's name and the company name, address, and phone number in the upper left-hand corner of each page.

5. Indicate by means of a release date when the story can be published. Write "For release on ...." in the upper right-hand corner of page one. Be sure to keep the release date in mind so that all of the "todays," "tomorrows," and "yesterdays" in your story make sense.

6. Send your stories to the papers well ahead of the release date; one day is considered a minimum.

7. Give the same news to all the papers at the same time, with the same release date (unless you have made arrangements with a paper for an exclusive story).

8. Work with the reporter who has your business on his beat instead of going over his head. If no reporter is assigned to cover your firm, send

---

2 Adapted from *Working With Newspapers,* by Gertrude W. Simpson, National Publicity Council, New York.

your releases to the city desk instead of to a reporter you know personally.

9. Notify the newspapers well in advance—at least three days—when special events are to be held which you want covered so that if reporters or photographers are sent to cover the story, there is plenty of time for the paper to schedule the assignments.

10. Never write a headline for your story. Leave space for it instead. Each newspaper has its own rules and styles for headlines; it has people on its staff whose job is writing them, and the homemade headline is a waste of effort. Above all, it is the mark of the amateur.

11. Don't hound the editor for space or complain to him that your story landed in the "wrong place." Don't berate him, either, for publishing the story of another business and omitting yours.

12. When reporters or photographers are invited to attend a special meeting, luncheon, dinner, or any other event of your business, provide a "press" table for them.

13. Always provide advance copies of speeches to reporters who cover meetings or other events. Better still, prepare a handout in which you state the purpose, occasion, names, and all the facts about the event; attach a copy of the main speech.

14. Don't overwrite, don't pad, don't use a lot of paper to tell a simple story. Nearly everyone can learn to write an acceptable "bare bones" story. If the editor thinks your story merits more space, he will ask for further material. If he doesn't, your effort to make the story seem bigger than it really is will cause him trouble in cutting or rewriting.

15 In writing stories for the newspaper, be wary of adjectives. Let events speak for themselves. Don't describe anything as pretty, inspiring, or delightful.

File of publicity clippings. A publicity-minded employer is always interested in keeping a file of the stories in which his name or the name of the firm appears. Make up such a file by clipping the publicity items as they appear and pasting them in a scrapbook or on sheets similar to those used for display ads (see page 232). Note the date of the item and the newspaper or other publication in which it appeared. The file of sheets is kept in chronological order, just as it would be in a bound scrapbook.

Chapter 16

Your Duties in a Property Management Office

A SMALL REAL ESTATE office rarely engages in property management on a large scale. It may take on the management of a few two-family homes, small apartment houses with or without stores, and the like. Whether or not it engages formally in property management, it will perform some of the work done by property managers on a large scale. For example, a small office rents property, prepares leases, and has contacts with owners and tenants. Therefore, what is given in this chapter is as useful to secretaries in small offices as to those who work in the property management department of a large firm.

Variety of duties. The work in a property management office is decidedly varied. It entails more personal contact with people, more record keeping, and more routine clerical duties than any other real estate activity. The duties fall into the following categories:

1. Dealing with people
2. Duties connected with renting, leasing, and tenant relationships
3. Duties related to repairs and maintenance
4. Rent collection
5. Reports to owners
6. Property management filing
7. Duties connected with getting new business

In this chapter we shall cover the first three categories of duties; in the next chapter we shall explain the last three categories. Rent collection will be treated in Chapter 18.

People with whom the Secretary Deals

Six categories. The people with whom the secretary may have to deal in building management work fall within six categories:
1. Personnel of the property management department
2. Personnel of other departments of the firm
3. Owners whose buildings are managed
4. Tenants of managed properties
5. Building employees
6. Suppliers of materials and services used in property management

Personnel of building management department. Whether a building management department is large or small, it performs the functions of renting space, collecting rents, taking care of the managed buildings, and servicing tenants. This work is divided among a number of people, depending upon the volume of property management done by the firm. Here are some of the people to whom the work of the department may be delegated:

The management executive. He guides the entire organization of the management department and is responsible for employee, tenant, and public relations.

Administrative assistants. The management executive may have assistants to whom he assigns such duties as taking care of taxes and insurance on the managed properties; purchasing supplies and services; and personnel, public, and tenant relations.

District managers or agents. Where many buildings are managed, the work of inspecting and supervising the physical property may be divided among a number of district managers. They make continuous rounds of the properties under their care. They may do some renting, collecting, and supervising of repairs. They are the contact men between the management department and the tenants and between the management department and the employees in each building.

Superintendents. There may be a superintendent for each building or for one or more buildings. The superintendent is the head of the operating staff of the building. The operating staff renders service to the tenants. The superintendent may do renting and collecting of rents.

Rent collectors. A special rent collector is sometimes employed.

Rental manager. Sometimes all renting and advertising are done by a rental manager.

Chief engineer. A large management firm may have a chief engineer to supervise work of a specialized character.

Relations with other departments of the firm. One of the advantages of having a property management department is that it is a feeder to other departments. An owner whose property is being well managed will use the firm's brokerage department when he wants to buy other property or when he wants to sell the managed property. The property management department helps the advertising department prepare brochures on income properties because it knows rental rates, leasing practices, costs, taxes, and the like. It helps the appraisal department for the same reason.

Some of the functions of property management may be done by other departments. For example, the renting may be done by the leasing department of the firm. In that case there will be a close connection between the management department and the leasing department. The accounting involved in property management may be done by the general accounting department. As all departments are part of one entity, the real estate firm, all employees in the management department must have the interests of other departments in mind and be completely cooperative.

Relations with owners. The management contract between the firm and the owner, when first entered into, is usually for a period of years; it is renewed thereafter for yearly periods unless either party notifies the other, within a specified number of days, that the agreement is to be terminated. Only if the interests of the owners are served will they continue to renew their contracts.

In dealing directly with the owners, or with any phase of your work that ultimately affects the owner, you must keep in mind the following four objectives of the owner in turning over the management of his property to your employer:

1. He wants to protect the money he has invested in the property.
2. He wants the largest possible net return from his investment.
3. He wants to see the value of his property increase.
4. He wants to be proud of the property he owns.

The secretary, of course, is guided in her relations with the owners by the policies of the firm. She is also guided by the desires of the owners. Some owners are vitally interested in every decision affecting their properties; others are interested only in results and do not want to be consulted except when absolutely necessary.

The aim of your employer is to keep the owners satisfied. By replying promptly to the owner's requests, notifying him of tenant changes if he wants that kind of notice, explaining unusual repairs to him, and by reminding your employer of the little things that might be overlooked, you can be invaluable in keeping the contact between the manager and the owner smooth and beneficial to both.

Relationship with tenants. The firm's relationship with tenants begins with the rental. At this point the secretary may have various routine procedures to follow, like writing for references. You therefore are quickly put into the position of knowing something about the tenants. You get to know more about them as the tenancy continues, through their rent payment record, requests, and complaints.

A capable renting agent explains the provisions of the lease and the regulations for the operation of the building at the time that the lease is entered into. By thus establishing a basis of confidence and understanding between management and the new tenants, he paves the way for a good tenant relationship.

As will be shown in Chapter 18, the firm's rent collection policies and procedures affect tenant relationships. Also, the manner in which requests and complaints are handled is vitally important. In a later section the practices the make for good tenant relationships in handling requests will be described.

In all dealings with tenants, the secretary must be courteous, patient, and tactful, no matter how difficult or irate the tenant is, for it is the aim of management to keep tenants satisfied.

Relations with building employees. The operating staff of the managed properties may include janitors, elevator operators, engineers, decorators, and others. Although these people are under the supervision of a superintendent, operating engineer, or operating manager, the relationships with the employees are the responsibility of the management executive or his assistants.

If you are secretary to the person who has this responsibility, any situation that creates an employee relations problem may come to your notice even before it is brought to your employer's attention.

In large organizations the operating staff payroll is usually handled by the bookkeeping department of the management firm, but in a small organization the secretary may keep the payroll records and prepare the payroll. The actual distribution of salaries is generally made by the superintendent of the building. Payroll records are described in Chapter 21.

Relations with suppliers. Suppliers are the people from whom your firm buys the numerous items that are necessary for the maintenance and repair of the properties managed. They include the people and firms that render such services as window cleaning, past extermination, general cleaning, gas, electricity, and the like.

A secretary to the person who has this purchasing responsibility may have contact with salesmen of firms who want to interest the employer in their products or services, or with representatives of the firms who are already supplying the management firm with their products or services. Relationships with such people were discussed in Chapter 2.

Duties Connected with Renting, Leasing,

and Tenant Relationships

Leasing and renting. A great variety of work may have to be done in connection with the renting and leasing of property. In large offices, special clerks may attend to some of these duties; in a small concern, the secretary may attend to all of them herself. The principal duties relate to (1) selection of tenants; (2) preparing and delivering leases; (3) maintaining good tenant relationships; (4) collecting rents; and (5) renewing leases.

Selection of tenants. The manager's objective in selecting tenants is to keep turnover down. This calls for careful investigation of the applicants for space. There methods of investigation are generally used, each of which may involve work for the secretary:

1. The tenant is required to file an application for a lease on a form furnished by the manager.

400 WESTFIELD AVENUE
ELIZABETH, N. J.
ELIZABETH 5-8100

TENANCY APPLICATION

...., 19..........

Location of Property : ....

Description : .... House; .... Floor; .... Apt. No.; .... Rms.; .... Car Gar.

Lease
Monthly Tenancy ☐ at $.............................. per mo. from..................... 19....... to .... 19.......

Deposit Herewith (at least one month's rent) $...................... Bal. $................. Possession .... 19.......

Water Rent Paid by ....

Electric Paid by ....

Gas Paid by ....

CONFIDENTIAL REPORT

Full Name of Applicant ....

Present Address .... For .... Years

Reason For Moving .... Present Rent $.....................

Present Landlord ....

Address .... Tel. ....

Last Previous Address .... For .... Years

Last Previous Landlord ....

Address .... Tel. ....

Occupation : Position and Title ....

Applicant Employed by .... For .... Years

Employer's Address .... Tel. ....

Applicant's Income $.............................. per month.

How Many Will Occupy Premises: Adults .... Children .... Dogs ....

Applicant Will Use Premises For: Residential .... Business .... Both ....

If For Business, Specify Exact Type ....

....

REFERENCES: Business references should be individuals or firms with whom you have been doing business over a
period of time, such as charge accounts, etc.

(Bank) .... Checking ☐
Savings ☐

(Business) ....

(Business) ....

Do You Own Real Estate? .... Where ....

Special Conditions and Repairs Requested by Applicant

....

....

....

To verify the above statements, I hereby direct the persons named above to give any requested information concerning me,
hereby waiving all right of action for consequences as a result of such information.
This application is subject to approval and acceptance by the owner or authorized agent. Until notification thereof no contract or tenancy shall exist, neither will I enter possession of the premises until one full month's rent shall have been paid by me.
r. e. Scott co.

(Signed) by ....   (Signed) ....
Representative   Applicant

Form 53

Figure 43. Tenancy Application.

250

2. References are followed up.

3. The tenant's credit rating is checked, if a commercial tenant.

The tenancy application. A rental application form, similar to that shown in Figure 43 is signed by the applicant, who must also submit payment of the first month's rent. Ordinarily the renting agent will see that all of the questions in the application are answered. If important information is omitted, you may have to telephone the prospective tenant and get the answers, or you may hve to write for the information and follow up the correspondence until the missing information is obtained.

Some application blanks are more complex than the one illustrated here. They may contain provisions and forms that entail office work on the part of the secretary.

Follow-up of references. It is usually the secretary's duty to follow up the references noted by the applicant in the application form. A printed form letter such as that shown in Figure 44 is used for this purpose in most offices. You merely fill in the name and address of the person to whom the request is to be sent and the name of the applicant. You keep the application in the follow-up file until the replies are received.

Checking credit of commercial applicants. The renting agent, or the credit department, must check the credit standing of business that apply for space in office buildings or commercial property, just as any firm checks the credit of a customer before selling a bill of goods. The Dun & Bradstreet Reference Book and reports may be used in the credit-checking process. A brief explanation of the Dun & Bradstreet services is given to familiarize the secretary with this method of checking credit.

Dun & Bradstreet, Inc. is a mercantile agency that gathers and distributes credit information about persons and firms engaged in all lines of business. The agency "rates" a business on the basis of information gathered by its reporters and correspondents about the owners and managers, giving consideration to their character and ability to make good on obligations. The ratings cover capital and credit. They are condensed conclusions that show, by means of symbols, (1) the range of a concern's estimated financial strength and (2) its grade of credit, reflecting past record, ability, and business prospects. Letters, from AA to M, are used to denote the capital classification; numerals, from A1 to 4, are used to denote the credit appraisal. The ratings are compiled in the well-known Dun & Bradstreet Reference Book.

Douglas L. Elliman & Co.
Inc.
15 East 49th Street
New York, N. Y. 10017
Plaza 3-9200

negotiating for an apartment through this organization and in accordance with the usual custom, references are required before occupancy may be given.

Your name was suggested among several others and we would appreciate your personal opinion concerning the desirability and responsibility of this prospective tenant. As an early decision is important, we would appreciate a reply as soon as possible. Be assured that any information given will be treated with the utmost discretion.

Thank you very much for your cooperation.

VERY TRULY YOURS,
Douglas L. Elliman & Co.
Inc.

W. S. SINEATH

WSS: jg

Figure 44. Letter to Follow Up References.

Sometimes the renting agent will ask Dun & Bradstreet for a report on the applicant. The report will give information showing: (1) history, including the background of the owners; (2) method of operation and fire hazard; (3) financial statement and comments; (4) trade reports showing how the company pays its creditors; and (5) a summary and rating.

The actual checking of the credit will be done by the renting agent, but the secretary may have to order the special report from Dun & Bradstreet. You keep the rental application in the follow-up file until the credit report is received.

A local credit agency may be used instead of Dun & Bradstreet. You will be informed by your employer of the name of the local agency and what procedure you must follow in getting a report on the applicant.

Preparing and delivering leases. If the investigation shows that the applicant will be a desirable tenant, the lease agreement is drawn up. An explanation of a lease is given in Chapter 11. The renting agent (or broker) must see that the lease is properly signed by the tenant. After it has been signed and returned, the lease is usually checked to see that no changes have been made in it and that the instrument has been properly witnessed. It is then sent to the owner to be signed.

A transmittal letter should accompany the lease when it is forwarded to the owner for signature, and instructions should be given as to where it is to be signed (see page 137). If the lease is to be signed by a corporation, it is usually advisable to explain exactly how the lease should be executed (see page 199). The executed lease is delivered in person to the tenant or is forwarded by mail.

Making records of leases. Each management office has its own system for recording the leases with tenants. Usually, a card record is used on which the essential data for each lease are entered. The card shows the name of the tenant, the building, apartment number, mailing address of tenant, rental terms, expiration date, data as to tax clauses, if any, and other important lease provisions. The filing of these cards and of the lease is covered at page 265.

In some organizations the record just described is kept in the book-keeping department, and a similar record is kept in the renting department.

Renewal of leases. From the lease records, the renting department knows when the leases will expire. It is common practice in some areas to have most of the leases for a particular building expire on the same day, say September 30. Even where this practice is followed, there may be some leases that expire at other times. The records must therefore be examined regularly to determine the expiration dates. Where necessary, a lease expiration date record can be set up for all leases that do not expire on the usual day.

Form letters are frequently used to ask tenants to renew their leases. The secretary's duties may include preparing these letters and following up for replies.

Preparing for good tenant relationships. Many management firms have adopted practices designed to gain the tenant's goodwill at the beginning of the tenant relationship. The objective of all such practices is to convince the tenant that the owner and the manager are interested in his housing problem; that he is getting, and will continue to get, the service he needs and wants; that prompt attention will be given to requests for emergency services.

Some firms use printed forms to transmit information about the lease and the work called for in it. The secretary may have the responsibility of seeing that this form is properly filled out and delivered to the tenant.

Keeping the relationship good. In addition to establishing friendly relations before and during initial occupancy, management must offer the kind of services during occupancy that will keep the tenants happy. A step in this direction is to send a message to tenants from the service department telling how to make requests for service. This is often done through a printed form which accompanies the lease.

A competent management will decide at the outset just what services can and should be furnished to the tenant. Such services should be offered promptly, willingly, and graciously. Also, it is advisable not to give one tenant some service that management is not willing to give all the tenants. Regardless of the extent of the service, it should be given with an air of graciousness.

The rent collection policies and practices of the firm are extremely important in maintaining cordial relationships with tenants. This subject is discussed fully in Chapter 18.

Duties Related to Repairs and Maintenance

The secretary's responsibility. Each management office has its own methods of dealing with repairs and maintenance. The secretary's duties therefore vary from office to office. Generally, however, her responsibilities may entail:

1. Handling tenant requests and complaints
2. Preparing orders for repairs and supplies
3. Follow-up
4. Filling and control forms

Handling tenant requests and complaints. You must know what the manager's policies are for the maintenance and repair of

			BUILDING		
DAILY REPORT				MAINTENANCE DEPARTMENT	
DATE	TIME CALL IN	ROOM	SERVICE REQUIRED	TIME CLEAR	

[Actual size 11″ × 8½″]

Figure 45. Service Request Record.

particular buildings. These policies may vary for the different buildings as they are determined by such factors as age, amount of income received from the building, the type of construction, the neighborhood trend, the character of the occupancy, and competitive conditions. You must also follow the procedures established by the firm for carrying out the policies. Although the procedures do not generally vary from building to building, there may be some differences due to variations in the operating staff setups for different buildings.

Tenant requests fall into three classifications: (1) the obviously unreasonable, which the building manager will refuse at once; (2) the obviously necessary, which he will fill at once; and (3) the questionable, which he will settle only after he inspects the property. It is the secretary's duty to get all of the information, if the request is made to her, and to assure the tenant that the request will have the immediate attention of the

---

REQUEST FOR REPAIRS OR ALTERATIONS

Class of Work ... .
Date Received ....
Address ....
Tenant .... Telephone..........
Owner .... Telephone..........
Address ....
Repairs requested by ....

Detail of Repairs Requested

....
....

[Original form allows additional space]

Estimate from	Date	Amount
Name		

....
....
....

Repairs authorized by ....Req. No.............
Contract let to ....:.....................Date...............
(Sign) ....

[Actual size 5¼″ × 9¼″]

Figure 46. Request for Repairs or Alterations.

No. 2000—REPAIR NOTICE
Printed and sold by Yeo & Lukens Co., Phila.

_____19____

To_____

_____

_____

Tenant desires the following repairs at

_____

_____

_____

_____

_____

_____

_____

_____

_____

We always advise prompt attention to request for repairs inasmuch as the neglect to these matters sometimes means the loss of the tenant and may result in personal injury for which the owner would be liable in an action for damage.

If you wish us to attend to the same please sign the order below.

_____

To_____

You are hereby requested to have the above repairs made and charged to my account.

_____

Figure 47. Repair Notice.

manager or other responsible person. Once the building manager receives the full information, you follow his instructions as to how to deal with the tenant so far as the immediate request is concerned.

Service request record for office building. Many requests for service come in from tenants of large office buildings. A record may be necessary for various purposes, such as follow-up to see that the request is filled, noting where the requests comes from and the like. The form shown in Figure 45 is adaptable for this purpose.[1]

Request forms. Many offices furnish their superintendents with forms for taking requests from tenants, like Figure 46.[2]

Getting owner's consent for repairs. It is usually necessary or advisable to inform the owner of any extraordinary repairs that are required and to await his approval before proceeding with the work. The form in Figure 47[3] is used for this purpose. The secretary makes a note to follow up the notice to the owner, if it is not received within a reasonable time. A duplicate copy of the repair notice, placed in the follow-up file, will serve as a reminder.

A simple letter, such as the following, can be prepared in multigraph form for use in advising owners of contractor's bids and asking for approvals.[4]

Dear Sir:

In re .... No. ....

Attached hereto find proposal covering ....

.... work to be done in ....

of the building mentioned about.

We submit the following contractors' bids:

.... $..........

.... $..........

.... $..........

and recommend acceptance of ....bid.

Kindly give this matter your usual prompt attention and send us your approval to proceed with the work.

Yours very truly,

..............................., Inc.

By ....

---

[1] Acknowledgment, Norris, Beggs & Simpson, Portland, Ore.
[2] Acknowledgment, Wakefield-Fries & Woodward, Portland, Ore.
[3] Acknowledgment, Arthur J. Parsons, Upper Darby, Pa.
[4] Acknowledgment, Harry U. Moser, Inc., Jersey City, N.J.

Some management firms have their superintendents make out a daily report that gives the firm a bird's-eye view of everything that happens at the property each day of the year. It serves not only as a daily report but also as a history of the firm's management efficiency.

Cumulative record of repairs. The secretary may have to keep records of all expenditures for repairs for a particular building and for repairs for individual occupancies. One such card is illustrated in Figure 48.

The cumulative record of repairs is particularly helpful in answering inquiries from owners about expenditures shown on the operating statement where bills are not submitted with the statement. It also serves in dealing with tenants and in handling questions of rent control. You make the entries on the cards from bills received, after they have been approved by the building manager.

Owner			Street								
Class..............			City								
Date	Repairs	Amount	Date	Repairs	Amount	Date	Repairs	Amount	Date	Repairs	Amount

[Actual size 8″ × 5½″]

Figure 48. Cumulative Repair Record.

Purchase orders for repairs and supplies. A complete and readily accessible record must be kept of every maintenance disbursement. The purchase of all repairs and supplies is therefore generally covered by a written purchase order. A verbal order, if given, should be confirmed by a written order on the same day. The order blanks should be numbered serially so that all orders can be accounted for. If the price is not known at the time order is given, an approximate price can be used. When a verbal order is given, detach a set of purchase order forms and place a pencil note on it to show what the order is to be used for. When the order is typed, you know from the pencil notation what property the material is for, vendor's name, work or material required, and the price.

It is usual to have purchase orders set up in triplicate, with the two copies in different colors. The original goes to the vendor. The first copy goes to the accounting department as a notice to hold a sufficient amount of the owner's funds until it is cleared by payment of the bill. Another copy is filed serially in a suspense file to serve as a follow-up to assure the prompt filling of the order and presentation of a bill.

In some systems, the first copy is sent to the superintendent of the building where the goods are to be delivered. When delivery is made, the goods are checked by the building superintendent against his copy of the purchase order. This checked copy is then returned to the building manager.

A form of purchase order is reproduced in Figure 49.

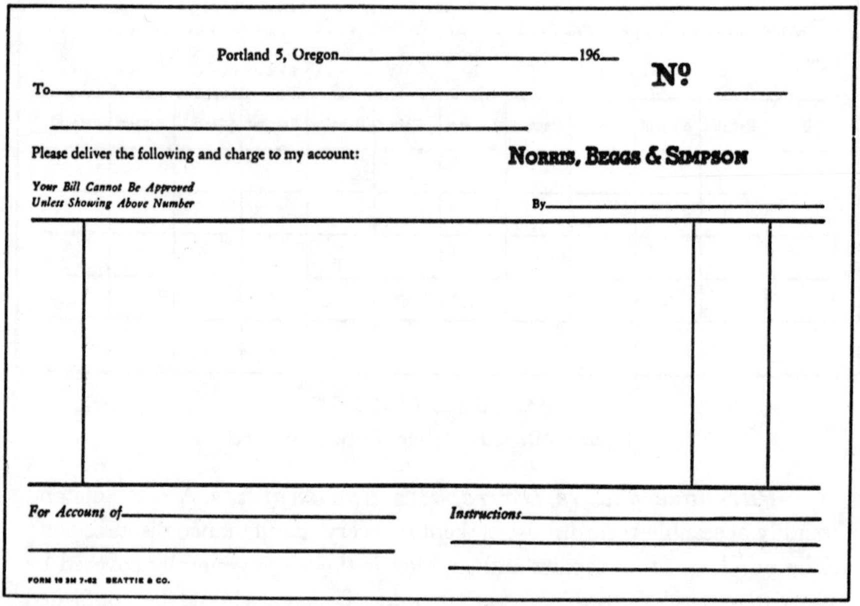

Portland 5, Oregon ________ 196__

Nº ____

To ________

Please deliver the following and charge to my account:

NORRIS, BEGGS & SIMPSON

Your Bill Cannot Be Approved Unless Showing Above Number

By ________

For Account of ________

Instructions ________

FORM 10 3M 7-62 BEATTIE & CO.

[Actual size 8″ × 6″]

Figure 49. Purchase Order.

Unpaid bills file. Some managers ask suppliers and those who render services to make out their bills in triplicate. When they are received, they are clipped together and placed in an unpaid bills file. When a check is sent in payment, two of the copies of the bill are enclosed with the check and a request is made that both be receipted and returned. One of the receipted copies is attached to the purchase order, which has been checked by the superintendent, and sent to the owner. The other receipted copy is attached to the office copy of the purchase order and filed in a bills-paid file. The unreceipted copy that was in the unpaid-bills file can be destroyed.

Follow-up. Close follow-up is required to see that tenants are advised of the disposition of their requests and complaints, that delivery dates are met, and that work is completed. Various systems may be used, but generally the type of follow-up file described at page 56 will meet all needs.

Filing and control of forms. The filing duties of the secretary vary with the kinds of files that are maintained. Management files are explained in the next chapter.

The secretary must be careful to see that the forms used in the management department are reordered before supplies run out. Before reordering, it is advisable to find out from the building manager whether any changes are to be made in them. For methods of storing forms, see page 71.

Chapter 17

Property Management Files—
Reports to Owners

In this chapter we wind up the secretarial duties entailed in property management. They include:

1. Filing property management data
2. Preparing reports to owners
3. Duties connected with getting new business

The Property Management Files

Variations in filing systems. The systems for filing management papers and records vary in different parts of the country, and from company to company. They depend to some extent upon the types of properties managed and the procedures used to carry out the various activities that give rise to the papers and records. Whatever system is established, however, it must be designed to take care of the following types of papers:

1. Correspondence with the owner
2. Correspondence with tenants
3. Property management agreements, contracts, and leases
4 Copies of operating statements sent to owners

5. Receipts for repair bills, taxes, insurance, and the like

6. Operating budgets, vacancy reports, rent schedules, and other miscellaneous papers

7. Special records maintained in the office

A management file for small properties. The simplest method of keeping the papers relating to small properties is to have one legal-sized folder for each property. The folders are marked with the address of the property, and all of the folders for named streets are then arranged alphabetically; those for numbered streets, numerically. If there are several houses on the same street, the folders for that street are arranged by house number. Dividers should be used for properties in different towns, so that each town has its own "property managed" files.

To make one legal-sized folder house all of the different kinds of papers relating to the property requires some improvisation. First, place an Acco metal fastener at the top of each side of the folder. Use the left-hand side for correspondence with the landlord and the tenant. Use the right-hand side for copies of the operating statements sent each month to the owner. The file will thus have no loose papers. All papers will be attached to the fasteners in chronological order. Second, get two red tie-string envelopes large enough to hold folded legal documents. Paste one of these lengthwise on each side of the folder so that it will rest under the attached paper. In the red folder under the correspondence, place all the legal papers to be kept in the file, like agreements, copies of leases, and other legal documents. In the red folder under the operating statements, place all receipted bills, rent records of tenants who have moved, and similar papers.

A management file arranged by owners. Sometimes property management files are arranged by owners. In this system a separate folder is made for each owner to house all of the correspondence with the owner, tenants, suppliers of material, and other papers pertaining to the property. The name of the owner and the address of the property is placed on the tab of the folder, and the folders are filed alphabetically by the names of the owners. For owners who have multiple properties, the file will consist of separate folders for each property.

A management file for large properties. Where many large buildings are managed, each having many tenants, the property managed files may be arranged by buildings, each building file occupying a large part of a drawer.

A separate folder is maintained for each tenant in the building, and all information pertaining to that occupancy is placed in the folder. The tab on the tenant folder would look like this:

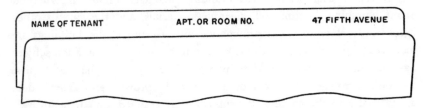

| NAME OF TENANT | APT. OR ROOM NO. | 47 FIFTH AVENUE |

Figure 50. Tab of Folder of Tenant File.

Other subdivisions of the buildings file may be created in this file for unpaid bills and for paid bills.

Dividers can be used to separate the files for each building. The arrangement of the files might be by street names, with numbers of the buildings in numerical order under each street, or it might be by numbers of the street addresses, with the streets alphabetized if there is more than one building with the same number.

For properties identified by the name of a building, like "Greystone Building," a separate subdivision may be maintained under a tab called "name buildings." The name buildings would be arranged alphabetically rather than by location.

File of leases. Some companies give each lease a filing number and file the leases in numerical order in legal-size steel files. Under such a system a cross-reference card must be made showing the name of each owner or tenant and the number that was assigned to the lease. When someone wants to use a lease, he refers to the card index by owner or by tenant, finds the number on it, and then gets the lease from the file.

File of lease information. A set of lease-information cards, similar to that described on page 253, is frequently kept to expedite the work of the leasing department. In the case of small properties, such cards might be filed alphabetically by tenants' names; in large multiple tenancy properties all the tenants might be grouped by buildings, with the tenants' names in alphabetical order under each particular building.

Card files of repairs expenditures. Card records of repair expenditures, such as those described on page 258, should be filed in the same way as the property managed files.

Address file of repairs. The secretary must keep on hand a file of the names, addresses, and telephone numbers of local repairmen who can be called upon to do the work required on the properties managed.

Maintenance file. The building manager retains information about plumbing, heating, oil, cleaning materials, and the various other items that relate to the maintenance and repair of the buildings he manages. This type of material is kept in a maintenance file Each subject has its own letter-size folder in which are placed the catalogues, pamphlets, articles, and other data that might prove useful. The folders are tabbed with the name of the subject and arranged alphabetically.

Rent control information file. As long as rent control laws are in effect, management offices must keep fully informed about them. A file of rent control information may be maintained in any subject file.

Plans file. An office that handles commercial properties may have a separate plans file. It is made up of folders for particular properties filed according to location. In each folder you place the plans showing the layout of the factory, loft, or whatever the property is that the office may hope some day to manage. The folders are made up as the plans are received.

Advertising file. A building management department may keep its own files of advertisements of specific buildings which it manages, and of institutional advertisements. The secretary would maintain this file in the same way that advertising files are kept in the advertising department. See page 236.

The prospect file for new management accounts. Every property management department should maintain a prospect file of possible new management accounts. Such a file generally consists of two parts: (1) a folder file for information on properties which the manager hopes some day to manage, and (2) a card file of owners of these properties.

Folder file. In this file you have a folder for each property. The folder should contain such information as:

1. Identification sheet carrying the following data
    a. Street address
    b. Legal description
    c. Name of owner
    d. Name of owner's present agent
    e. Photograph of property

2. Description of the physical property
3. Floor plans, if available
4. Itemized classification of rental units
5. Latest rent schedule, if available
6. Lease schedule, if a commercial property, showing
    a. Names of tenants
    b. Type of business
    c. Amount of rent paid
    d. Lease expiration
7. Sales history and previous owners
8. Construction data
9. Architect
10. Construction contractors
11. Value
    a. Original cost
    b. Assessed value
12. Newspaper clippings about the property
    a. News stories
    b. Advertisements

Card file. Cards 4″ × 6″ or 5″ × 8″ should carry such information on the owners as:

1. Owner's name
2. Business address and telephone
3. Residence address and telephone
4. Occupation, business, or profession
5. Position and title
6. Age
7. Nationality
8. Represented by what law firm
9. Served by what accounting firm
10. Bank connections
11. Club memberships
12. Church membership
13. Hobbies
14. Served by what real estate men
15. Properties owned
16. Who is likely to inherit the property

Tie-up of folder file and card file. The folder file can be arranged by property addresses; the card file, alphabetically. Since the folder file shows who the owner is, the card can be easily located. Similarly, since the card file shows the properties owned, the information about them can be easily located in the property folders.

Prospective tenants files. This file is maintained to help the manager find tenants for the properties he manages when space becomes available. The arrangement of this file is generally by types of properties. Any of the classifications listed below may be further subdivided according to size of space the prospect may want, or into three subgroups—prospects for low-priced, medium-priced, and high-priced space.

1. Prospects for residential property
   a. Single family homes
   b. Unfurnished apartments
      i. One bedroom
      ii. Two bedrooms
      iii. Three or more bedrooms
   c. Furnished apartments
      i. One bedroom
      ii. Two bedrooms
      iii. Three or more bedrooms
   d. Residential hotels
   e. Resort hotels, cottages, homes
2. Prospects for commercial property
   a. Vacant
   b. Retail
   c. Wholesale
   d. Office buildings
   e. Professional or specialized offices
3. Prospects for industrial property
   a. Vacant
   b. Light manufacturing
   c. Heavy manufacturing
4. Prospects for farm property
   a. Vacant
   b. Grain
   c. Dairy
   d. General

Sources of names. The secretary may have various duties connected with selecting names for the prospect file. For example, she may have to watch the newspapers for the following items:

1. Births, betrothals, marriages, and deaths
2. Organization of new companies

3. Expansion of existing companies

4. Moves by important commercial tenants

5. Acquisitions of wealth through inheritance

6. Promotions, appointments to public office, and other indications of financial success

In addition, the secretary may have to keep records of answers to advertisements which the firm places in newspapers and trade magazines, as well as the records of persons coming into the office in search of renting accommodations. Names of prospects may also be collected by watching advertisements in the trade magazines in which the firm advertises office or other commercial space.

Information on prospect cards. The information placed on the prospect card varies with the kind of space for which the person or firm is a prospect. For example, a prospect card for tenants for office building space may include such information as the name and address of the firm, the name of the person to see, and the credit rating of the firm.

Preparing Reports to Owners

Records required for monthly operating statement. The business manager must give a report to the owner of each managed building at regular intervals, usually monthly, showing the rents collected, rents in arrears, expenses paid, and the balance due the owner. He must remit to the owner the balance due as shown by the statement. To prepare this report, it is necessary to keep careful records of all income and disbursements. Large organizations generally have a trained bookkeeping staff to do this work. In a small office, the secretary may have to keep all of the records. The explanation that follows is intended for such a secretary.

No bookkeeping training is necessary to keep the records that are the basis of the report to owners. It involves merely knowing how to keep bank accounts, entering receipts of funds and payments of bills, and preparing the report from the records. These subjects are discussed in the following paragraphs.

Separation of management funds. A separate bank account is always kept for the moneys received in connection with managed properties and for the payments made from them. The funds must never be mixed with your employer's personal funds or with the funds of the firm. In large organizations that manage many buildings, separate bank accounts are opened for each building managed, and code systems are set up to identify each account. In a small office, such as we are concerned with here, which manages only a few small properties, one special bank account for the managed properties is usually sufficient. It is in the nature of a trustee's account, as the funds are held in trust for the owners. The account is carried under a special name to identify it as a management account.

Handling the bank accounts. To handle the bank account properly, you must know how to endorse checks, make deposits, make withdrawals, and reconcile a bank statement. These subjects will be explained in connection with the handling of bank accounts generally in a real estate office (see pages 320–325).

Recording rents received. Recording the rents received consists of making an entry in the rental book, and another in the cash book to show the deposit of the funds. (For rent receipts given to tenants, see page 280.)

The rental book. When rent is received from a tenant, it is entered in the rental book which is maintained for all of the managed buildings. The rental book is a ring binder in which there are pages for each tenant, similar to those shown in Figure 51. The reverse side of the sheet carries the record for May through December. The book is divided into as many subdivisions as there are properties managed. The sheets are arranged alphabetically under each property by the names of the tenants in the building.

You will notice from the illustration that each record sheet serves for six years. When a tenant moves, the sheet is taken out of the rental book and filed in the property management file for the property. A new sheet is made up for the new tenant.

The cash record. A cash record must be made to show the receipt of rents by the days on which the money is deposited in the bank. This record is made in an ordinary journal ruled with two columns. The first column is for the amount of the individual entry; the second column is for the amount deposited, or the total of the entries on the day of deposit.

Make the entries when you are ready to make the deposit. Show for each entry in the explanation column the address of the property, the

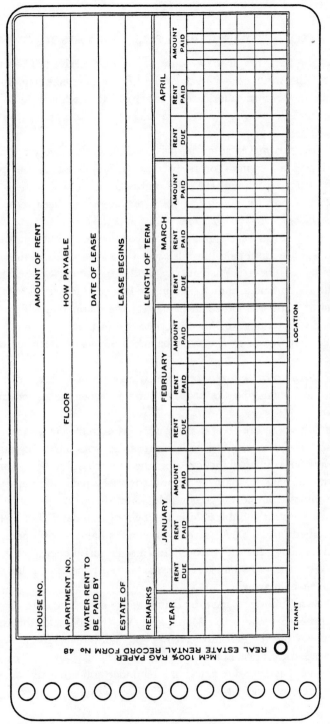

Figure 51. Real Estate Rental Record.

271

name of the tenant, and the amount of the rent received. Then total all of the receipts for the day and enter the total in the deposit column.

This cash record takes care of receipts; the checkbook takes care of disbursements. No other records are necessary for preparing the reports to owners.

Paying repair, service, and other bills. Every bill incurred in managing an owner's property must be approved by the property manager before it is paid. He will approve a bill only after he is certain that the materials for which the bill is rendered have been received and that the labor performed has been satisfactory.

In some offices, bills are paid as soon as they are approved. In others, they are kept in an unpaid-bills file, which is a subdivision of the property managed files. On a particular day of the month all of the approved unpaid bills are paid and then filed in the bills-paid folder. As we shall see on page 274, the method used may affect the manner in which the disbursements are entered on the report to the owner.

The preparation of checks in payment of bills is described on page 322.

Paying real estate taxes. Owning property involves payment of taxes, and managing the property for the owner means looking after the taxes.

Usually there are several taxes, such as a county tax, a village tax, and a school district tax. Tax bills are received from the taxing authority. They show clearly what they are for, the assessed value of the property, when the tax must be paid, to whom it must be paid, the penalties that will be imposed if the tax is not paid when due, and the discount that will be allowed if the bill is paid in full by a certain date. Usually tax bills are presented in two halves. If only one half is paid, there is no discount; no bill is rendered for the second half. In some jurisdictions, payment can be made quarterly. Failure to receive a tax bill is no excuse for delay in payment or nonpayment.

The secretary may have to maintain a tax reminder record for all of the properties managed. A simple method is to make the reminder notations on the regular desk calendar or in the diary at the beginning of the year. All properties managed in a particular town or city will have the same tax payment due dates; one reminder notice for all such properties is therefore sufficient.

Paying salaries and wages to the operating staff. Some secretaries have the responsibility of preparing the payroll for employees of the managed buildings. In large management departments, the bookkeeping department attends to this. Preparation of a payroll is more or less the same whether it is for the employees of managed buildings or for employees of the real estate office. Preparation of the office payroll is discussed in Chapter 21.

Paying social security taxes. If you are handling the payroll for building employees, you may have to pay social security taxes. These taxes are explained on page 330.

Paying insurance premiums. The property manager has the responsibility for seeing that the buildings he manages are properly insured. If the real estate office has an insurance department, the secretary to the building manager has nothing to do with this aspect of property management. The insurance department handles all of the details and merely submits the bills to the property manager.

If there is no insurance department, the building manager will have an insurance broker or brokers with whom he places all insurance. The insurance broker usually attends to the renewal of expiring policies well in advance of the expiration date. However, it may be the secretary's duty to see that the renewals are received. Some card record system to call attention to expiration dates is therefore essential. What you write on the card will vary with the type of policy. The following, however, are the minimum essentials to be noted: (1) type of coverage and expiration date; (2) identification by company and policy number; (3) agent's name; (4) insured; (5) property covered; (6) amount of premium.

The insurance bills must be approved by the building manager before they are paid.

Paying mortgage installments and interest. The property manager is responsible for seeing that interest on mortgages on managed properties is paid when due and that any installments on principal are met as required by the mortgage. The secretary must therefore maintain a reminder record of these due dates. A card for this purpose is illustrated in Figure 5 on page 55.

Paying commissions to real estate men, management fee, and amount due owner. After the report to the owner has been prepared, and approved by the building manager, checks are drawn in payment of any commissions owned to the real estate salesmen, the management fee, and the amount due the owner.

Preparing the report to owners. Each real estate office has its own printed form of report to owners. It may be called a "realty operating statement," a monthly "statement of receipts and expenditures," or some other name. The forms vary as to the manner in which the receipts and disbursements are itemized. A typical form is illustrated in Figure 52.

The report is always prepared in duplicate. The original is sent to the owner, and the copy is filed. To fill out the form, where such records as were described in the preceding section are used, do the following:

1. From the rental book, enter the receipts of rent in the upper part of the form, and total the amount of receipts. Itemize any receipts other than rent, and total those receipts. (It simplifies the record keeping if all rents are made payable by the tenants on the first of the month.)

2. From the check stubs for the month, enter the checks applicable to the property in the appropriate disbursement lines. Make a mark in red on the check stub to show that the item has been entered on the statement.

3. Enter the commissions earned by the salesmen for renting. Memoranda of these items are kept by the secretary during the month.

4. Calculate the management fee, according to the percentage of total receipts to which management is entitled. The management contract fixes the percentage.

5. Total the disbursements and subtract them from the total receipts. The difference is the amount which must be remitted to the owner with the statement.

Entering disbursements from a paid-bills file. Some offices, as shown on page 272, pay all bills on a certain day of the month and then put the paid bills in a paid-bills file. Under this system, it is not unusual for the secretary to make the disbursement entries on the operating report from the paid-bills file instead of from the checkbook. The paid bills are then attached to the report which is sent to the owner.

Approval of report and transmittal. When the report is completed, have it examined and approved by the manager. You are then ready to draw the checks for payment of the commission to salesmen, the management fee, and the balance due the owner. In some offices the procedure may call for a requisition to be signed by the manager before these checks can be signed.

Send the original of the report to the owner with the check for the

Property Management Department

REALTY OPERATING STATEMENT

Prepared by

Property:

Owner:

Period: from   to

RECEIPTS

Unit	Name of Tenant	Monthly Rate	Arrears At Beginning	Amount Paid This Month	Arrears At End
	Totals				

Item

1. Rents Collected per above Schedule . . .   . $ _____

2. Other Receipts (Itemize) .   .   .   . _____

Total Receipts . . . . $ _____

DISBURSEMENTS

3. Commissions for Renting—To   .   .   .   . $ _____ ____

4. Decorating . . . . _____

5. Electricity . . . . _____

6. Extermination   .   .   .   . _____

7. Fuel (Coal #_____Tons) (Oil #_____Gallons) . . . . _____

8. Gas   . . .   . _____

9. Insurance   . . . . _____

    .   .   .   . _____

10. Management Fee_____% of Total Receipts . . . . _____

11. Mortgage Payments—Interest_____% on $_____ for_____ months _____

12. Repairs   . . . . _____

    .   .   .   . _____

13. Salaries   . . . . _____

14. Supplies and Equipment . . . . _____

15. Taxes $_____ for _____ Quarter 19_____ .   .   .   . _____

16. Water—Period Covered _____ to _____ _____

17. Security Deposit. . . . . _____

18. Sundry   . . . . _____

    .   .   .   . _____

Total Disbursements . . . . . $ _____

Form 62   Balance—Check Herewith . . . . $ _____

Figure 52. Report to Owner.

amount due him. It is not necessary to send a letter of transmittal with the report unless some special matter is to be taken up with the owner at the same time.

Duties Connected with Getting New Business

How new accounts are obtained. The property management department has two principal ways of getting new management accounts: (1) by direct, personal solicitation, and (2) by advertising.

In his efforts to get new accounts through personal solicitation, your employer makes use of the prospects file which is explained at page 266. You may have charge of this file. You may also have to make appointments with prospects, write letters to them, and keep records of information your employer obtains about them.

Making a favorable impression upon prospects. Your employer must "sell" the prospect on the use of the firm's building management services. He will generally prefer to conduct the interview with the prospect in his own office rather than in the prospect's office or home. You must have in mind, therefore, that when the prospect comes for an interview he is going to be affected by what he observes of the activity, orderliness, and organization of the manager's office. You can be of great help in seeing that the prospect gets a most favorable first impression.

You can place before your employer the files he will need in speaking to the owner. You can see that his desk is clear of all extraneous material; that the prospect's chair is in place before he arrives; that the room is neat and comfortable. The way in which you receive the prospect when he arrives; how you handle interruptions during the interview; how quickly you can bring to your employer any information he asks for during the interview, all enter into the prospect's judgment of the efficiency of the office. Efficiency, remember, is the keynote to satisfactory property management services. The principles discussed in Chapter 2 on meeting the public should be applied to owners.

Assisting with advertising for new accounts. In advertising for new management business, the firm may use display advertising in newspapers and trade journals or direct mail advertising. The secretary's duties in assisting with advertising were explained in Chapter 14. One point with which the secretary should be familiar is particularly important in property management advertising. It is the use of testimonials. The building manager can make very effective use of letters from owners who commend the firm for its satisfactory services. Sometimes these letters are received voluntarily; other times the manager requests them. Keep a file of the testimonial letters and also place in it memoranda of letters that might be developed into testimonials.

Chapter 18

Collecting Rent

IN EACH REAL ESTATE office where rent collection is one of the functions, a rent collection procedure suitable for the type occupancy of the building, is set up. In some buildings it may be possible to collect nearly all of the rent by mail. In another it may be necessary to have a rent collector at the building the day the tenant gets his pay. The secretary attends only to those parts of a rent collection procedure that entail office work.

The Secretary's Duties

Whatever the rent collection system may be, there are likely to be the following types of office work:

1. Billing
2. Preparing rent receipts
3. Recording receipts of rent
4. Following up delinquent tenants with collection letters or telephone calls

Billing. Monthly rent statements are not usually sent to tenants in houses, duplexes, or small commercial properties. In the case of office buildings and large apartment houses, it is common practice to send tenants a printed form of statement of rent and miscellaneous items due. Time-saving devices are generally provided for this operation. For example, the statements are sent out in window envelopes, and they are addressed on an Addressograph machine. More than one copy may be made of the statement form, the extra ones to be used for recording the receipt of rent and for follow-up letters.

It may be your responsibility to see that the statements are sent out on time. If the rents are payable one month in advance on the first day of each month, the statements must reach the tenant's office or home on the morning of the first of the month.

Figure 53 is an example of a rent statement.

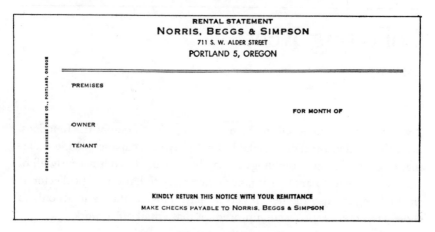

Figure 53. Form of Rent Bill.

Preparing rent receipts. All real estate offices use some form of rent receipt to be given to the tenant either upon request or when collection is made by a collector. A form of receipt that is suitable for rent or other items is shown in Figure 54. The rent or item for which the payment is made is explained on the two blank lines. In the case of rent, include the address and show the period covered by the payment. Thus, "in advance and commencing March 1 and ending March 31 at noon."

A type of rent receipt book useful for recording moneys brought into the office is illustrated in Figure 55. The book is large enough to hold eight receipts on a page. Each page has a duplicate copy so that as a receipt is made out and extracted from the book to be given to the payor; a copy of the receipt remains in the book.

Individual rent receipt books are sometimes used, especially where collections are made by a collector. A page from such a rent book is shown in Figure 56.

$_____   _____*19*__

*Received from*_____

_____*Dollars*
100

_____

_____

*No.*_____   _____

Figure 54. Ordinary Receipt Used for Rent Collection.

EARL S. KESTER, Realtor 519 Linden St. Allentown, Pa.			No. _____
Received payment from _____ Date _____ 19 __			
	Rent	Insurance	Sundries
Remarks:	Received by		

Figure 55. Rent Receipt from Rent Receipt Book.

Date Due	Amount Due	Signature	Date Paid	Amount Paid	Balance

[Actual size 3¾ × 5½]

Figure 56. Page from Individual Rent Book.

Recording receipts of rent. Rents collected must be accounted for and turned over to the owner of the property. How this is done is described in Chapter 17.

Sending Out Delinquency Notices

Rent follow-up practices. In many offices, a follow-up system is established that provides for the mailing of printed notices or reminders that the rent is past due. If all rents are due on the first of the month, a first delinquent notice may go out on the 5th; a second notice on the 10th; on the 13th there will be a follow-up by telephone or letter. In some offices, not more than one or two letters are sent to tenants who have not paid their rent when due.

When it is apparent that a tenant will not or cannot pay his rent, he is served with a dispossess warning. The dispossess proceedings are conducted by an attorney, who must be furnished with all of the facts.

Systems and use of judgment. Your office might have an excellent follow-up system, so far as its mechanics are concerned, but if you do not use discretion in carrying out the system, it will not bring the desired results. Some of the systems actually begin with the exercise of judgment by the secretary or whoever is doing the rent follow-up.

Suppose, for example, your employer is managing a building in a low-rent area. He has set up a system under which a rent card is prepared for each unit and followed up by due dates. When the due date arrives you are supposed to place the card in a delinquent section, but no follow-up action is to be taken on these cards until you say so. How will you decide when to follow up? First, you should observe the tenant's paying habits. Second, you should observe how long he has been delinquent. Having taken both facts into consideration, you should place the card in position for follow-up on a certain date. The steps provided by the follow-up system can then be taken. Hardship cases would, of course, fall out of the fixed schedule for collection.

To take another typical case, suppose your employer is collecting rent from office tenants among whom are physicians. Experience has shown that these physicians send out their statements on the first of the month and that they pay their rent after they have made their collections. It would be advisable, under the circumstances, to allow the physicians until the tenth of the month before following up, even though the procedure called for earlier follow-up of other tenants.

Now suppose your employer is collecting rents from tenants in an apartment house, and you know that the tenants usually pay their rents out of their pay checks. Pay day varies from business to business. Therefore, you must observe the rent-paying habits of the tenants. If a tenant's record indicates that he has been paying his rent consistently for a period of time on about the 12th or 15th of the month, you would not send him a reminder until, perhaps, the 16th or 17th of the month.

Basic follow-up rules. The secretary who has to carry out the rent collection procedure of the office should bear in mind two basic rules:

1. The follow-up once begun should not be relaxed. The tenant should not be given a chance to forget that his rent is past due and that it must be paid promptly.

2. If a letter contains any threat of action, that action should be taken at the time indicated. For example, if a letter says that legal action will be taken unless the rent is received by the 20th, the tenant should not be sent another letter saying that he will be given just five more days— unless, of course, the tenant has asked for more time and it has been granted to him.

When the tenant asks for more time. Frequently a tenant will ask for more time until certain money that he is expecting is received. Just as frequently the money does not arrive on the day set, but the tenant is sure that in a few more days he will have it. The secretary should refer such cases to the building manager, who must decide whether the tenant is merely bluffing or is really telling the truth about the payment time.

In such a case, the building manager might ask the tenant to give some security for the rent. Actually he is not so much concerned about obtaining the security as he is in observing the tenant's reaction to his demand. If the tenant is sincere, he will be glad to give any reasonable security. But if he refuses the manager's request, something is wrong. The tenant wants the office to have faith in his story, but he is not willing to back it up with any evidence of his own good faith. The manager will probably begin immediate action to dispossess the tenant.

Get request for extension in writing. If a tenant asks for an extension of time, it might be advisable to have the tenant write out his request. This practice eliminates misunderstandings and provides a definite businesslike arrangement. The request should indicate that the tenant will make payment of a certain amount on a certain date if he is granted a temporary extension.

Examples of Rent Collection Notices and Letters

Initial rent collection notices. The following are samples of first notices suitable for mailing to those tenants who have not paid their rent.

IMPORTANT

We regret the necessity of calling attention to your past due rent. It is now requested that the unpaid balance of $.....................be paid immediately. (*R. E. Scott Co., Elizabeth, N. J.*)

*   *   *

IMPORTANT NOTICE

Our records show that you have not paid your rent which was due and payable at this office on the first day of the month in accordance with the terms of your lease.

We hope that this matter will receive your prompt attention. (*Swan-Lorish, Inc., Chicago, Ill.*)

Second rent collection notices. The following are samples of notices suitable for mailing to tenants who received a notice similar to those given in the preceding group and who several days later are still delinquent.

FINAL NOTICE

We have extended every opportunity to you to pay the balance due us. We now regret to inform you that unless payment is received in full before the close of business........................appropriate legal action will be reluctuantly taken. (*R. E. Scott Co., Elizabeth, New Jersey*)

*   *   *

We have previously called to your attention that we have not as yet received payment of your rent for the current month. In again checking our records we find that payment has not been received and as your remittance is now long overdue, it is most important that payment be received without further delay. We will therefore appreciate it if you will give this your immediate attention. (*Waguespack, Pratt, Inc., New Orleans*)

*   *   *

FINAL NOTICE

Payment of your delinquent rent in the sum of $.............must be made to this office before....................(*Heyer-Kemmer, Inc., Philadelphia, Pa.*)

*   *   *

Your rent payment in the amount of $. . . . ., which was due in our office on . . . ., has not been received although a "reminder" was mailed to you on the . . . . of the month.

We must now advise you that unless payment in full is received by return mail, we will take such action as we deem necessary to fully protect the interests of the lessor. (*Keyes Company, Miami, Florida*)

Final communications before attorney takes over. The rent collection procedure generally ends with a formal notice to the delinquent to vacate, or some other similar type of notice that gives the tenant warning that he is to be dispossessed. Usually this is a printed or mimeographed form similar to that shown in Figure 57. If this notice does not bring in the rent, the attorney takes the necessary legal steps.

NOTICE TO VACATE

. . . .
. . . .
. . . .

You, ..., are hereby notified that you are in default in the payment of rent pursuant to the agreement under which you, as Tenant, hold the following described premises:

and you are further notified that. . . . ., the Landlord to whom said money is due in the sum of . . . . Dollars, ($. . . . .), from the . . . . day of . . . ., 19. . to the . . . . .day of . . . ., 19. . demands and requires the payment of all such rent now due, or the possession of said described premises within three (3) days from the date of the delivery to you of this Notice.

This notice is intended as a compliance with Section 83.20, Florida Statutes, 1951.

PLEASE GOVERN YOURSELF ACCORDINGLY.

Dated at . . . ., Florida, this . . . . day of . . . ., 19. . . .

THE KEYES COMPANY, Agent for

. . . .
Lessor and Owner

Figure 57. Notice to Vacate

Chapter 19

How You Can Help the Appraiser

As SECRETARY to an appraiser you may have many of the secretarial duties that have been covered in previous chapters. Here are duties that relate specifically to appraisal work. What you may be called upon to do as secretary to an appraiser depends upon (1) the amount and kind of appraisal work your employer does; (2) what kind of assistance he desires; and (3) what special assistance you may be qualified to give.

How Appraisers Work

Type of work done by expert appraisers. A man who devotes all of his time to appraisals of property and is well-known in his profession may receive orders for appraisals from property owners, banks, lawyers, insurance companies, Federal government departments, municipalities, housing authorities, and others. The appraisals may be for different purposes—selling, buying, fixing inheritance taxes, condemnation, planning civic improvements, and so on. There may be appraisals of apartment houses, office buildings, stores, garages, hotels, motels, factories, or any other kind of property. He may be employed to appraise a one-story building or an entire area comprising hundreds of units and embracing numerous kinds of properties. The more recognition the appraiser has earned for his work and the greater the variety of appraisal work he does, the more important are the projects he accepts and the more exacting the work. Such an appraiser is frequently called upon to testify in court as to the value of property in dispute.

The time and effort consumed in making appraisals and preparing reports vary with the assignment. For example, in making an appraisal of extensive properties for the Army, the appraiser may exert the utmost effort to render an appraisal report that is complete in every detail. In making an appraisal of a dwelling for a small estate, he will prepare a less elaborate and shorter report. The opinion of value, however, will be as sound as that made for a property of great value.

The expert appraiser may accept assignments in different parts of the country. He may share an appraisal project with another appraiser, doing one part of the valuation job while the other appraiser does another portion.

Type of work done by the average appraiser. The average appraiser may take on appraisal work from time to time while he carries on other kinds of real estate work like brokerage, leasing, and building management. Such an appraiser usually does not take on large appraisal projects. Nevertheless, he goes through very much the same steps as the expert in preparing his appraisals.

Kind of assistance the appraiser expects. Every appraiser expects his secretary to be able to assist him in the following ways:

1. Find out from the person who orders the appraisal to whom it is to be addressed, how many copies are required, what special forms, if any, are to be used if the appraisal is made for a financial institution or governmental body, and any other special instructions concerning the appraisal report.

2. Order all necessary photographs, photostatic copies of maps, articles, and other art work that is to be included in the report. The secretary does this upon instructions from her employer.

3. Take dictation of the report and transcribe it accurately.

4. Make corrections of grammatical errors, punctuate, and capitalize in accordance with accepted rules of good writing.

5. Type the report with the utmost attention to accuracy, arrangement of the material, spacing, tabulation, and the like. The original and the copies must be physically attractive and appeal to the client through its craftsmanlike preparation.

6. Check all mathematical computations to be certain of accuracy.

7. Prepare simple diagrams of property location.

8. Prepare a table of contents of the report.

9. Get together the material on the appraiser's qualifications.

10. Assemble the original and the copies and bind them in the covers provided for the purpose.

11. Maintain all appraisal files in systematic order.

12. Supply her employer with any material from the files needed for the appraisal on which he is working.

13. Keep an index of names of people referred to from time to time.

14. Keep the appraiser's kit in order.

15. Keep records of work done for accounting purposes.

Other ways in which the secretary may assist the appraiser. A few years of experience in general real estate practice, familiarity with the work of the appraiser, a good educational background, and native intelligence have qualified some secretaries to do more than what is generally expected of appraisers' secretaries. They actually make some of the studies that are necessary in arriving at an opinion of value. For example, one of the factors entering into an appraisal of the value of a building is the complete history of sales or other transfers of the property to be appraised, for a period as far back in some cases as twenty years. Part of this sales record may be in the office files; part may require a search in published or public records. Such a search is ordinarily made by assistants specially trained in this field who work closely with the appraiser. A secretary who knows how to do this work and come up with a complete record of every sale or transfer of interest, showing the date; the parties to the transaction, what part of the sale was made for cash, what part on mortgage, and what the selling price was, may do this operation for each appraisal by herself. Obviously, such an assistant is invaluable to the appraiser, particularly if he has no one else to do the leg work for him.

A few women have become good appraisers in their own right through the experience of working with an expert appraiser. Some of them are qualified to turn out a complete report. Certainly, appraisal work is a field in which women, especially college graduates, can make important strides not only as assistants but as qualified appraisers.

Scope of chapter. In most positions, the secretary to an appraiser needs to know the following: (1) what kind of appraisal data are collected and kept on file for repeated use and for use in arriving at valuations of specific properties; (2) how to keep appraisal files; (3) how to prepare the written report. The first two subjects are covered in this chapter. Appraisal reports are covered in the next chapter.

Collecting Appraisal Data

Kinds of data collected. An appraiser collects and retains whatever data may prove useful in his appraisal work. For example, he collects data about (1) the city, (2) trends of the community, (3) the site, (4) specific kinds of properties, (5) costs of construction, (6) expense items, (7) income, and (8) other factors. Some of the material is of a general nature that can be used over and over again, and some applies to specific properties. How both types of material are filed will be explained in the next section.

Library of appraisal publications. Every successful appraiser collects and keeps readily available a library of atlases, maps, books, periodicals, and other publications containing appraisal information.[1] These volumes are usually kept in bookcases or on shelves within easy reach of the appraiser. It is the secretary's responsibility to keep the appraisal library in order. She must see that the books are arranged by authors and that the periodicals are kept chronologically. The secretary should be able to put her hands quickly on any book or publication her employer asks for. You will be able to do this only if you familiarize yourself with the publications in his library and refuse to allow any book to be taken away from his office without a written note of who borrowed it and the date.

Keeping records of books and periodicals. Although few secretaries go to the trouble of keeping a card record of the books, periodicals, atlases, and maps that make up the appraisal library, such a record is worth maintaining.

To establish the record, supply yourself with ordinary 3 × 5 cards. Make up a card for each book now in the library and place on record the author, title, publisher's address, and year of publication. As a new book is acquired, make up a card for it; if it is purchased, include the price. If there are many books to be catalogued, it might be well to prepare a second card for each, with the title in the principal position.

---

[1] Stanley L. McMichael, *McMichael's Appraising Manual* (Englewood Cliffs, N.J.: Prentice-Hall, Inc., 4th ed. 1951).

Arrange all of the cards alphabetically. Titles and authors will be in the same alphabetical file.

In the same way, make up a record card for each of the periodicals, showing the years for which you have complete volumes. As current numbers are received, enter the date of the issue on the card. Thus, if an issue is missing, you can tell by consulting the card whether it was received. This card should also show the date the subscription expires and the price of the subscription. The expiration dates should be entered on your calendar (see page 47). Arrange the periodical cards alphabetically by title. Keep them separate from the catalogue of books because you will use them more frequently to enter receipts of current issues

Also make up a record card for each atlas or book of maps in the appraisal library, indicating the title, the publisher, the publisher's address, or other source. Note on the card the date on the map; you may want to follow up each year to see whether later editions have been published.

When books or maps are to be used away from the place where they are kept, make a note on the record card of the person who took it and the date. Find out from the borrower how long he expects to keep it and follow up to see that it is returned. When it is returned, erase the memo you made on the card when it was borrowed. You may, if you wish, keep the cards for the books that are out in a separate section of the box in which the record cards are kept.

Historical data on specific properties. Appraisers have need for historical data on specific properties, such as when transfers took place, what mortgages were recorded, when they were satisfied, and the like.[2] In a number of cities there are publications that report such information. In places where there are no publications of this kind, a search must be made of the public records to gather this information when it is needed. A brief description is given below of three real estate publications in different parts of the country to acquaint you with the way in which real estate transactions are reported. Your office may subscribe to one of these publications, or to similar ones in your part of the country.

New York City: In New York City, the *Real Estate Record and Builders Guide* (usually referred to as *Record and Guide*), published by

---

2 The selling department is also interested in these data. See page 68.

F. W. Dodge Corporation, reports weekly all real estate instruments recorded in Manhattan and the Bronx. They include conveyances, leases, mortgages, assignments of mortgages, and satisfied mortgages. The publication also reports sales, mortgage loans, and other items. Figure 58a is part of a page from the *Record and Guide,* showing how conveyances are reported. Every three months a quarterly is published in which the recordings noted in the weekly issues of the magazine are accumulated. All items pertaining to a particular street are placed together. At the end of the year all of the recordings in the four quarterly issues are accumulated in proper sequence in one volume. Files of annual volumes and current issues are retained permanently by subscribers.

> **Wadsworth ter, 49-55** (8:2170-368), ws, 494.6 s Fairview av, runs s100 to Tunnel xw116.1 xn105.6xe116 to beg, 5-sty apt; Haft Assets Corp (Abbott R Monness, pres), 32 Cushman rd, White Plains, N Y, to 7-9 East 85th St Corp, 18 E 41: B&S: CaG; mtg $85,750; Feb4; Feb6'52; A$40,000-135,000.
>
> **Wadsworth ter, 65-71** (8:2170-410), ws, 294.6 s Fairview av, runs s100xw116xn37 to Fairview av xne69.10xe89 to beg, 5-sty apt; Haft Assets Corp (Abbott R Monness, pres), 32 Cushman rd, White Plains, N Y, to 7-9 East 85th St Corp, 18 E 41; B&S; CaG; mtg $85,-750; Feb4; Feb6'52; A$41,000-135,000.
>
> **Wadsworth ter, 65-71** (8:2170-410), ws, 294.6 s Fairview av, runs s100xw116xn37 to Fairview av xne69.10xe89 to beg, 5-sty apt; 7-9 East 85th St Corn (Abbot R Monness, pres), 32 Cushman rd, White Plains, N Y, to Haft Assets Corp, 18 E 41; B&S: CaG; mtg $83,-750: Feb5; Feb7'52; A$41,000-135,000.
>
> **Washington pl, 12-16** (2:546-15), sec Greene (No 240), 114.3x96.2, 13-sty apt & strs; Jos P Tolins, 14 Washington pl, to Helen Carner, 859 Forest av, Rye, N Y; B&S: CaG: 10% pt: mtg $——: July21; Feb6'52: A$115,000-780,000 (R S $1.10).

Figure 58a. Excerpt from "Real Estate Record and Builders Guide" (New York City) reporting Conveyances in Manhattan.

Chicago: In Chicago, *Realty & Building,* a weekly published by Realty & Building, Inc., reports real estate sales, real estate transfers, trust deeds and mortgages, foreclosures and receiverships, new leases, and other data. Figure 58b is part of a page from *Realty & Building* showing how real estate transfers are reported. An indication of the consideration involved may be derived from the amount of revenue stamps, shown as RS in the items reported. Thus, if the publication shows that each 55 cents in revenue stamps represents $500 in value, or less, the value of the first item reported in Figure 58b would be $8,000 [$8.80 ÷ 55 × $500].

HYDE PARK

LAKE PARK AVE 360 ft N of 46th St E fr 22x180; Murata to Shigemi Chakuno; RS $8.80; 2/4.

LAKE PARK AVE 380 ft N of 49th St E fr 50x132; Rosenberg to Joe Feferman et al; RS $13.20; 2/4.

KENWOOD AVE 223 ft S of 55th St E fr 38x175; Salisbury to Jesse F Jenkins; RS $18.15; 1/10.

DANTE AVE NE Cor of 85th St 29x125; Kay Builders Inc to John F Healy et al; RS $19.25; 1/24.

COMMERCIAL AVE 280 ft S of 87th St W fr 25x140; Ginsberg to Julius L Kahn; RS $13.20; 1/14.

ANTHONY AVE SE Cor of South Park Ave 58x272; South Chicago Sav Bk to Elaine Wallace; RS $94.60; 1/29.

AVALON AVE NW Cor of 81st St 30x122; Olson to Edmund T Walsh et al; RS $19.25; 12/19.

BENNETT AVE 29 ft S of 89th St E fr 30x125; Rapka to Theodore L Kardaras et al; RS $17.05; 1/30.

Figure 58b. Excerpt from "Realty and Building" (Chicago) reporting Real Estate Transfers

Fresno County, California. The *Daily Real Estate Report and Abstract of Records,* published by M. S. Webster Sons, daily, except Saturdays, Sundays, and legal holidays, reports Fresno County real transfers and transactions. They are shown under such headings as deeds, deeds of trust, mortgages, crop mortgages, chattel mortgages, contracts to sell, releases, assignments, leases, homesteads, and others.

Clippings of historical data. Some firms that subscribe to the *Record & Guide* and similar publications clip from each issue the items for the counties in which they operate, and paste them on 4" × 6" cards, which they call history cards. (Two copies of each issue of the publication are, of course, needed to maintain this file.) A separate card is made for each individual property and the address of the property is noted in the upper right-hand corner. Thus they maintain their own cumulative data. The cards are filed by location.

A similar file is maintained by the Real Estate Board of New York, Inc. Members may consult this file, and frequently do so to save the time required to trace the history of a particular property through many volumes of *Record and Guide.*

Sales records. The appraiser is always interested in the price at which properties in his territory have been sold. Some offices therefore keep card records of sales showing the address, a brief description of the property sold, sales price, terms and date of sale. All sales reported by local organizations such as the real estate board, or the Multiple Listing Service, or by newspapers and other publications, are entered on thi record. Sales made by the firm are also recorded in this file.

A common practice is to clip from the newspapers in the territory all sales reported in the real estate news section of the dailies or weeklies and to paste the clippings on 8″ × 12″ sheets. The address of the property is noted in the upper right-hand corner, and the sheets are filed by location. In one office in which this practice is followed, the sheets are transferred at the end of the year to large cumulative binders and consolidated with the previous years' records of the same properties. Thus, in the consolidated binder all of the sheets for a particular property are arranged by years, the earliest year first.

Keeping the Appraisal Files

Kind of material kept in appraisal files. Probably no two independent appraisers maintain exactly the same types of files or filing system for appraisal material. However, they do all have the following kind of material to be filed.

1. Data of a general nature that are used over and over again in appraisal work.

2. Data relating to particular properties.

3. Correspondence relating to individual appraisals and working papers used in making the appraisals.

4. Appraisal reports submitted to clients.

Most of the appraisal material is kept in letter-size filing cabinets.

In addition, there are cross-reference card files to help locate the filed material. The systems described below are typical of filing methods used in appraisal offices.

The general appraisal data file. The general appraisal data file is a subject file, arranged alphabetically. A folder is made for each class of property that the appraiser may be called upon to evaluate. There may be folders entitled "elevator apartments," "hotels," "office buildings," "garages," "cemeteries,' and the like. (See classification of property at page 63.) Also, there may be folders called "census and population," "city planning," "zoning," "sanitary regulations," "taxes," "heating," "air conditioning," and so on. Also, there may be folders with the names of cities in different parts of the country for which data have been accumulated.

As papers are filed, a notation of the name of the folder in which they belong should be placed on them. Then, if anything is taken from the file it can be replaced in the proper folder quickly.

Appraisal data on particular properties. This file is made up of folders bearing the addresses of particular properties or the names of the buildings or accounts. Thus, the appraisal data files of a leading New York appraiser are divided into numbered avenues, east streets, west streets, named streets, named accounts, named buildings for Manhattan, plus files for Queens, Bronx, Brooklyn, Westchester, Connecticut, New Jersey, and other states. All west streets, for example, are numerically arranged, with house numbers following in proper order.

In each folder are placed any data relating to the property, with a notation of the address on each paper. Folders for all of the buildings for which data have been assembled are kept in this file whether or not an appraisal has been made of the property. When an appraisal is made, the folder represents the working papers used in making the evaluation. In it is also placed a copy of the appraisal report.

Correspondence and working papers for particular appraisals. Correspondence relating to individual appraisals is never filed in a general correspondence file. It is usually kept with all of the working papers used in making the appraisals and is filed with the report, or separately from the report, as described below.

File of appraisal reports. You must be able to locate appraisal reports by (1) the name of the property or owner, (2) the location of the property, and (3) the type of property. The reasons are obvious: When your employer wants to see a certain appraisal report, you have to be able to find it for him if he remembers only the name of the client, the location, or the type of property. When he has to appraise a special type of property—say, a garage—he may want to see some of the other appraisals he has made of garages. Any system of report filing must therefore have a cross-reference file.

The reports may be filed separately from the working papers or together with them. The file itself may be made up of flat legal-sized folders or of pocket folders open at the top. Bulky appraisal reports are usually kept in red expansion envelopes. If pocket folders are used, all of the papers are folded to fit into the pocket, and the identification data are written on the face of the pocket. If flat folders are used, the identification data are placed on the folder tab. If red expansion envelopes are used, the identification is typed on a label and pasted on the envelope.

Appraisal reports are generally filed by location, chronologically, or by number.

Location filing. The folders, pockets, or envelopes are filed by the location system used in the office. This may be alphabetically by streets, by building number, by block and lot numbers, or any other location system (see page 62).

Chronological filing. Each appraisal report is placed behind the previous report, thus forming a chronological file. This system is often combined with a location system. Thus, the reports may be filed chronologically by district, county, or other area.

Number filing. Each appraisal report is given a number, which is placed on the tab of the folder, face of the pocket, or face of the envelope, along with other identification data. The folders, pockets or envelopes are arranged in numerical sequence. The file is thus a chronological file since the latest number is that of the latest completed appraisal.

Cross references to appraisal reports file. When a report is ready to be filed, all of the necessary cross references are prepared, either on cards or in a loose-leaf book. At the same time, a memorandum is prepared to notify any other interested departments that an appraisal has been completed on the designated property.

Cross-reference cards. When a numerical system of filing reports is used, at least three cross-reference cards must be prepared to locate the appraisals by client, type of property, and location. Each card contains the same data—number, name of client, type of property, location of property, date—arranged to facilitate the filing. One card is filed alphabetically by client, one by type of property, and one by location.

When a location system of filing is used, two cross-reference cards are sufficient—one for the type of property and one for the name of the client.

Loose-leaf book. Some appraisers prefer to keep a cross index of appraisals in a loose-leaf book rather than on cards. The book is divided into as many sections as are necessary to supply the required cross references. Thus, one part of the book would be arranged by location (alphabetical streets, east side streets, west side streets, and the like). Another part of the book would be subdivided into types of property. A third part would be alphabetical by names of clients. When an appraisal report is completed, the record is made in each of the applicable sections. The loose-leaf sheet contains the same data as the cross-reference card described above.

Although a loose-leaf record may appear more compact and easier to handle than a card record, it does not have the flexibility of a card record, or allow for exact alphabetical arrangement of the entries. However, the amount of appraisal work is rarely so voluminous as to require exact alphabetizing of cross references.

Records of court testimony. Only the most experienced, confident, and skilful appraisers are likely to want to appear as expert witnesses in court cases. In this type of work, the appraiser does not write an appraisal report but does put into writing, for his own use, any of the data that he is likely to want to refer to in his testimony.

Ordinarily, there is no record in the appraiser's office of the exact testimony he gave in all court cases. He may have some of the records. If your employer wants a record of his testimony, he may arrange with the court reporter at the time of the trial to make a copy for him. Upon delivery of the record, payment is made to the reporter. If no copy of the testimony is obtained at the time of the trial, and later your employer wants to obtain one, get in touch with the lawyer by whom he was employed and ask him to procure it.

Material relating to testimony might be filed in a section of the appraisal file devoted to court matters, or in the files of data on specific properties.

Index of names. The secretary should keep an index of the names, addresses, and telephone numbers of individuals to whom the appraiser is likely to refer repeatedly. In this index would be listed the names of attorneys for whom the appraiser has worked, realtors in different areas men in key positions to whom he can refer on specific jobs, and the like.

The appraiser's equipment. The appraiser may use various items of equipment in his appraisal work. The secretary should see that the kit is well supplied with the necessary materials and that all of the items are at hand when needed. These items might include: a steel tape; a steel rule; a small drawing board; a file board with clip to hold papers on which to take notes; a camera; a magnetic compass; a traffic counter; a slide rule; a flashlight; a set of small drawing instruments; colored pencils; bottles of red ink and black India ink; a box for erasers, blotters, stamps, rubber bands, and so forth; an ice pick to hold one end of a tape when making building measurements; and finally, a stout envelope containing an assortment of the appraiser's stationery.[3]

Keeping records of appraisal fees. The secretary is responsible for keeping a record of all appraisal fees earned by her employer. A simple note book ruled as shown in Figure 59 is adequate for this purpose. If the fee is not fixed at the time the appraisal is ordered, the amount of the fee is left blank until it is determined. Items such as taxi fares, telephone expenses, and the like are not entered in this record. Make a note of them on your reminder calender and add them to the invoice.

You must follow up to see that the fees are collected. The reminder to be sent will depend, of course, upon the particular circumstances. Get instructions from your employer if there is any question as to what

RECORD OF APPRAISAL FEES						
DATE WORK DONE	ADDRESS OF BUILDING	TO WHOM BILLED AND ADDRESS	FEE	DATE OF BILLING	DATE COLLECTED	REMARKS (SPLIT-UPS)

Figure 59 Record of Appraisal Fees

---

[3] Stanley L. McMichael, *McMichael's Appraising Manual* (Englewood Cliffs, N.J.: Prentice-Hall, Inc., 4th ed. 1951), p. 603.

tone to use in writing for the fee. You need not ordinarily follow up public bodies as you would individual clients. The payment routines of public offices are usually prescribed and, unless there is some question that holds up the approval of the invoice, payment will be forthcoming.

In a large organization, the secretary may have to conform with the accounting department's procedures for billing clients for appraisal fees. A common procedure is for the secretary to prepare a voucher and send it to the accounting department. The latter prepares the invoice and returns it to the secretary to be forwarded by her to the client with a letter or a copy of the appraisal report.

Chapter 20

How to Prepare an Appraisal Report

AFTER AN APPRAISER has made an investigation, study, and analysis of the factors affecting the value of the property, he prepares a report to substantiate his valuation. This report may cover only a few pages, or it may run into ten, twenty or even hundreds of typewritten pages. The size depends upon the complexity of the appraisal and various other considerations. From the viewpoint of the person who has to put into finished form the material dictated, written, or assembled by the appraiser, the appraisal report presents essentially the same problems whether it is a simple or elaborate one. We shall treat here the following aspects of the secretary's work in preparing the final appraisal report:

1. Importance of the appearance of the report
2. The form of the report
3. Preliminary study of what is to make up the report
4. Paper
5. Hearings
6. White space—margins, spacing, and numbering within the report
7. Tables and other symmetrical arrangements
8. Figures in the text
9. Maps, photographs, diagrams
10. Numbering pages

11. Title page
12. Table of contents
13. Binding or fastening
14. Statement of appraiser's qualifications
15. Letter of transmittal
16. Appraiser's certificate

The appearance of an appraisal report is important. An appraiser may spend days or weeks in diligent investigation, study, and analysis to arrive at a valuation of a property. Unless the report in which he presents his opinion reflects the quality of effort that went into the appraisal, the appraisal may be misjudged. A carelessly prepared report will hurt the appraiser's reputation; an excellently prepared report will augment his prestige. It is up to the secretary to make each report an example of quality workmanship. Bear in mind that your employer will use his reports to attract new clients; that to him each report is a selling brochure and should therefore have the finish, style, and perfection of an outstanding piece of display advertising. If you apply the instructions given in this section, you will be able to produce an artistic report of which your employer will be proud.

The suggestions given in this chapter supplement those given in Chapter 7, which deals with improving your typing efficiency generally You are advised to review Chapter 7.

The form of the appraisal report. Each appraiser works out his reports in his own way, varying the presentation of the data to fit the type of property he is appraising. Many appraisers take great pride in being completely original in the arrangement of the data contained in each report. Others have a more or less standard arrangement for appraisals of particular types of properties. Thus, apartment house appraisals follow a certain pattern, office buildings another pattern, and so on.

Banks, other lending institutions, and governmental bodies sometimes prescribe the form of the appraisal report. If they furnish printed blanks, the report is prepared by filling in the required details directly on the form. Otherwise, the report follows the prescribed form but is typewritten on the paper used for other appraisal reports. A filled-in form requires the closest attention to fitting the material in the allotted space The instructions on pages 103 and 188 should be closely followed.

An employer who is just beginning to do appraisal work will probably study the samples of appraisal reports reproduced in various textbooks and will pattern his first reports on suggested models. As he gains experience, he will deviate more and more from any model until he develops his own report presentation.

Dictation and typing. Some appraisers are able to dictate an average report from beginning to end in the order in which the subject matter is to be presented. Others, not quite so skilled in dictating or in appraising, might work on different portions of the report and later indicate the order in which the topics discussed are to be presented. In any case it is well to have in mind, when typing the report, that when the work is all done it will be arranged in its final order. Therefore, if the discussion of a subject takes up about two thirds of a page, start a new page for the discussion of some other phase of the work.

Your experience with your employer will tell you whether you ought to make rough drafts of the notes you transcribe or whether you can transcribe them directly on report paper. A highly skilled appraiser, working with a competent secretary, might produce a finished report without a rough draft and with only occasional retyping of a page.

The Secretary's Responsibilities

Study shorthand notes and written material. Before you transcribe your notes or type any handwritten or rough draft prepared by your employer, go over the material with these purposes in mind:

1. To see that each sentence makes sense. If you cannot understand something that was dictated or written, do not hesitate to ask the meaning of the sentence or paragraph and have it clarified.

2. To correct mistakes in English.

3. To punctuate correctly.

4. To identify the headings and subheadings so that you can visualize the report in final typewritten form. Headings and subheadings are always used to introduce each new subject or factor discussed in the report.

Select paper. Reports are usually typewritten on heavy substance, white letter-size paper (8½″ × 11″) or on legal-size paper (8½″ × 13″). The practice in the particular office may be to use legal-size paper only for appraisals prepared in connection with a legal action, or for inheritance tax purposes. The original and copies to be delivered to the client are made on report paper; office copies may be made on lightweight paper of a good quality.

Many appraisers have special report paper with the name of the firm printed across the top or in the upper left-hand corner. The name on the sheet offers protection against unauthorized replacements of any page of the report.

An appraiser may also have sheets specially printed with headings and subheadings for certain portions of the report; information applicable to a particular appraisal is typed in the spaces provided in the form.

Some appraisers use a printed appraisal certificate, with blanks for the insertion of the name of the applicant, address, location of the property, valuation, date and signature of the appraiser. (See page 317).

How to arrange headings. The body of a report is divided into topics and sub-topics with headings. In setting up the headings, keep this thought in mind: *Topics of equal importance should be given equal emphasis.*

How to show emphasis. Emphasis is shown in typed material by centering and by the use of caps, spacing, underlining, or a combination of these techniques. Headings of the same relative importance should be identical in form.

Patterns of headings. In typing a report, make a pattern of the style of headings that you intend to use throughout the report.

The following pattern is adequate for the average report:

TOPIC HEADING
SUBDIVISION HEADING
Minor subdivision heading

If the report requires more breakdowns, the following pattern may be followed:

TOPIC HEADING
SUBDIVISION HEADING
Subordinate Heading
Minor Heading
Least important subdivision heading

Note that when the letters are spaced, there is a double space between words. Use triple space between a center heading and the text that precedes it; use double space between the heading and the text that follows.

If upper and lower case is used, capitalize only the important words. Only the first word in a minor subdivision heading is capitalized.

Topic headings are always centered on the line; other headings may be either centered or written at the left margin. (See discussion under "indentation"; see page 102 on "how to center headings.")

How to word headings. The wording of the headings is dictated by the appraiser. They should be uniform in grammatical construction, if possible. For example, if a subtopic is introduced with a participle, other subtopics in the same topical discussion should be introduced with a participle.

Since the factors entering into an evaluation vary with the type of property and purpose of the appraisal, the headings naturally vary from report to report. A simple appraisal report on an apartment property, for example, might have the following topic headings, centered on the line.

Description of improvements
Condition of improvements
Building measurements
Depreciation
Physical value
Rentals received as of March 1, 19. .
Estimated fair rental income
Estimated deducations from rent
Estimated average rent collections
Rentals per room
Estimated fair average operating expenses
Valuation analysis

Use white space. The secret of preparing an attractive report is to allow ample white space on each page. White space is obtained from the margins, spacing between paragraphs and topics, and skilful placement of tabular and other symmetrical material on the page. The following discussion of margins, spacing, and arrangement of tabular matter should be closely observed. Some employers may favor an even greater amount of white space in their reports than is supplied by the spacing here suggested. You should, of course, modify the rules given to suit the wishes of your employer.

Leave space for ample margins. Use ample and uniform margins at top, bottom, and sides. A 1½ inch margin is appropriate, *exclusive* of the part of the page that is used for binding. Thus, if ¾ of an inch is used for binding, the bound edge (left side or top if on legal paper) has a margin of 2¼ inches instead of 1½ inch.

The first page of the report (and the first page of each part, if the report is presented in parts) should have a 2½ inch margin at the top.

See page 184 for instructions on how to end each page the same distance from the bottom.

How to space the report. The discussion portion of an appraisal report is usually single spaced, with double space between paragraphs, and triple space before each main center heading.

Numbering within the report; indentation. Portions of a report may make use of numbering and lettering schemes, in addition to headings, to simplify the reading. There are no fixed rules as to numbering schemes, but the following three patterns will ordinarily be adaptable. Notice that, whatever the scheme, topics of equal importance are given equal emphasis in the arrangement. Whatever scheme is selected, follow it consistently within the report.

	Pattern 1		Pattern 2		Pattern 3
	I.	I.		I. ....
1.		1.		A. ....
	(a)	A.		1. ....
	(b)	B.		2. ....
	(1)		(1)		(a) ....
	(2)		(2)		(b) ....
2.		2.		B. ....
	II.	II.		II. ....

Observe the following rules within the numbering and lettering scheme:

1. Follow Roman numerals and Arabic numerals with a period.

2. Do not use a period after a number or letter in parentheses.

3. Use double space between paragraphs carrying a number or letter just as you would between other paragraphs.

4. Determine how far you will indent each of the groups in your numbering and lettering scheme, indenting each successive group at least five spaces more than the preceding group, and maintain the same indentation plan throughout the report. Thus, in Pattern 1 the left-hand margin of paragraphs lettered (a), (b), etc. would be indented at least five spaces more than paragraphs numbered 1, 2, and so on, and the left-hand margin of paragraphs numbered (1), (2), and so on would be indented at least 10 spaces.

5. Indent the first line in a main paragraph 10 spaces.

6. Indent the first line in an indented paragraph five spaces more than its own left-hand margin, or use the block form.

How to type tabular matter and symmetrical arrangements. Anyone who has to type an appraisal report should be experienced in typing tables, for a great variety of them may be presented. Complete instructions for typing tables are given on page 104. Here we shall offer a few additional pointers that apply to setting up tabular and other symmetrical arrangements.

Numerous items under a side heading. To make the items stand out, indent the carry-over lines two or three spaces. *Example:*

Interior
    Vestibule and lobby—marble walls and floors, ornamental plaster ceilings
    Upper floor corridors—cement floors covered with rubber tile, plaster walls and ceilings, painted
    Doors—bucks hollow metal, doors kalamein with glass panel
    Washrooms—one men's and one women's on each floor; tile floors and 4'6" wainscoting; each contains two wash basins and two toilets (all fixtures are modern)

Numerous side headings on one page. When there are a number of side headings on a page, each beginning at the left-hand margin and each followed by a discussion, align the discussion to begin at the same point on the typewriter scale for each item. To do this, count the number of letters and spaces in the longest side headings and add several spaces to produce white space between the side-heading and the discussion. For example, assume that the following side headings are to appear on the page:

        Type
        Floor size
        Location
        Year completed
        Layout
        Exterior
        Construction
        Roof
        Vestibule and lobby

> Upstairs halls
> Stairs
> Elevators

The longest item, *vestibule and lobby*, has 19 letters and spaces. Assuming that the tabulation of items is set at 20 on the typewriter scale, the discussion for each of the items might begin at 42 on the scale.

Alignment of like data. When there are number of paragraphs with similar data, each with the same kind of information, like address, dimensions, stories, percentages, and the like, align the similar data on the same tabular stops. *Example:*

500 Central Avenue   100′ × 100′   26-stories
    sold June 19   , for indicated consideration of $1,360,000.
    Assessed valuation $1,200,000. Ratio of price to A.V.   114%

42 East Boulevard   50′ × 100′   8-stories
    sold January 19   , for indicated consideration of $640,000
    Assessed Valuation $500,000. Ratio of price to A.V.   128%

A computation. Align all symbols such as %, @, $. *Example:*

Mortgage band rate   66.6% @   4% = 0.02664
Equity band rate   33.3% @ 10% = 0.03333
                                      0.05997—say 6%

Column of figures with addition. When a column of figures is added, put a line below the last item, space once, enter the total under the line, and draw a double line below the total. Subtotals may be placed in the next column on a line with the last item of the column added.

ESTIMATE OF PHYSICAL VALUE

Land:	222.25 ft.	@ $100.00 =	$ 22,000.00
Building:	855,000 cu. ft. @	.38 = $325,000.00	
Less Depreciation—		@ 40% = 130,000.00	195,000.00
			$217,000.00

Dollar signs and ciphers. The dollar sign ($) is placed with the first item in a column of values and again in the total. If the dollar figures are presented in two or more columns, the first item in each column should carry a dollar sign ($). In tabulations you may or may not use ciphers for cents, but if any sum in a column has cents, use ciphers for all other sums in the column.

What to do with figures in the text. Spell out all numbers under ten; at the beginning of a sentence spell out all numbers whatever they may be. Use figures for distances, dates, percentages, and sums of money. For sums of money unaccompanied by cents, omit the period and ciphers after the number of dollars.

Maps, photographs, and diagrams. Almost every appraisal report has some maps, photographs, sketches, and diagrams in it to enhance the value of the report. The number and kind of depend upon the type and size of the property, the importance of the report, and other factors. The cost of making the illustrations is included in the appraiser's fee. In ordering the photographs and other art work, you should be careful to indicate the exact dimensions of the illustrations. They usually look better if they are the same size as the report page.

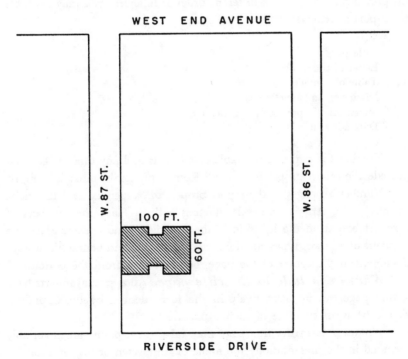

Figure 60. Diagram of a Building Location.

You will probably not be required to make complicated diagrams of property location, but you may very well undertake to prepare simple ones for the average report. The diagrams need not be drawn to scale, but the building should be placed in its approximate position on the street. Figure 60 is a diagram of a building location that any secretary can prepare herself.

How to number pages. Before you number the pages of the report, be sure that it is assembled in the exact order in which your employer wants the report to appear. Find out exactly where the maps, diagrams, and other exhibits are to appear. Their placement depends on the report. Frequently one photograph is put at the beginning of the report to give the reader a visual idea of what the appraiser is trying to do. Additional photographs may be put at the back of the report, along with plot plans, surveys, and other exhibits. If the report is large, it may be divided into two parts under two separate covers.

Unless your employer instructs you otherwise, or you observe from his previous reports that a different order is followed, you may assemble the report as follows:

> Title page
> Letter of transmittal
> Table of contents
> Discussion and conclusions
> Statement of appraiser's qualifications
> Data addendum

Number the pages of the table of contents and any other pages that precede the report proper with small Roman numerals, thus: i, ii, iii, iv.

Number all pages of the report proper, the appendix, and the index (if any) with Arabic numerals, starting with 1. Place the numbers of a report bound on the left side in the top right-hand corner. Place the numbers of a report typewritten on legal-size paper and bound like a legal document in the center of the page, one-half inch from the bottom.

What to include in the title page. All appraisal reports have a title page, set up attractively in the form desired by the appraiser. Figure 61 is an example of such a page.

Whatever form the title page may take, these points are invariably included in the presentation: the name of the person or organization for whom the appraisal is made, the location of the property, and the name of the appraiser.

WM. A. WHITE & SONS

APPRAISAL

of

900 CENTRAL AVENUE
Borough of Manhattan
City of New York

for

THE YOUTH LIFE INSURANCE COMPANY
345 Main Street
New York 12 New York

by

WILLIAM MacROSSIE
Senior Vice President

Wm. A. WHITE & SONS
51 EAST 42nd STREET
NEW YORK, NEW YORK   10017

May 17 19--

Figure 61. Title Page of an Appraisal Report.

The items on the title page are centered horizontally on the available space, exclusive of the part taken up by binding or fastening. With a left side fastening, allow ¾ of an inch for binding. The centering point on the typewriter scale is then moved 7 spaces to the right of the actual center for *pica* type and 9 spaces for *elite.*

Separate each item on the title page by a least four line spaces to give the page a balanced appearance, but use only two spaces between the lines of an item.

Arranging table of contents.

Arranging table of contents. A table of contents is a listing of the contents of the report with the page number on which each item listed begins, indicated in the right-hand margin. It always appears immediately before the report proper begins. As you look at the page numbers, they are in exact numerical order. The table of contents is prepared after the report is completed and the pages numbered.

Center the table of contents horizontally and vertically. Double space a short table of contents and single space a long one. If the report is divided into numbered parts, center the number and title of each part, leave a double space above and below the part title, and single space the topics under each part.

Entitle the page "TABLE OF CONTENTS" in the center of the line, and write "Page" at the right where the page numbers are to appear. Then list each principal topic, writing each at the left-hand margin and using periods for leaders to carry the line all the way over to where the page number is to be inserted. If you space between the periods, always begin the dots at an even number on the typewriter scale so that they will be aligned. The table of contents may show subtopics under a main topic; in that case the subtopics are indented five or ten spaces and all subtopics begin at the same indentation.

An *index* has three characteristics that distinguish it from a table of contents: (1) it is an alphabetical arrangement of the subjects covered in the report; (2) it is more detailed than the table of contents; and (3) it appears at the back of the report. Only voluminous appraisal reports are indexed; all reports have a table of contents. *DO NOT CALL A TABLE OF CONTENTS AN INDEX,* or vice versa.

Binding and fastening.

Binding and fastening. Many appraisers present their reports to clients in leather-covered binders, stamped in gold with the name of the client for whom the appraisal was prepared, the location of the property, and the name of the appraiser. Office file copies are bound in manila folders and labeled in the same way. Use brads, paper fasteners, or staples for fastening, or lace with a cotton lace.

If the report is prepared on legal-size paper, it is bound with a backing sheet of thick paper like any legal document (see page 186), folded, labeled, and fastened as described at page 188.

Stating appraiser's qualifications. It may be the practice of your employer to include with each report a statement of his qualifications and experience as an appraiser. Such a statement would include among other pertinent personal information:

1. The appraiser's name and address
2. The name of the company with whom he is associated
3. Position in the company
4. Schools attended; degrees; honors
5. Business and professional association memberships
6. Offices held in business and professional associations
7. Books, articles, and other writings by the appraiser
8. Experience; types of appraisal work done; most important appraisal assignments completed; courts in which he has acted as an expert witness
9. A list of appraisals of properties similar to the one with which the report deals

As each appraisal report is completed, show your employer the statement of qualifications included in the last previous report and ask him for changes. Attach to the copy a reminder of any additional accomplishments that you think he may want to add to the statement.

This type of statement is frequently used in contacting prospective clients. It may therefore be convenient to have a supply multigraphed or printed, covering items 1 through 8, and to insert a copy in the report instead of rewriting the information for each report. In that case, item 9 would be prepared on a separate sheet.

What to do about the letter of transmittal. Every appraisal report is accompanied by a letter of transmittal. It is usually the secretary's duty to find out from the applicant for the appraisal exactly whom the report is to be addressed to. The transmittal letter should be dated the day it is sent. Include on a line with the salutation, in the center, a reference showing the location of the appraised property.

The transmittal letter is dictated by the appraiser. It is generally brief and covers the following points: (1) in response to whose request the valuation has been made; (2) identification of the property by street

WILLIAM J. DEMOREST
VICE CHAIRMAN OF THE BOARD

PETER GRIMM
CHAIRMAN OF THE BOARD

LOUIS SMADBECK
PRESIDENT

DIRECTORS

FRANK P. ANDERSON
JOHN C. BOHLING
IAN G. M. BROWNLIE
JERRY L. COHEN
WALTER A. DAVIS
WILLIAM J. DEMOREST
EDWARD F. GALLAHER
PETER GRIMM
HENRY HOF, JR.
DONALD JONES
ROBERT T. LAWRENCE
WILLIAM MacROSSIE
JOSEPH T. MIRTL
JACK L. NUNBERS
LOUIS SMADBECK

WM. A. WHITE & SONS
ESTABLISHED 1868
REAL ESTATE

NEW YORK

51 EAST 42ND STREET
MURRAY HILL 2-2300

50 BROAD STREET
DIGBY 4-3797

110 EAST 56TH STREET
PLAZA 5-0700

APPRAISAL DEPARTMENT
WILLIAM MacROSSIE, M.A.I., C.R.E.
SENIOR VICE PRESIDENT

MAIN OFFICE
51 EAST 42ND STREET
NEW YORK 17, N. Y.

May 17, 19--

The Youth Life Insurance Company
345 Main Street
New York 12, New York

Gentlemen:

In accordance with your request, and for the purpose of appraisal, we have inspected the following described property:-

900 CENTRAL AVENUE
Borough of Manhattan
City of New York.

We have considered pertinent data affecting the valuation, including location, type, use and earning power of the subject property, the rentals, sales and asking prices of comparable properties, the trend of the neighborhood and of business conditions generally.

As a result of our study and analysis we are of the opinion that the market value of the above mentioned property, as of May 17, 19--, is

EIGHT HUNDRED TWENTY-FIVE THOUSAND ($825,000.) DOLLARS

of which amount ONE HUNDRED FIFTY THOUSAND ($150,000.) DOLLARS is allocated to the value of the land.

Figure 62.

WM. A. WHITE & SONS

The Youth Life Insurance Company 2- May 17, 1965

A report is attached hereto and made a part hereof. The valuation is expressly made subject to the conditions and comments appearing on such pages.

Very truly yours,

Wm A. WHITE & SONS

William MacRossie
Senior Vice President

WMacR:lmh

ALL INFORMATION FURNISHED REGARDING PROPERTY FOR SALE, RENTAL OR FINANCING IS FROM SOURCES DEEMED RELIABLE. NO REPRESENTATION IS MADE AS TO THE ACCURACY THEREOF AND IT IS SUBMITTED SUBJECT TO ERRORS, OMISSIONS, CHANGE OF PRICE, RENTAL OR OTHER CONDITIONS, PRIOR SALE, LEASE OR FINANCING, OR WITHDRAWAL WITHOUT NOTICE.

Figure 62. (Cont)

RICHARD J. LEYDEN
REAL ESTATE APPRAISALS
INSURANCE VALUATIONS
FIRST NATIONAL BANK BUILDING
CHICAGO

TELEPHONE FRANKLIN 2-9557

CERTIFICATE OF APPRAISAL

Richard J. Leyden does hereby certify that upon application for valuation by:

_____

_____

the undersigned has personally examined the following described property:

_____

_____

and that he is of the opinion that on_____
the

This valuation is contingent upon the following conditions:
This appraisal is to be used in whole and not in part. No part shall be used in conjunction with any other appraisal.
No responsibility is assumed by the appraiser for matters which are of legal nature, nor is any opinion on the title rendered herewith. Good
title is assumed.
This property has been appraised as though free of all liens and encumbrances unless otherwise stipulated.
The appraiser herein, by reason of this report is not required to give testimony in court with reference to the property appraised, unless
otherwise previously arranged.
The undersigned appraiser has no present or contemplated future interest in the property appraised and the compensation for making the
appraisal is in no manner contingent upon the value reported.
This appraisal has been made in accordance with the high standards of practice of the American Institute of Real Estate Appraisers.

Date_____   Signed_____

                                             Signed_____

Figure 63.

number and legal description; (3) the appraiser has made a careful personal investigation of the premises, has analyzed the property, its environs and the general neighborhood, and as a result of such examination is of the opinion that the property as of the date stated in this recital is worth a specific sum in dollars and cents.

Always center the valuation on a separate line so that it stands out in the letter.

The transmittal letter is personally signed by the appraiser, who signs the report at the same time and in the same way. If the appraiser is a member of the American Institute of Real Estate Appraisers, the letters M.A.I. are placed after his name. An example of a transmittal letter is shown in Figure 62.

Appraiser's certificate. Some appraisers use a special printed or typewritten form of appraiser's certificate in which they certify their opinion of the value stated and set forth the underlying conditions and assumptions. An example of a certificate of appraisal is reproduced in Figure 63.

If a special form of certificate is not used, the transmittal letter serves as the certification of value. The report itself enumerates the underlying conditions and assumptions.

Chapter 21

Keeping Accounts
in a Small Office

Every real estate office, large or small, must keep accurate books of account. Without them the owners, whether they do business as individuals, partners, or a corporation, cannot report their Federal and state taxes properly and cannot run their business efficiently.

Who keeps the books? In large organizations, trained accountants and bookkeepers keep the accounting records. Secretaries who perform the functions described in this book have nothing to do with the actual books of account, though they may have a good deal to do with the records of transactions that find their way into the books.

In a small office, the secretary often has the responsibility of keeping the books that record the receipt of income and the disbursements. If these records are kept accurately, the owners can tell at any time how the business stands financially, and they can meet the requirements of the Federal and state tax laws.

Must the secretary know bookkeeping? To keep the bookkeeping records of a small office the secretary does not have to be a trained bookkeeper. She merely has to be instructed by someone who knows how the books are kept, and she must understand the instructions well enough to follow them. A public accountant is generally employed in such offices to audit the books periodically, make up the financial statements at the end of the year, and prepare the tax returns. He may be the one who instructs the secretary, or someone who has already kept the records may do so.

Scope of this chapter. It will help a secretary to take on the responsibility of keeping the records if she has a basic understanding of what this work generally entails. The purpose of this chapter is to give you that basic understanding. No attempt will be made to explain any one system completely because the systems vary from office to office. However, whatever system is used, you will generally find it necessary to know the following:

1. How to keep bank accounts
2. How to handle petty cash
3. How to keep the payroll records
4. How to keep a record of all real estate transactions
5. How to keep records of cash income and disbursements

How to Keep Bank Accounts

Sources of moneys received. Most real estate businesses receive money from the following sources. This money must be placed in bank accounts.

1. *Commissions and fees.* This is the money that is earned for selling properties, negotiating leases, making appraisals, managing property, and performing other services. The funds belong to the business. To be sure, part of the commission will have to be paid to the salesmen, and maybe to co-brokers, but these are debts of the business that will be paid out of the moneys received. A real estate business must have a bank account for funds that belong to it.

2. *Deposits from buyers.* The moneys received from buyers as deposits do not belong to the firm. The deposits are held in trust until released to the owners. They might be held, for example, until a mortgage commitment comes through.

Such deposits must not be mixed with the firm's funds. There are various ways in which such funds are kept separate from the firm's, but the usual one is to have a separate "trustee account" at the bank.

3. *Deposits and rent from lesees.* Rent deposits and rent collected from tenants do not belong to the firm. These funds must be deposited in a bank account maintained for managed properties, as explained on

page 269, or in the trustee account. Eventually these moneys are turned over to the owner.

What you should know about bank accounts. To handle bank accounts properly, you should know:

1. How to endorse checks
2. How to make deposits
3. How to make withdrawals
4. How to prepare a reconcilation of a bank statement

Each of these aspects of bank accounts is treated below.

Endorsing checks. Always endorse checks on the back, across the left end. Place the endorsement as near to the edge of the check as possible because checks may be endorsed several times. Make the endorsement correspond *exactly* with the name of the payee. If the name of the payee is not correct, endorse the check as it is made out and then write the correct name under the first endorsement.

Making deposits. In the space provided on the deposit slip, type the name and address of the account exactly as they are carried on the bank's records. Then list the items that are to be deposited. Always make a carbon copy of a deposit slip so that you will have a detailed record of your deposits.

Place the original deposit slip and items of deposit, with the deposit slip on top, in the pass book. Hand them to the receiving teller at the bank. The teller will keep the deposit slip for his records and will enter the amount and date of the deposit in your pass book. Many banks do not enter the deposits in pass books, but use a special form of deposit slip and give the depositor part of it as a receipt. Other banks issue receipts similar to cash register receipts. These temporary receipts must be kept at least until the bank statement is received.

Depositing checks. You should examine a check carefully before depositing it to see that it is properly drawn. If the check is post-dated, or if there is a discrepancy between the figures and the written amount, the bank will not accept the check. When an improperly drawn check is received, do not deposit it but take the matter up with the person from whom you received the check.

If a check bears a notation or endorsement to the effect that it represents payment in full, do not deposit it without your employer's approval unless the check is actually for the full amount of the account.

Endorse the checks and list them individually on the deposit slip.

Some deposit slips call for an identification of each check by its A.B.A. transit number or by the place where it is payable. The small printed number that appears on the face of the check, for example $\frac{1-8}{210}$, is the transit number assigned to a bank by the American Bankers Association. Banks do not insist that the depositor identify the checks, but they do insist that he itemize them.

A check is a cash item. If a deposited check is not paid by the drawer, the bank charges it back to the account of the depositor.

Using a checkbook. The bank supplies check forms for making withdrawals. Checks bound in book from with three or more checks to the page are convenient for office use. It is desirable to have the name of the account printed on the checks and to have the checks and stubs numbered before they are bound. The bank sometimes charges for the special printing and numbering of checks.

After all the checks in a checkbook have been used, paste a label on the outside cover, giving the name of the bank, title of the account, and dates on which the first and last checks were drawn. Number the books. This procedure facilitates finding a stub.

Reordering checkbooks. It takes about three weeks to get a new checkbook printed. Therefore, estimate the number of checks that you write in three weeks and order a new book in ample time to avoid running out of checks. The printer usually inserts a form for reordering near the end of the bound book. Complete this form and send it to your bank when you reorder, but do not depend upon the form as a guide as to *when* to reorder. The number of the first check in the new book will follow the number of the last check in the previous book, in numerical sequence.

Preparing the check stub. Before writing a check, fill out the stub with the number and amount of the check, the date, the name of the payee, the purpose for which the check is drawn.

In the case of trustee bank accounts and accounts for managed property funds, the stub should show the name of the owner of the property, the address of the property, or any other identifying information. Make each stub specific enough to enable you to include the item properly in whatever records you have to prepare from the check stubs.

Writing the check. Always write checks on the typewriter or in ink in a clear, legible hand. Observe the following procedure:

Stubs. Fill out the stub before writing the check.

Number. Be sure that the number on the check corresponds to that on the stub. If the numbers are not printed on the checks, number consecutively all checks and stubs when you begin to use a new checkbook.

Date. Date the check the exact day on which it is drawn, or on the previous day if it is drawn on Sunday or a holiday. The bank will honor checks that are dated on Sunday or a holiday, however.

Payee. State clearly and accurately the name of the party to whom the check is payable. Do not prefix the name of the payee by a title, such as "Dr.," "Judge," "Rev.," or "Mr." If the payee is "Mrs. John E. Browne," include "Mrs." before the name, but if the payee is "Mrs. Ella Browne," do not include "Mrs."

If the check is payable to the officer of a club or society in his official capacity, follow his name with his office—"John E. Browne, Treas."

Amount. State exactly in figures and words the amount of the check. Write the figures close to the dollar sign that is on the check, separating the cents from the dollars with a decimal point, thus, $1,254.53 or $1,254.00. Do not separate the cents from the dollars with a space, for spaces make alteration of the check easier.

In writing out the amount, express cents as fractions of 100. If there are no cents, use the word "no" as the numerator of the fraction. The following are approved forms for writing out amounts in checks:

One Thousand Two Hundred Fifty-Four and 53/100 ....Dollars
One Thousand Two Hundred Fifty-Four and no/100 ....Dollars

If it is necessary to write a check for less than a dollar, enclose the figures in parentheses, and precede the amount written out in words with the word "Only." Thus:

Pay to...... ...... John E. Browne...... ..$ (53¢)
Only Fifty-Three Cen.s ....Dollars

Blank spaces. Fill in all blank spaces before or after the name of the payee or of the amount with hyphens, if the check is written on the typewriter. Draw a straight line in the spaces if the check is written in ink.

Signature. The signature should agree exactly with that shown on the signature card at the bank

Totaling deposits, withdrawals, and carrying forward.
Each page of stubs in checkbooks bound with three or more checks to
a page has a date column and a deposit column. At the top of the
deposit column is space for entering the balance brought forward from
the preceding page. Enter all deposits on the stub, inserting the date of
each. When all the checks on a single page have been used, compute
the balance to be brought forward to the next page. Do this by adding
the deposits on the page to the balance brought forward at the top of
the page; enter the total at the bottom of the column in the space marked
"total deposits." Then add the column of the amounts of checks drawn,
enter the total of checks drawn at the bottom of the page, and bring
the total over to be subtracted from the total deposits. The difference
is the balance to be brought forward to the next page.

Getting the bank statement. Ask the bank how often it sends
statements, together with canceled checks, to depositors. If the bank
does not render monthly statements unless requested, enter a permanent
request to have statement and canceled checks sent to you as of the
close of business the last day of each month.

Reconciling bank statement and checkbook. Upon receipt
of the bank's statement, reconcile the balance shown by the bank with
the balance shown by your checkbook as of the date of the bank statement. Here are the steps necessary to reconcile the bank statement with
your checkbook balance:

1. The bank statement shows all withdrawals against, and deposits
to the credit of, an account. When a statement is sent to you, the canceled
checks are arranged in the order in which the items appear on the
statement. Compare the amount entered on the statement with the
amount on the check. If there is a discrepancy, call the bank immediately.

2. Arrange the canceled checks in numerical order.

3. Beginning with the first check, compare the amount of each
canceled check with that shown on its stub in the checkbook. If the
amounts are in agreement, put a check mark in front of the amount
on the check stub. (If they are not in agreement, you have made an
error and will have to adjust your balance accordingly.) Also compare
the name of the payee on the check with the name on the stub.

4. Make a list of the outstanding checks—those that have not been
paid, as indicated by the stubs that do not have check marks on them.
Show the number and the amount of the check on this list.

5. Enter the service charges and debit memos and subtract the totals from the balance shown by your checkbook. This is your actual balance and is the amount with which the balance shown by the bank statement must be reconciled.

6. Check the deposits shown on the bank statement against those shown on your stubs. Make a list of deposits not shown on the bank statement. If deposits that the bank has received are not entered on the statement, get in touch with the bank immediately.

7. Some bank statements have a form of reconciliation printed on them. If they do not, make the reconciliation on a separate sheet or on the back of the stubs of checks written the last of the month, as follows:

Reconciliation, June 30, 19—

Bank statement balance		$1,385.45
Add late deposit		865.80
Total		$2,251.25
Checks outstanding:		
734	$200.00	
742	16.50	216.50
Balance		$2,034.75

This amount should be the same as the balance shown by your checkbook after you subtracted service charges and debit memos (see Step 5).

If your checkbook balance and the bank balance are not reconciled after you have taken the foregoing steps, you have made an error in your stubs (or the bank has made an error). Check carefully the addition and subtraction on each stub and, also, the balance carried forward from stub to stub. This will reveal any error you have made and you can then adjust the final stub to show the correct balance.

After the reconciliation has been made, O.K. and initial it. Put the reconciliation, the bank statement, and the canceled checks on your employer's desk if he is interested in seeing them.

Petty Cash

The petty cash fund. Every office needs to have a small amount of cash (bills and coins) on hand to pay for minor incidental expenses. A petty cash fund is established for this purpose. The size of the fund will vary according to the demands made upon it, but it should be large enough to last a few weeks or a month. The fund is created by drawing a check on the employer's bank account in favor of petty cash for the amount of the fund.

Keep the petty cash fund in a cash box in a safe place because you are responsible for it. Never mix this money with your own funds; never make change from it unless you can make the exact change; *never* borrow from it.

As each expenditure is made, no matter how small, make out a receipt slip showing the date, the amount, and the purpose for which the disbursement was made. The record should be sufficiently specific to enable you to classify the expenditures so that they can be entered in the proper expense accounts. Have the person to whom the payment is made receipt the slip. Keep the slips in the cash box.

Reimbursing the petty cash fund. When the cash remaining begins to run low, take the slips out of the cash box, and assemble them according to expense classification, such as stamps, carfare, and the like. Total each classification, staple the slips together, and put them in a "petty cash reimbursement envelope." On the face of the envelope make a summary record of the expense classifications and the amounts for each. Draw a check for the amount of the disbursements. That is the amount necessary to bring the petty cash fund up to its original figure. Attach the petty cash reimbursements envelope to the check when you give it to your employer for his signature. Mark the envelope "Paid— (*date*), Ck. No. . . . . ," initial, and file it. Cash the check and place the currency in the cash box.

The procedures for getting the expenses shown in the expense classifications on to the books of account may vary from office to office. That is a detail, however, that will be explained to you by the accountant.

The Transaction Record Book

Purpose of transaction record book. Some record must be made of each real estate transaction that occurs in order to be sure that the commissions earned are received and that salesmen's and co-brokers' commissions are paid. The record might also be used for following up other details, for example, reporting to the Multiple Listing Service.

It is simple to set up such a record, if one is not already maintained in your office. Get an ordinary journal in a stationery store. Rule up the facing pages as shown in Figures 64a and 64b. When you are informed of a transaction, make the entry in the columns that apply to the transaction.

Such a record is not necessarily part of the regular books of account. In other words, it does not take the place of the books in which records are made of cash receipts and expenditures.

RECORD OF TRANSACTION

DATE	PROPERTY ADDRESS	TYPE OF DEAL	AMOUNT OF DEAL	NAME OF MORTGAGER TENANT OR BUYER	NAME OF MORTGAGEE LANDLORD OR SELLER

Figure 64a. Transaction Record Book (left-hand page).

RECORD OF TRANSACTION

COMMISSION RECEIVED		COMMISSION PAID								NET TO COMPANY	REPORTED FOR MULTIPLE LISTING
AMOUNT	DATE	AMOUNT	DATE	EXCLUSIVE	AMOUNT	DATE	CO-BROKER	AMOUNT	DATE		

Figure 64b. Transaction Record Book (right-hand page).

Cash Income and Disbursement Records

Terminology used in keeping books of account. When you hear such words as "account," "journal," "ledger," and the like, you should know what they mean. Although they are sometimes used loosely by untrained bookkeepers, you should know what their technical meanings are.

Account. An accounting record maintained in a ledger to which entries are posted from books of original entry in the form of debits (at the left) and credits (at the right). The difference between the totals of both sides of the account is known as the balance. The account assembles all transactions relating to the subject identified in the name of the account.

Books of original entry. The journals in which financial transactions of a business are originally recorded. Books of original entry are contrasted with books of subsequent (or secondary) entry known as ledgers.

Cash receipts journal. A book of original entry in which the receipts of cash (deposits in bank account) are recorded.

Cash disbursements journal. A book of original entry in which disbursements of cash represented by checks drawn are recorded.

Ledger A book in which the financial transactions of a business are classified by separate accounts, each bearing its own name. Entries in the ledger are made by posting from books of original entry The ledger may be a bound book, loose-leaf book, unbound looseleaf sheets, or a card record.

Cash receipts and disbursements records. The books of account are always adapted to the needs of the business. Thus, in a real estate office there will be columns in the cash receipts journal and in the cash disbursements journal to classify the receipts and disbursements. In Figure 65 is a cash receipts journal with columns to indicate how much of the commissions received were for sales, leases and rents, management fees, and so on. In Figure 66 is a cash disbursements

CASH RECEIPTS

DATE	ADDRESS OF PROPERTY	COMMISSIONS RECEIVED						
		AMOUNT	SALES	LEASES AND RENTS	MANAGEMENT	APPRAISAL	GENERAL	
							ITEM	AMOUNT
	TOTALS							

Figure 65. Cash Receipts Journal.

journal with columns to show whether the payment was for payroll, commissions to salesmen and co-brokers, expenses, and so on.

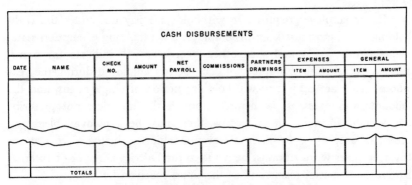

							EXPENSES		GENERAL	
DATE	NAME	CHECK NO.	AMOUNT	NET PAYROLL	COMMISSIONS	PARTNERS DRAWINGS	ITEM	AMOUNT	ITEM	AMOUNT
	TOTALS									

Figure 66. Cash Disbursements Journal.

In some offices a separate record is maintained for entering moneys received that make up each bank deposit. A record similar to this was described on page 270. Where such a cash record is kept, it is used in conjunction with the cash books illustrated in Figure 65 and 66. Entries in the cash record are carried over in detailed form to the cash receipts journal. The entries of disbursements are made from the stubs in the checkbook.

How to Keep the Payroll Records

What is involved. If you are responsible for making out the payroll, you must know something about the tax and other laws of the Federal government and the state in which your office is located. This is true even though you are the only employee. You must also know who is an employee within the meaning of the law and who is not. In most cases, real estate salesmen are not employees.

A very brief explanation will be given here of the laws affecting the payroll, merely to acquaint you in a general way with the requirements. For actually keeping the payroll records, you will need more detailed information. You can always get this from the particular taxing or governmental authority.

Federal income tax withholding at the source. Employers must withhold from each payment of wages made to their employees an amount representing a proportionate part of the employee's approximate income tax liability for the year (assuming the employee's entire income is from wages).

Every employer required to withhold and pay tax under the withholding provision must keep his employee's withholding exemption statements (Form W-4) and such other records as will indicate the name, address, social security number of each person employed during the year whose wages are subject to withholding; period of employment, and the amounts and dates of payments. Although the law does not prescribe any specific form for these records, they must be kept available at all times for inspection by internal revenue officers. Furthermore, returns covering taxes withheld must be made to the District Director of Internal Revenue on special forms and at the times specified by law.

State and local income tax withholding. Many of the states that impose income taxes on individuals have some provision with regard to withholding taxes from wages received. Some of these states require withholding only in the case of nonresident employees, while others make no distinction and require withholding from residents and nonresidents alike. State laws vary as to the amount to be withheld, exemptions, time for filing reports, payments, and so on.

Cities in Kentucky, Pennsylvania, and Ohio (as well as cities in other states) require employers to deduct and withhold income tax on salary and wages.

Federal old age, survivor and disability insurance benefits. The Federal Insurance Contributions Act imposes taxes which support the old age, survivor and disability benefits payable under the Social Security Act, as well as medical care for the aged. All employers of one or more persons for any period of time, however short, in non-exempt employment are subject to the law and are liable for the taxes Employees also are taxed. Each employer is responsible for deducting the employee's tax from wages and must show such deductions on his payroll records. Both employer and employee taxes are remitted by the employer.

State unemployment insurance laws and disability benefits laws. The state unemployment compensation laws conform to the standards specified in the Federal Unemployment Tax Act. The state laws vary, however, from one another and from the Federal law in many important respects. For example, each state law sets forth the number of employees an employer must have to be subject to the law, the types of employment which are exempted, and the inclusion or exclusion of part-time or seasonal employees. Whether or not employee contributions are required and the amount of benefits to be paid are also matters that vary from state to state.

In all of the states, however, unemployment taxes (contributions) are based upon the employer's payroll.

Six states (Alabama, Alaska, California, New Jersey, New York, and Rhode Island) require that the employee make contributions that are deductible from wages. In all of these states except Alabama the contributions are either entirely for sick benefits or partly for sick benefits and unemployment insurance. The employee tax must be computed and deducted from the wages every time wages are paid.

Federal wage and hour law. The Fair Labor Standards Act of 1938, as amended, establishes a specific minimum wage per hour for all employees covered by the Act. The law also sets maximum hours of 40 per week, but it imposes no absolute maximum number of hours which an employee may work in a work-week. It merely requires that the employer must pay one and one-half times the regular rate of pay for all hours in excess of 40 per week, unless the employee is exempt. (Some states also have wage and hour laws.)

Many real estate businesses are not subject to this law, but those whose activities take them out of the state might well be. You employer should get the advice of his attorney as to whether he is subject to this law.

Record requirements. All Federal "payroll" laws require employers to keep records of certain information concerning their employees. The importance of these record-keeping requirements should not be underestimated. Severe penalties may be imposed for failure to comply. You can find out what records must be kept by writing for the regulations issued by the government department that administers the particular law.

The payroll records. All kinds of payroll record-keeping devices are available at local stationers and office supply companies. They are made up to fit the requirements of the particular state. Each real estate office selects a system that is best suited for its size. Generally, the records include (1) a payroll sheet and (2) individual earnings records. With these two records; you can meet the requirements of the law. You can also easily inform employees at the end of the year, or when they leave, of their total earnings and deductions, as required by law

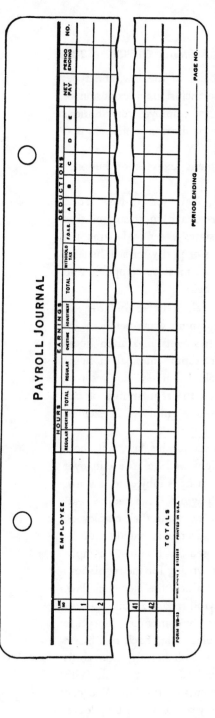

Figure 67. Payroll Journal.

Figure 68. Employee's Individual Earnings Record.

The payroll sheet. The payroll sheet is made up for each pay period, and shows the amount of compensation paid to each employee. It is usually a columnar form that provides for listing the following information under appropriately entitled column headings—employee's name, gross pay, deductions (individually listed), total deductions, net pay, period ending, and check number. It should have columns for regular and overtime hours worked and the hourly rate, if the business is subject to the Federal wage and hour law. The payroll sheet provides complete information for disbursing the net amount of compensation due each employee and for completing the current entry on the individual earnings record. A form of payroll sheet or "journal" is shown in Figure 67.

Individual earnings records. A record of earnings for each employee is indispensable in any system, principally because information as to earnings must be readily available to the employer and the employee for the preparation of the various tax returns. The form provides space for an entry for each payroll period during the year and enough vertical columns for entering gross pay, individual deductions, and net pay. The form usually provides for quarterly totals, a summary, and grand totals for the year. A form is shown in Figure 68.

Real Estate Terms and Phraseology[1]

1. Parties involved.

a. PRINCIPAL: Generally, the word means chief or most important. Specifically it may mean the person employing an agent or broker; a sum of money as distinguished from the income earned by this money.

b. VENDOR: One who disposes of property by sale.

c. VENDEE: One who buys.

d. BROKER: One employed in negotiating the sale, purchase or exchange of land for a commission contingent on success.

e. AGENT: A person acting on behalf of another, called his principal.

f. COMMISSION: A sum or percentage allowed an agent for his services.

g. GRANTOR: The seller of property when he conveys the land and title.

h. GRANTEE: The purchaser of property who accepts the deed.

i. ASSIGNEE: One to whom some right or interest is transferred.

j. MORTGAGOR: One who borrows money and pledges real property as security for repayment of the loan by giving mortgage thereon.

k. MORTGAGEE: A creditor acquiring an interest in the land of a debtor for the purpose of securing the debtor's personal obligation.

[1] Robert Kevin Brown and Elbert E. Sturgess, Sr., *Real Estate Primer* (Englewood Cliffs, N.J.: Prentice-Hall, Inc., 1961), pp. 223–231.

l. LANDLORD: The lessor or owner of the property in fee who leases his property to a tenant or lessee.
   1. LESSOR: The landlord. (See above)
   2. LESSEE: The tenant who occupies rented property.

2. **Listings—First step in a sale.**
   a. OPEN LISTING: Permission granted a broker to offer for sale or lease property on a non-exclusive basis.
   b. EXCLUSIVE LISTING: The right given to a broker by a property owner to sell the property to the exclusion of any and all other brokers.
   c. EXCLUSIVE RIGHT TO SELL: Right given by an owner to a broker to sell the property to the exclusion of all others.

3. **Preliminary matters in a sale**
   a. MEETING OF MINDS. When the parties to a proposed contract reach an agreement upon the price, terms and all other essential conditions preliminary to the execution of a contract, they have had a meeting of minds.
   b. CONSIDERATION: Something which suffices to make an informal promise legally binding, usually some value given in exchange for a promise or property.
   c. OPTION: A contract by which a landowner gives to another person, for a consideration, the right to buy the land at a fixed price within a specified time.
   d. BINDER. An agreement in writing for the sale and the purchase of real estate, usually brief in form and with a nominal deposit. Contains only most important provisions. More generally, a preliminary draught of a contract executed by the party sought to be bound and containing all the essentials of a contract.
   e. CONTRACT OF SALE: An agreement in writing between competent parties, upon legal consideration, for the sale or exchange of real estate.
   f. INSTALLMENT CONTRACT: An agreement providing for the payment of a specified amount in periodic installments, as a condition precedent to the purchaser receiving his deed.
   g. FORFEIT: Something to which the right is lost by breach of contract, such as the deposit money which a purchaser may default in failing to carry out a contract of sale.

4. **Types of holding—ownership and leasing.**

   a. FEE SIMPLE: Complete ownership, subject only to Eminent Domain (5c).

   b. JOINT TENANCY: Tenure by two or more persons of an estate by unity of interest. The survivor takes the whole estate.

   c. TENANCY IN COMMON: An estate in land held by two or more persons who are not husband and wife. On the death of either party, his interest will go to his heirs or to persons named in his will.

   d. UNDIVIDED INTEREST: Fractional ownership.

   e. TENANT: The person who acquires the right to the use and occupation of the premises for a definite period at a fixed rental.

   f. LEASE: A contract between a landlord and a tenant for the use and occupation of the landlord's property for a specified term by the tenant, who in consideration thereof, pays rent.

   g. LEASEHOLD: The tenant's interest on a property created under a lease.

   h. TENANCY AT WILL: A tenancy which may be terminated by either party whenever he wishes to do so.

   i. TENANCY AT SUFFERANCE: A tenancy where a person has been lawfully in possession of premises (as under a lease), but has remained in possession after his right to possession has expired.

   j. SUB-LETTING: The act of an original lessee to rent all or part of the premises to another, called the sub-lessee, who becomes fully bound by all the covenants of the lease on which the original lessee is held.

   k. PERCENTAGE LEASE: A lease wherein the tenant is required to pay as rental a specified percentage of the gross income from the total sales made upon the premises.

   l. GROUND RENT: The rental paid on a lease made for a parcel of land for a term of years or perpetually. (Perpetual ground rents are now forbidden by statute.)

   m. LIFE ESTATE: (Life Tenant): An estate in land limited in duration to the life of the owner of such an estate or the life of another.

   n REVERSION: The right of a grantor to recover title or possession of land upon termination of the estate granted, such as the right of a lessor to recover possession of leased property upon the termination of the lease, with all the subsequent rights to use and enjoyment of the property.

5. **Restrictions on Ownership.**

a. RESTRICTION: A limitation of the use of property, such as to location, character, cost or type of improvements and occupancy. RESTRICTIVE COVENANT: A clause in a deed by which there is an agreement between seller and purchaser in regard to certain restrictions as to the use of the property, and which is binding on all subsequent owners.

b. ZONING: A municipal ordinance regulating the use that may be made of each parcel of land.

b-1. BUILDING CODE: An exercise of the municipality's policy power by which the manner in which buildings are erected and the materials used are controlled by the municipality for the well-being of the public.

c. EMINENT DOMAIN: The power of a municipal, state, federal government or Public Utility to take property for public use by condemnation proceedings.

c-1. CONDEMNATION: The legal proceeding by which private property is taken for public use or destroyed in the interest of the public welfare.

d. COURTESY: (Curtesy) The right which a husband formerly had in his wife's estate at her death and which is now replaced by her husband's statutory interest under the Intestate Laws.

d-1. DOWER: A wife's right under the common law to possession during her lifetime of one-third of the real property or to one-third of the income from the real property owned by the husband at the time of his death. Now replaced by the wife's interest under the statutes relating to intestacy.

e. EASEMENT: A right acquired by the owner of one parcel of land to use the land of another for a special purpose.

f. ENCROACHMENT: The unauthorized occupation of one's property usually by a building, wall, fence or other structure and usually unintentional as the result of inaccurate surveying.

g. ENCUMBRANCE: Any outstanding claim or lien of record against specific property, or any legal right to the use of the property by any person not the owner.

g-1. CLOUD ON THE TITLE: Any encumbrance, charge or claim against property which makes it legally impossible for the owner to convey a marketable title.

h. LIEN: A hold or claim upon the property of another as security for some debt or charge.

i. MECHANIC'S LIEN: A lien given by statute to contractors and subcontractors who perform labor or furnish material in the improvement of real property to obtain security for their compensation in the event it is not paid when due.

j. MORTGAGE: An instrument in writing or contract pledging as security specific real property for the repayment of a loan.

k. RIGHT OF WAY: As a privilege to pass or cross, it is an easement over another's land.

l. POLICE POWERS: The power of the sovereign or government to regulate the conduct of men and the use of property in the interests of the public welfare, as, for example, the authority exercised by a governmental agency to restrict the use of realty so as to protect the well-being of the citizens.

m. WAIVER: An intentional relinquishment of some right or interest.

6. **Title investigation.**

a. ABSTRACT OF TITLE: A condensed history of the title, consisting of a summary of the various links in the chain of title, together with a statement of all liens, charges, or encumbrances affecting a particular property.

b. TITLE INSURANCE: An insurance policy issued by a title company in which, for a premium, the company obligates itself to insure against defects of title not set forth in the policy.

7. **Survey.**

a. SURVEY: An accurate mathematical measurement of land and any buildings thereon by the aid of instruments.

b. APPURTENANCES: All those rights which go with the land, although not necessarily within the area described.

b-1. RIPARIAN RIGHTS: All rights accruing to the owner of land abutting upon a navigable water course, in the stream and the land thereunder between high and low water marks.

c. FRONT FOOT: A means of determining the value of land by placing a price per foot on its width at the front and assuming an average depth, usually of 100 feet.

    d. ACRE: A unit of land measure, equal to 43,560 sq. ft. or 1/640 sq. mile.

    e. METES AND BOUNDS: A description of the property by measurements and directions.

    f. SUB-DIVISION: The taking of raw land and laying it out in lots and sometimes putting in streets, sidewalks and other improvements.

8. **Evaluation.**

    a. APPRAISER: One who, by virtue of specific training, is qualified to express an opinion of value.

    b. APPRAISAL BY CAPITALIZATION: A valuation reached by capitalizing rents received from improved land, less a reasonable charge-off of those items required for maintenance.

    c. APPRAISAL BY SUMMATION: A valuation reached by estimating the reproduction cost of an improvement, less accrued depreciation and obsolescence, and adding value of underlying land.

    d. APPRAISAL BY COMPARISON: A valuation reached by comparing the sale price of similar properties in similar neighborhoods.

    e. ASSESSED VALUATION: The value assigned to a piece of property by taxing officials for the purpose of levying taxes.

    f. ASSESSMENT: Charges upon real property benefited by local improvements to pay all or part of such improvements.

    g. CUBAGE: The actual space within the outer surfaces of the outside walls of a building and contained between the outer surfaces of the roof and the finished surface of the lowest basement floor.

    h. DEPRECIATION: The loss in value of buildings or land resulting from age, physical decay, changing conditions in neighborhoods and numerous other causes.

    i. ECONOMIC LIFE: The estimated remaining number of years during which a property may be considered to be profitably used.

    j. MARKET VALUE: The amount which a person willing to buy would pay to a person willing to sell, neither acting under compulsion and both exercising intelligent judgment.

    k. OBSOLESCENCE: Loss of building value due to structural, economic or social changes.

    l. REPRODUCTION COST: The amount of money required to replace a building on the current market.

    m. OVER IMPROVEMENT: An improvement which is not the highest-best use for the site on which it is, placed by reason of excess in size or cost.

9. Financing.

a. EQUITY: The interest of an owner of real property represented by the difference between its market value and the aggregate amount of the mortgages and other liens.

b. MORTGAGE: An instrument in writing or contract pledging as security specific real property for the repayment of a loan.

c. MORTGAGEE: A creditor acquiring an interest in the land of a debtor for the purpose of securing the debtor's personal obligations.

d. MORTGAGOR: One who borrows money and pledges real property as security for repayment of the loan by giving mortgage thereon.

e. BLANKET MORTGAGE: A mortgage placed on two or more properties with no specific amount attributed to each property.

f. BOND: The evidence of indebtedness and the promise to repay money borrowed usually accompanying a mortgage.

g. PRINCIPAL NOTE: A promissory note which may be one of several secured by a deed of trust for real estate. (In many states a note or notes and the deed of trust are used in lieu of a bond and mortgage.)

h. AMORTIZATION: Regular periodic payments made on account of the principal during the term of a mortgage.

i. DEFAULT: Failure to perform an act or obligation legally required, such as to meet payments scheduled on a mortgage loan or to comply with provisions of a sales agreement.

j. FORECLOSURE: A legal action taken by a mortgagee when a mortgagor is in default of his mortgage payments, with the intention of the mortgagee acquiring ownership of the property or the amount of his claim at public sale.

k. JUNIOR MORTGAGE: A mortgage subject to others superior in lien.

l. JUDGEMENT: A court order resulting from action at law directing a debtor to pay a creditor amounts found due creditor, and which become a lien on real property.

m. PURCHASE MONEY MORTGAGE: The seller's lien in the form of a mortgage given by buyer to seller against the property sold, to secure the payment of the balance of the purchase price.

n. REDEMPTION: The right to pay off or discharge a mortgage or the right to buy back within the period provided by statute, a property that has been sold for taxes or a municipal claim.

o. TRUST DEED: A form of mortgage where the borrower conveys the land not to the lender, but to a third party, in trust for the benefit of the holder of the note or notes that represent the mortgage debt.

p. USURY: Rate of interest which is in excess of the legal rate.

q. RELEASE: An instrument in writing giving up, relinquishing or surrendering a right or claim.

10. **Closing.**

a. ESCROW: A contract, deed, bond or other written agreement deposited with a third person, by whom it is to be delivered to the grantee on the fulfillment of some condition, upon which last delivery the transmission of title is complete.

b. CONVEYANCE: The transfer of the title to real property from one person to another. Also called a deed.

c. SEIZIN: A covenant in a deed that the grantor owns and is in possession of the property and has good right to sell it.

d. QUIT-CLAIM DEED: One which purports to relinquish or release to another only the garntor's present interest in the land, if any.

e. SPECIAL WARRANTY DEED: One in which the grantor covenants only against the lawful claims of all persons claiming by, through or under him.

f. GENERAL WARRANTY DEED: One in which the grantor covenants and warrants the title against all claims of all persons whatsoever.

g. HABENDUM CLAUSE: A clause in a deed which specified the kind of an estate conveyed, such as a fee, for life or a term of years.

Index